Strategic and Systems Thinking:
The Winning Formula

Systems...the Basic Unit of Life

"Systems Thinking:

Following the Natural Order of the World... in Our Work and in Our Lives"

**Systems Thinking
is
the only universal and integrated organizing framework
of the 21st Century**

—by—
Stephen Haines
Founder and CEO
Haines Centre for Strategic Management

Publisher's Cataloging-in-Publication

Haines, Stephen G.
 Strategic and systems thinking : the winning formula
 / by Stephen Haines.
 p. cm.
 Includes bibliographical references.
 LCCN 2007905124
 ISBN-13: 978-0-9779786-0-1
 ISBN-10: 0-9779786-0-5

 1. Organizational effectiveness. 2. System theory.
 3. Strategic planning. I. Title.

 HD58.9.H35 2007   658.4'01
                             QBI07-600215

Haines Centre Book Series on Business Excellence

The Haines Centre Book Series on Business Excellence is based on the Systems Thinking Approach® to Strategic Management; Our Only Business.

It is based on 50+ years of Scientific Research on Systems Thinking, the "the Natural Way the World Works". The Haines Centre does not do original research, but are world-class experts on the interpretation and translation of this Best Practices Research of others into the simple, common sense and practical applications that come from Systems Thinking.

The framework for this Series is built on the Malcolm Baldrige National Quality Award: Criteria for Performance Excellence as analyzed and extended by the Haines Centre into the 21st Century Systems Thinking Organizing Framework of Seven Hexagons of Organization Functioning. It includes the following books—and continues to grow:

Hexagon #1: Strategic and Systems Thinking (The Winning Formula)
Hexagon #2: Reinventing Strategic Planning into Strategic Management (The Systems
        Thinking Approach®)
Hexagon #3: Leading Strategic and Cultural Change (The Systems Thinking Approach®)
Hexagon #6: Enhancing Your Strategic IQ (Winning Strategies from A to Z)

Testimonials

This is a groundbreaking framework that integrates the three pillars that twenty first century organizations will need to thrive and survive: Strategic Thinking, Systems Thinking, and Change Management. It's the best system out there for managers and human resource practitioners to manage the people side of the organization.

Tom Land, Ed.D.
Dean of Training and Professional Development
Nova Southeastern University, Fischler School of Education and Human Services

As individuals and organizations move from *actions* to manage parts and move into the *thinking* **and** *actions* of managing relationships, they will also discover a corresponding higher level of team work and organizational effectiveness. Lacking this insight, organizations will continue to manage parts, as if they "fly in close formation" and suffer from the corresponding inefficiencies. Those in search of the new world view of systems thinking and thirsty for the greater implications of "thinking and acting together" will find great joy in "Strategic and Systems Thinking," by Steve Haines.

Bill Bellows
President
In2:InThinking Network

Strategic and Systems Thinking: The Winning Formula takes the average business professional on an enlightening ride! Quite often theories are overwhelming, cumbersome and difficult to apply to real-world situations. Instead, we now have a book that introduces us in easy A, B, C...steps how to shift away from analytical ways of deciphering our organizations to relational thinking. This type of thinking allows business leaders, to develop an easy and effective way to fully integrate and create holistic ways to lead organizations, with the most collaboration. The real life examples of company experiences with Strategic and Systems Thinking throughout the book give readers practical explanations that can be applied to their individual company situations. All leaders should add this book to their "must reading list" who are tired of fads and strategic planning theories, and instead open to making a systems-wide change that involves the entire organization completely on-board with future change.

Jodi Waterhouse
Manager, Corporate & Professional Education
University of San Diego

The Strategic and Systems Thinking Book is a comprehensive, holistic approach to Strategic Thinking, Planning and Strategic Management. In a very condensed and organized manner, the book outlines the key components of building a sustainable Strategic Management process. We have used the process for three years and the systems thinking approach has helped us build better strategies and measures of success and also aligned our entire organization to be Strategic Thinkers. The result is that we have a clearer sense of direction and purpose and we are prioritizing and executing initiatives that deliver the most Strategic and Operational value to our customers.

Marc Miller
VP of Strategic Planning
Guadeloupe Valley Telecommunications Corporation
San Antonio, Texas

THEORY AND APPLICATIONS OF SYSTEMS THINKING
Systems Thinking is the "the Natural Way the World Works".

Systems Thinking is the best, most universal, integrated organizing framework and language available

Systems Concept #1: Seven Levels of Living and Open Systems
(Systems within Systems within Systems)

Strategic Thinking Applications:
- Seven Rings of Focus and Reality—Problem Solving, Team Building, etc
- Six Natural Levels of Leadership Competency
- Six Natural Levels of Human Resource Management Competency
- Cascade of Planning and Change

Systems Concept #2: Twelve Characteristics and Natural Laws of Living Systems here on earth

Strategic ThinkingApplications:
- Best Practices Characteristics vs. Traditional Human and Group Dynamics
- Top 10 Everyday Tools for Daily Problem Solving
- Top 10 Everyday Tools for Strategic Thinking

Systems Concept #3: Basic Systems Model/Simplicity of Systems Thinking
(Six of the 12 Natural Laws above)

Strategic Thinking Applications:
- The Systems Thinking Approach® to Strategic Management
- Backwards Thinking: Five Questions and Phases
- ABCs Strategic Thinking Template
- Systems Solutions vs. Problem Solving only
- Many, many other applications to Strategic Management:
(Planning-People-Leadership-Change to Deliver Customer Value)

Systems Concept #4: The Natural Cycles of Change

Strategic Thinking Applications:
- Rollercoaster of Change (It is natural, normal and highly predictable)
- Many, many applications: The only Change Framework/ Model you need to know Individual, Interpersonal, Team, Cross Functional, Organization-Wide Change (20+ Theories of Change and they are all the same)

Preface

Systems Thinking is based on 50+ years of scientific research by the Society for General Systems Research on the 12 Characteristics of life on earth, leading to the natural way the world works.

Strategic Thinking is the application of Systems Thinking to today's issues, problems, and challenges. That is what this book is all about—research and applications for every aspect of our work and lives!

Today's world is one of rapid change, driven greatly by the enormous changes in technology, particularly those in computers in telecommunications, miniaturization, lasers, advanced materials, and biogenetics. Our capabilities on and beyond this planet have experienced unprecedented advances due to the many unbelievable technological discoveries, inventions, and applications that have led to the generally accepted view of our era as the 'Information Age.'

At the same time, however, our North American society has become less and less a 'civilized' one. Our 'moral statistics'–including crime, drugs, health, education, safety, values, etc.–have gotten progressively and dramatically worse. In addition, our corporations have undergone incredible downsizing, layoffs, and failures—size no longer seems to make companies immune from trouble, witness GM, United Airlines, and AT&T to name a few.

Further, Corporate America's CEO level greed has been rampid, witness Enron, Fannie Mae, and Tyco, again to name just a few. In addition to the world-wide war on terrorism that preoccupies so much of our time, money, and energy.

In the short-hand of the day, 'high tech' has not been accompanied by the 'high touch' as predicted. Chronic problems abound.

It is our strong belief–supported by substantial data and examples–that we are now entering the 'Systems Age.' With the use of technology applied to systems such as computers, and in networks of systems, such as the Internet, we are indeed already there. Same thing with our global world interdependent system. There can be no question that these technologies and their systems applications have changed our lives for the better. **However**, until we as leaders apply this same 'systems thinking' to our humanity, our organizations, our social lives, and our global society, progress will suffer. Thomas Friedman's best seller, *The World is Flat*, has incredible detail on this global system.

The analytical, fragmented, mechanistic approaches of the past 100+ years have taken us as far as we can go.

Analytic, reductionist or linear (either/or) thinking as the approach to today's complex, intertwined organizational, societal, and global problems has fragmented and alienated so many of us nearly to the point of losing our status as a civilized society and corporations in North America. If you find this difficult to believe, look at the startling moral statistics today that are outlined in Chapter 1–then see if you agree.

So...what can be done about this state of affairs? How can we lead our organizations and communities to a brighter future in the 21st Century? Can we find useful answers on the far side of this complexity that are elegantly simple enough to work? We are concerned about it all–yet we continue to be uncertain about how to successfully handle these chronic problems. We flip from quick fix to quick fix.

Even our political leadership has seemed just as misdirected for years on these chronic problems. In the '90s, Ross Perot appeared to want to be the United States' leader and political savior. However, he backed away, lost credibility, and Bill Clinton, a Democrat, was elected President in 1992. George Bush was defeated for the U.S. Presidency. Yet less than two years later in the 1994 elections, Democrats lost all across the board–Senate, Congress, Governors, State Houses, etc. In 1996, the "come back kid", Bill Clinton won again. Bob Dole won the moral high ground and still he lost the election. In 2000, George W. Bush was elected President while terrorism was kept below the radar screen. He then had to deal with the aftermath of 9/11 and has led us into two quagmires called Iraq and Afghanistan.

Now in 2006, history has repeated itself and the Democrats have retaken the House and the Senate.

I believe that bouncing from one quick fix solution to another will never enable us to lead a lasting reversal of our organizational, societal, and moral decline. **Only by true systems thinking will we find the profound change needed in the way we think and approach these problems**. Systems Thinking is an approach that is currently being tried, at least partially, in many successful projects, in almost every scientific discipline, and in many business operations.

My hope for this book is that it will provide us with a new leadership framework and a practical, even simplistic, systems framework that allows us to think at a higher systems level so we can begin to "clarify and simplify" the way we see these chronic team and organizational issues...and then provide the leadership that will produce the solutions to these complex systems problems in a more holistic and successful way.

While there is never just one right answer, we at the Haines Centre for Strategic Management know that there is a better way to think, to lead, and to orient our lives, teams, and organizations. We believe we can act in a more systemic way, with more clearly defined solutions. Please join me in our work-in-progress, a continuing search for practical (i.e. Far side *Elegant* Simplicity) tools that work and 'make a difference' to us as individuals, teams, and organizations.

Stephen Haines
Haines Centre for Strategic Management
Founded in 1990

Acknowledgments
"Make a Difference"

This book reflects a lifetime of thinking and caring about people and organizations, as well as my long-term adult experiences and learnings regarding "systems thinking" as a better way to make sense out of the overwhelming problems we face in today's global world, planet, and living system.

My caring and concern for others is manifested in the rallying cry of "make a difference" that my wife, Jayne, and I have implemented in our own Strategic Life Plan. This concern was initially instilled in me through my parents, Virginia and George T. Haines, Jr., who raised me in small-town America (Pleasantville, NJ), with all its positive community and patriotic values.

My mother's parents, Reverend Harold G. Gaunt, D.D. and his wife, Suzie-Lou, as well as my father's parents, George T. Haines and his wonderful wife, Ada, ('Nanna' to us kids) also helped craft my values and concerns for others. They were then honed through four tough years at the United States Naval Academy in Annapolis, MD where I graduated with the now Legendary Leadership Class of 1968

To all six of my parents and grandparents, I dedicate this book in the hope that it can make a difference in the lives of future generations including my daughter, Monica and my grandson, Sebastian.

Thanks:

I would also like to thank two people without whom this book would never have been completed.

First, is Katie McCoy (Kate Brausen to some of you). She and I wrote - and re-wrote - and re-wrote this book together to get it "just right"—it being a very difficult job for a "work in progress" and a lifetime pursuit of understanding and learning practical applications to systems thinking.

Last, but most important, I would like to acknowledge my wife Jayne (Reed) Haines. She is our Business Manager - but even more importantly for this book - did the hard job of editing - and editing - and editing the final manuscript.

To both of you, thanks is inadequate to describe my appreciation for your invaluable help!

Stephen Haines
2007

About the Author

Stephen Haines

"CEO, Entrepreneur and Strategist...Facilitator, Systems Thinker, and Author"

Stephen Haines is *the world leader on the System's Thinking Approach®
to Strategic Management.* He has used Systems Thinking as his orientation to
life since the late 1970's. He is now president and founder of the Haines Centre
for Strategic Management® and an internationally recognized leader in strategic
planning, leadership, and strategic change. He has over 30 years of diverse
international executive and consultant experience in virtually every part of the
private and public sectors.

Mr. Haines was formerly president and part owner of University Associates
(UA) Consulting and Training Services. Prior to that, he was executive vice
president and Chief Administrative Officer of Imperial Corporation of America,
a $13 billion nationwide financial services firm. He has been on eight top
management teams with organization leadership for operations, planning, human
resources, training, organization development, marketing, sales, communications
public relations, and facilities. These organizations include Marriott Corporation
(two divisions), Exxon Enterprises (Qyx), MCI, Sunoco (Sun International)
and Federal Home Loan Mortgage Corporation (Freddie Mac), and Imperial
Corporation of America.

A U. S. Naval Academy engineering graduate with leadership, strategy,
and foreign affairs expertise as the U.S.N.A.'s Western Vice President for the
Legendary Leadership Class of 1968. Mr. Haines has completed his course work
and dissertation for an Ed. D. in management and educational psychology from
Temple University and a Master's in Organization Development with a minor in
finance from George Washington University.

Mr. Haines has written 14 books and 11 volumes of the Haines Strategic
Library (over 7,000 pages). He has taught over 80 different type seminars and is
in demand as a keynote speaker on CEO and Board of Directors issues. He has
served on a number of boards and is the past chairman of the board of Central
Credit Union.

The Haines Centre *for* Strategic Management is an unusual international mix
of master level consultants and trainers with 38 offices in 20 countries

The Author may be contacted at:

Haines Centre for Strategic Management
1420 Monitor Road
San Diego, CA 92110-1545 U.S.A.
Telephone: 619-275-6528
Fax: 619-275-0324
www.hainescentre.com
E-Mail: stephen@hainescentre.com
www.StephenHaines.com

Table of Contents
Strategic and Systems Thinking:
The Winning Formula

Systems Thinking: Following the Natural Order of the World in Our Work and in Our Lives

LIST OF FIGURES

Introduction

Strategic and Systems Thinking:
The Winning Formula

Systems Thinking: Following the Natural Order of the World in Our Work and in Our Lives

> "Preparation, discipline, and talent—
> working within a system—
> is the **winning** playoff formula."
>
> — *Michael P. Mitchell, St Louis*
> Sporting News, May 1994

Systems Thinking

From theory ⇒ to practice
From complexity ⇒ to simplicity
From confusing complexity ⇒ to elegant simplicity
From tradition ⇒ to innovation
From analytic/reductionistic thinking ⇒ to systems thinking
From mechanic ⇒ to organic thinking
From parts ⇒ to the whole
From tactical ⇒ to strategic thinking

THINK

"Thought," said IBM's founder, Thomas J. Watson, Sr., "has been the father of every advance since time began."

The one-word slogan "THINK" has appeared in offices and plants throughout the company since the early 1900s.

PARADIGMS AND BELIEF SYSTEMS

"Who the hell wants to hear actors talk?"
—Harry Warner, Warner Brothers Pictures, 1927

"Heavier-than-air flying machines are impossible."
—Lord Kelvin, President, Royal Society, 1895

"Sensible and responsible women do not want to vote."
—Grover Cleveland, President, 1905

"Babe Ruth made a mistake when he gave up pitching."
—Tris Speaker, Baseball Player, 1921

Think Differently

*"We don't need to think more,
we need to think differently!"*

—Albert Einstein

Introduction

There's no question that the revolutionary changes we face in today's organizational and global world and system has created and is still creating tremendous shifts in our lives, our institutions, organizations, and in our global economy. It's unlikely we will see an end to those changes in the foreseeable future. So far, we have not discovered a working map that can help us find our way through this maze of turbulence and chaos in our teams and organizations. We have continued to see a slow moral decline for us as a society over the past 25 years. Our 'moral statistics" are those chronically unresolved problems we read about in the newspapers and see on TV day after day or read in Scott Adam's Dilbert daily cartoon strips highlighting organizational and management mishaps (of which there are many).

> *"Problems that are created by our current level of thinking can't be solved by that same level of thinking "—Albert Einstein*

Who will be the leaders that guide us through this maze of problems, into a saner, more civilized era? Who will we look to, to create the map that will direct us? If we look at every other era in human history, the leaders were not necessarily the most unique, gifted, or powerful individuals of the day. More often, they were normal, everyday individuals—ordinary people and managers, with extraordinary drive and desire to see their organizations and world become better, richer, more welcoming to contributions of wide and varied origins. People just like you and me all across the Internet.

As in those other eras, I believe each of us has within us the capacity to become leaders in our own right—leaders who have the potential to take the best our teams and organizations have to offer and shape it into workable solutions for our current struggles. These leaders, however, need to be equipped with new and better ways to think about these chronic issues, i.e. a fundamental shift in our awareness. As leaders, we need to develop a different, more fluid, clear, and simple way of thinking that doesn't try to control external forces, but rather encourages working *with* and *in* the natural systems that make up our world. To that end, *Strategic and Systems Thinking: The Winning Formula* consists of three main parts:

Part I: Analytic Approaches to Systems Problems... *We've gone as far as we can*

Part One explores what's going on with the leadership in society and organizations today—the complexities, fragmentation, alienation, chaos—i.e., "change" in every sense of the word. It looks at the failure of society, organizations, and even of us personally, to find solutions for the chronic problems that face us. Despite our wonderful "high tech" Information Age, there is a terrible dichotomy with today's serious problems such as, terrorism, greed, crime, education, teenagers, poor management, bureaucracies, unresponsive big government, and health care.

One fundamental problem in facing these changes is the singular, almost naive form of solutions we chose based on our reductionist and analytic thinking. We're looking for *the fad,* stubbornly searching for the *one right answer* that will magically resolve issues with one fell swoop. At best, this usually results in only partial solutions, at worst, it just creates new ones. As a result it doesn't come close to providing any paradigms and long-term frameworks that will result in root cause solutions for better management and leadership.

Reductionist or analytic thinking is defined as breaking problems down into their smallest elements, then problem-solving each one separately and independently. For those of us who were trained in the scientific method, as I was (i.e., engineers, doctors, dentists, lawyers, accountants, scientists, etc.), it is the dominant paradigm of our time. However, it has taken us as far as it can. Command and control doesn't get it done, as it cannot handle problem-solving each and every chronic problem separately. Since our organizations and world are now too *inter*dependent and complex for independent and separate problem-solving, this approach cannot take us any further along the road to organizational and societal success.

The good news is what is beginning to happen now, in spite of—or perhaps, because of—today's far-reaching struggles, I call it "partial systems thinking". It's attempting to solve problems by looking for linkages between issues and events, trying to find patterns of occurrences to which we can apply more integrated solutions. Even so, it's still only a partial answer, it is in essence, a laundry list of related, yet eclectic, topics and issues. Ultimately, it will not give us as leaders the systemic and long-lasting, more holistic solutions we need to best meet the many chronic interdependent challenges of our rapidly changing lives, organizations and world.

Think about it from a personal perspective. As individuals (or living systems), our maturity levels progress from *de*pendence to *in*dependence, to *inter*dependence—the highest level of human wisdom and awareness. We in organizations and as a society need to continuously begin moving our leadership toward this highest level of awareness…and thus, the need for true systems and *inter*dependent thinking to solve these chronic problems.

Systems Thinking follows the extensive research and science of General Systems Theory (GST). The biologists and General Systems theorists attempted, from the 1920's to the 1970's, to discover the basic characteristics of natural and living (i.e., organic) systems. In Systems Thinking the *whole is primary and the parts are secondary.* In analytic, mechanistic, or reductionist/sequential thinking, by contrast, *the parts are independent and primary, and the whole (and its purposes or relationships) a distant second.*

Part II: Systems Thinking for 21st Century Success

Part Two addresses the dichotomy of societal and organizational changes, proposing that, as leaders, we understand and accept that they create both chaos *and* opportunity. It analyzes many aspects of our current and complex organizations and puts forth new, systemic ways of thinking about and resolving its many-layered issues.

As modern-day leaders, we can trace our progress from the Agricultural Age through the Machine and Industrial Ages. We label our current age as the Information Age because the immediate, predominant change comes from the information and knowledge advances in computers and telecommunications that are reshaping our global economy and world connectedness. This has the effect of causing vast changes, as our world shrinks and reshapes itself (becomes *Flat* as Thomas Friedman's book states).

What's coming on the heels of the Information Age is a rapidly expanding biogenetics industry. Since we are now riding in the 21st Century on genetics research, as well...does that follow we are also soon entering the Genetics Age?

If we want to successfully lead the healing of our organizational fragmentation and alienation discussed in Part I, we must search for tools and responses that can be applied not only to the current problems that we're dealing with, but to the larger natural living systems within which we exist, as well. Information and telecommunications are part of the answer. So are biology and the 21st Century's biogenetic research and applications. However, they are not the only answers for us.

In reality, all of the technological and biological progressions we are currently experiencing—internet, computers, satellites, networks, lasers, mapping the human genome, gene splitting, etc.—have one common thread. They are all systems and types of systems that exist and are changing—all the while embedded in larger and larger interdependent systems—ultimately, the earth as the largest living system.

Thus, Part Two will look at General Systems Theory (GST) to see how it applies to the problems that today's leaders of all types are dealing with. While it was developed by biologist Ludwig von Bertalanffy and four Nobel Prize Winners in the 20th Century, its usefulness is coming more fully into its own in the 21st Century.

Systems Thinking

Systems Thinking is defined as being a more holistic and yet...elegantly simplistic way of thinking that precedes our actions.
It is based on a complete view of the complex relationships within the entity we are discussing, along with its purposes and roles within its larger external environment.

Reshaping the rules and frameworks of our organizations and society according to Systems Thinking means more closely following and being more in tune with the simplicity of our natural laws and world. In other words, it means acknowledging and viewing our global world as an intricate, interdependent complex network of living systems within living systems within living systems. Again, the common thread is that every issue, every problem we face as leaders is embedded in its own system which exists—and changes—while embedded in other larger and more complex interdependent systems.

As leaders, following this natural order will also mean acquainting ourselves intimately with these key systems concepts in order to move beyond this seeming complexity to some natural and elegantly simplistic useful concepts

First, we'll need to recognize and use each of the Seven Levels of Living Systems in which we exist to fully solve today's seemingly intractable problems.

Secondly, we will need to fully understand the Twelve Characteristics of all Living Systems and their predictable "systems dynamics". These characteristics exist all around us, and their dynamics will become obvious as we learn to look for them.

Thirdly, all systems can be described as being in a circular framework within their environment—as an "input-throughput-output" process, with a feedback loop providing the next round of inputs.

In essence, it will be the paradigm shift of our own awareness of these concepts that will allow us to realign our thinking, and lead in more natural ways to better outputs, outcomes, and solutions to our personal and organizational issues.

General Systems Theory's research and conclusions provide us with marvelously simplistic vehicles and frameworks that can be applied to virtually any issue in human nature: individually, team-wise, organizations, and society. As we've said, in studying solutions to any problem, the *whole* is paramount; its parts are secondary and important only as they help achieve the outcomes of the whole system. This clarity and simplicity is in direct contrast to today's analytic, sequential or reductionist thinking, which considers parts or single elements primary and independent, with the whole system coming in a distant second.

If we truly seek the needed leadership with which to live and thrive today, we can only do so through a fundamental paradigm shift in our thinking. Though "paradigm" is an overused term, it has value in its meaning. A paradigm, after all, sets rules and establishes boundaries by which we conduct our day-to-day lives. Through reductionist and sequential thinking, and an analytic or mechanistic approach, we've set artificial rules and boundaries that are inaccurate and no longer useful or in harmony with society's needs or the natural world in which we live. This thinking has taken us as far as we can go in our mass production, complex industrialized society.

We are actually in the early stages of developing this Systems Age; we just don't know it yet. Ever since the astronauts first glimpsed Earth from afar—and provided some of us with new pictures of our planet—our awareness has changed dramatically. We now see the Earth for what it is—a fragile, living system, floating in a vast universe, a universe beyond our imagining. It was at this point, I believe, that the Systems Age first caught our imagination and our awareness. It has since become commonplace for our children as they are already growing up with "spaceship earth", the Hubble Telescope, and pictures of the stars well beyond our complexity on earth.

The Systems Age will eventually make us and our leadership aware of these common systems threads and interdependence. It is about rising above all of our seeming complexity and chaos for a new, more enduring awareness and perspective. Using a holistic simplicity and framework for better thinking, this is the only kind of framework that can assist us in discovering that Strategic and Systems Thinking **is** The Winning Formula. We need desperately to develop some valid and integrated solutions to our fragmented and deep-seated complexities, bureaucracies, and chronic problems—thus leading us to a more civilized, effective, and vibrant 21st Century.

Part III: It's Everywhere, It's Everywhere! Systems Solutions to Systems Problems

To paraphrase Albert Einstein, leadership cannot solve today's problems with the same level of thinking that created those problems initially. That is precisely why, if we look at the reductionist/analytic/mechanistic/sequential thinking that helped create society's and organization's current fragmentation, separatism, and alienation, we realize that an entirely new way of thinking is needed to improve or even possibly eliminate today's intractable problems. It is a higher level or "helicopter view" of life.

Peter Drucker said that, rather than 'reform' something that is already not working, we instead need to *rethink* what it is we're trying to accomplish from a higher and broader level.

> "Every agency, every policy...every activity,
> should be confronted with these questions:
> 'What is your mission?'...'Is it still the right mission?'...
> Rethinking is not primarily concerned with cutting expenses...
> but substantial cost savings always emerge as a byproduct."
> —*Peter Drucker*

In Systems Thinking, Drucker's questions on mission are the *very first questions to be addressed*—as well as thoroughly understood and agreed to—before moving on to anything else involving any system, be it an individual, a team, organization, or society. Systems Thinking is a helicopter view of the world that follows the elegantly simple logic of first asking ourselves where we want to end up (our output, purpose, goal, vision, mission, etc.) *before we* continue following or changing our current path. It causes us, in effect, to **think** *backwards* from the future and the destination we desire and then work forward in the right way to achieve it. As a result this creates a common sense reality check of whether we are really doing what we need to in order to reach the desired outcomes in our lives, teams, organizations, etc.

Part Three will look at how to apply this Systems Thinking Approach®

through the three key systems concepts stated earlier (plus a fourth key concept):

- **Concept #1**: *The Seven Levels of Living Systems*—that make up our world and how we as leaders need skills to work at each of these levels. Particular attention is given to how we personally approach our own lives as individuals and as leaders in pursuing self mastery. Self mastery is a prerequisite to all else that follows in this book.

- **Concept #2**: *The 12 Systems characteristics that lead to a set of "Standard Systems Dynamics"*—at all *Seven Levels of Living Systems.* These standard dynamics make behaviors quite predictable in all living systems. These characteristics are in a web of relationships that are quite visible and understandable (i.e. elegantly simplistic) when viewed from this higher, helicopter view, or Far Side of Complexity.

  The internal workings of any organization or society are so complex now, that they are like a Rubik's Cube—with over three trillion moves, most of them wrong. Thus producing a **Rubik's Cube Effect** of negative *unintended consequences* of analytic thinking which we will discuss throughout this book.

- **Concept #3**: *The Basic ABC Systems Framework*—*that* describes all living systems in operation. The use of the five A-B-C phases or locators of any living system again simplifies systems without losing their essential properties. Thus the many issues in our "organization as a system" level can be more effectively dealt with. Issues such as department/team and cross-functional teamwork, strategic planning, product and business development, being customer-focused, business process re-engineering, quality, service and speed, downsizing, and other major organizational issues become easier to understand and deal with effectively. Again, there are many different kinds of organizational systems at this level—churches, private corporations, community organizations, not-for-profit, government, military, and the like—each requiring different approaches, but all within the same ABC systems context and dynamics, as we shall see.

- **Concept #4**: *Changing systems all undergo the same "Rollercoaster of Change™".* The change cycle is the same no matter what the level of change we are viewing. The words and applications may seem different at the surface level, but at the underlying human dynamics and systems level they are the same process. We have identified over 20 change theories and they are all the same—this Rollercoaster.

  Specific examples will be provided—not only of why Systems Thinking is needed to deal with all these chronic issues in our fragmented organizations and society above—but also how a systems approach can make the difference between day-to-day complexity and chaos versus simplicity, long-term progress, and positive solutions. It will also look at how organizational managers and leaders need to think and work with the leaders in our organizations and in communities as they play key roles in nurturing much-needed and long-lasting changes.

Part IV: "Feedback, the Breakfast of Champions"

Part Four concludes with a close examination of why feedback is the key to learning and to the entire systems process. It shows why it is imperative for us as leaders to look at feedback as a gift, rather than something we avoid. Finally, it provides some techniques for leaders to implement systemic change, such as superordinate goals, participative leadership, search conferences, parallel involvement processes, and Change Leadership Teams involving all key stakeholders.

Part Four also includes an Epilogue and some last thoughts regarding our dismaying statistics and our fragile planet as a whole. It takes an optimistic view, due to the sheer volume of scientific disciplines that are all beginning to converge toward this Systems Age. Systems Thinkers and leaders are emerging in almost every scientific discipline imaginable—over twenty-five that the author alone has identified.

In its entirety, *Strategic and Systems Thinking: The Winning Formula* is a **work-in-progress** to find an entirely new way to lead our complex and fragmented organizations and society of ours through all of our multi-faceted challenges. The old way is broken and we must fix it using new ways that work. While we are in a high-tech world of tremendous growth and progress, our civilized organizations, and society are in terrible shape. Many managers are at a loss as to how to lead effectively. Our government is at a loss on how to win the global war on terrorism. The old road maps are either gone or no longer work.

If we truly want to become a "high tech" *and* civilized society of organizations and people that can see our global marketplaces and environment bloom and flourish, we must learn about and fully understand the elaborate network of systems—human, biological, electronic, and mechanical—at all seven levels—that hold it together.

An ancient Buddhist proverb observes that "the thicker and deeper the mud, the more beautiful the lotus blooms." We must be willing to look honestly at that 'mud—all the changes, fragmentation, complexity, and chaos that is occurring within our organizations and society—and then seek to understand them in a more holistic and yet elegantly simplistic and practical way.

Understanding the issues from a higher view, a helicopter view, is better than either giving up or just working harder doing what we already know isn't working. Only then will Systems Thinking become the language and fuel with which we can be transformed to lead in a more constructive, guided and holistic way. If we look at our lives, our leadership responsibilities, and our global organizational networks of systems from this perspective, maybe we can better guide ourselves and our institutions toward a future of our own positive design. The solution is not through mechanistic re-engineering and all the other singular management fads and quick fixes of the day, but through rethinking and reshaping our policies, programs, practices, and perspectives within our interdependent natural world of living systems. Only then will the possibility of a better and brighter future emerge.

When all is said and done, what other viable choices do we have? The old management and societal ways aren't working, no matter how hard we try, how much information we have, how strong our command and control is, how big and technically advanced our military is, or how fantastic the Internet is. In light of this, we *must* change our paradigm from mechanistic, sequential, reductionist, and analytical thinking from knee-jerk single management solutions—and change our continued **in**dependent approaches to today's **inter**dependent social and organizational chronic problems. Systems Thinking and systems solutions are the way out of our current complexity and chaos, over to the simplicity on the far side of complexity. To paraphrase: **And if not us...who? And if not now... when? And if not Systems Thinking...how?**

In other words, as Jacques Cousteau so eloquently put it when describing a world gathering of astronauts in his foreword to Kevin Kelley's book, *Home Planet: "From their exceptional journeys, they all came back with the revelation of beauty. Beauty of the black sky, beauty and variety of our planet, beauty of the Earth seen from the moon, girdled by a scintillating belt of equatorial thunderstorms. They all emphasized that our planet is one, that borderlines are artificial, that humankind is one single community on board spaceship earth. They all insist that this fragile gem is at our mercy and that we must all endeavor to protect it."*

What we have—in ourselves, our teams, our organizations, and our world—is both a gift and a responsibility that is, in the end, worth our finest effort.

Let's begin...

Systems Thinking Research = Strategic Thinking Applications

It is about:

- Clarity and Simplicity
- Meaning and Purpose
- Focus and Direction
- Desired Outcomes
- Relationships and Feedback!

Part One

Analytic Approaches to Systems Problems...

We've Gone as Far as We Can

Voyage of Discovery—New Eyes

"The real voyage of discovery consists not in seeking new landscapes but in having new eyes".

—Marcel Proust

"To attain knowledge,
add things every day.

To attain wisdom,
remove things every day.

—Lao-tzu

CHAPTER 1

The Failures of Fragmented Organizations...
There is no quick fix...OR free lunch!

That today's revolutionary change has turned our organizational and societal infrastructure—and our managers and leaders—on their heads is obvious to even the most casual observer. To say that our underlying values and corresponding behaviors as organizations and as a society are also changing would be a gross understatement. In some ways, we are becoming a society of individuals—an entity in which loyalty to self far outweighs loyalty to any larger group or organizations. Leadership and "heroes" have become almost an endangered species despite all the rhetoric.

Those things which concern us today are also far different than the things that concerned us in earlier times. Precisely how far apart they are is glaringly obvious when we look at the five most extreme problems of American teachers over the past half-century. Ken Adelman, a columnist for the San Diego Union-Tribune, contrasted what today's American teachers saw as their students' top five problems, as compared with teachers of fifty years ago.*

It is an extremely telling, albeit alarming, list:

1940's	1990's
1) talking out of turn	1) drug use
2) chewing gum	2) alcohol abuse
3) making noise	3) pregnancy
4) running in the hall	4) suicide
5) cutting in line	5) rape

* "Why do Americans feel so bad?"—Ken Adelman, San Diego Union-Tribune

Indeed, we all see the statistics and acknowledge that crime is alarming. Drugs and weapons have become so pervasive in schools that one in 10 students admits to carrying a weapon and some stay home because they fear for their safety. Yet we're continually overwhelmed, on a daily basis, by the unprecedented level of violence and global terrorism involved in today's random and drive-by shootings, bombings, murder, and more.

The internal dangers which cause the disintegration of our societal, organizational, and universal infrastructures—creating a sense of loss, an increasing inability to focus, and a lack of clear direction and leadership that permeates all aspects of our lives—are far more insidious and difficult to remedy than the more obvious and external dangers of times past. The corporate downsizings of the '90s and 21st Century, and the outsourcing and global competition have left millions of American careers in ruins, a strongly negative "survivor syndrome" and a tremendous loss of loyalty by American workers.

If we look at how much really changes in our organizations and society from one year to the next, it seems a minor amount, maybe not even worth making a fuss over. However, when we look at not only how much has changed over the last fifty years—but also at the types of things that have changed so dramatically—we recognize that it's time to stop kidding ourselves that, "Everything's really OK...we just have to wait it out..."

Everything is most definitely not OK, neither in our organizations, our society, nor in our personal lives. It's time to stop playing ostrich, and take our heads out of the sand for a long, honest look at exactly what's changed and why. This book is about a Paul Revere-type call to arms, a sounding of our inner alarms that connect us to those things that keep us alive and vital and productive for ourselves and our society.

It's only human, to be sure, to shy away from those things that confuse, dismay, trouble, or threaten our status quo. As leaders, all of us at one time or another have delayed making a particular decision, sacrifice, or behavioral change that, in the end, we knew was inevitable.

It's a little like that old fable of the emperor's new clothes. A tailor appealed to the emperor's vanity enough to convince him that he was wearing a new suit made of such priceless fabric that mere mortals could not see it, when in fact he was wearing no clothes. All the people in the kingdom were so intimidated by the possible result of contradicting the emperor in his belief that they convinced themselves that he really was wearing a fine new suit—they just couldn't see it. Out of the entire kingdom, only one small child was brave (or unworldly) enough to state the obvious, thus exposing the tailor's fraudulent claim—and sending the emperor dashing for cover.

In many ways, this is what is taking place in our global marketing and society today. We're frightened by the ever-increasing speed of change we don't understand, and for which we have no easy answers. We're covering our eyes and refusing to see, at least for the moment, that the emperor isn't wearing any clothes. While this is natural and understandable, avoiding our more serious modern issues may exact from us a price that we as leaders, as organizations, and as a society can't afford to pay.

The 'Boiled Frog' Syndrome

I liken this state to the story of the Boiled Frog. In *Shaping Your Organization's Future* (from Pfeiffer & Co., San Diego, CA), there is a metaphorical tale that involves a laboratory-controlled test. In this, a frog is tested in water levels of varying heat to determine at what point the water becomes too hot for the frog to adapt. The upshot of it is that the frog is so superior in its ability to adapt to the ever-increasing heat; it eventually is scalded and dies.

I believe the metaphor of the Boiled Frog is indicative of the state of our existence today. Many of us have trouble seeing evolutionary change until it is too late. We tend to believe that "It's not happening in my life, so why should I worry?" The answer is, it's happening to all of us, whether we see it before our eyes or not.

Think about it for a moment. Even if you live a comfortable middle-class life and have a job in a good organization, this terribly unbalanced world we've been describing impacts your everyday life in ways you may not realize. How much, for instance, are you required to spend on home and automobile protection and liability insurance to keep your home covered in the event of crime? You probably have a nice wardrobe and belongings, as well; how much do you think the price you paid for these things reflects the billions lost each year in business—employee theft and shoplifting? How much change do you have to deal with at work? Does change leave you overwhelmed, stressed out and worn down?

I could go on, but I think you get the picture. We've become so proficient at adapting to each rapid-fire change that comes our way—personally or professionally—that we've neglected to check the water temperature. In every arena of society, the water is getting hotter and hotter. If we adapt too much more, we could become as boiled and as dead in the water as that unfortunate frog in the chemistry lab. We are in danger of adapting ourselves and our world right out of existence.

To really appreciate the enormity of problems facing us—and the bankrupt approaches with which we as managers and leaders have been attempting to solve them—I believe we must take the time to look at all the fragmentation and failures around us on a number of levels…government…society…organization…community…and individually.

Level of Governmental Fragmentation

U.S. and Canadian governments are bending under their own pressure-cooker issues, such as welfare spending, health care reform, tax cuts, social security, budget deficits, and more. Canadian communities and the families that dwell within them are suffering an increasing inability to define themselves in terms of economic and social security—all exacerbated by the Quebec separatist question, concerns over Western Provinces alienation, and volatile Constitutional issues.

The picture doesn't improve a whole lot in the U.S., either. The borrow-and-spend binge of the last six years has burdened the U.S. with problems that will frustrate its growth for years. In many respects, we've grown too big and cumbersome for our own good. A clear example of this would be our federal income tax code, which started out at a 1% rate and a few pages at the turn of the 20th century, growing to more than 5,000 pages now.

Looking back over the centuries, said Peter Drucker in Post-Capitalist Society, our government:

"…has evolved into the primary agent for all social problems and tasks—to the point where national income is seen as belonging to government, with individuals entitled only to whatever government is willing to let them have."

"The [nation state], however, has been less than successful. It has not redistributed income. It has not controlled recessions...and the social programs it has operated have been failures.

It has spent itself into impotence — with little to show for it.

Looking back over the last fifty years, we see that the North American political structure has gone from strength and world leadership to volatile governmental issues and questionable decisions. The U.S. of the '60's—with its abundant natural resources, its tightly woven infrastructure of land, air, and sea roads, strong manufacturing and agricultural base, inexpensive skills, cheap energy, abundant technical leadership with an educational system to back it up, and seemingly limitless financial resources—seems only dimly related to the 21st Century United States.

Unemployment—and underemployment—levels, reduced revenues with simultaneous, increased expenditures, budget deficits and tax increases have many states in the grip of a vicious cycle of economic decline. If the dollar loses value worldwide, the federal government's massive deficit will almost certainly result in a severe decline in our standard of living.

In questionable attempts to constrain the deficit, Social Security and other trust funds—funds earmarked specifically for future retirement income—have been used to reduce the deficit. This 'deficit monster' has created a 'smoke-and-mirrors' effect of actually reducing our annual deficit—all while virtually wiping out baby boomers' retirement funds. This leaves future generations with the responsibility for funding boomers' retirement funds. It also creates a pyramid-like scheme that in other situations has put many people in jail for fraud.

This game of 'borrow Peter to pay Paul'—in which federal budget deficits have eroded the economic base has started a vicious cycle of economic decline that comes with no printed instructions on how to resolve it.

In his newsletter, Perspective, U.S. Senate Chaplain Richard Halverson quoted 18th Century historian, Alexander Fraser Tytler, in his book, The Decline and Fall of the Athenian Republic: *Ministries Today, March/April, 1991

"A democracy cannot exist as a permanent form of government. It can only exist until the voters discover that they can vote themselves money from the Public Treasury. From that moment on, the majority always votes for the candidates promising the most benefits from the Public Treasury with a result that a democracy always collapses over loose fiscal policy, always followed by dictatorship."

"The average age of the world's greatest civilizations has been 200 years.

Former governor of Colorado Richard D. Lamm was quoted in The Futurist magazine, saying, "Every once-great nation in history thought itself immune from decline, and, up to now, none of them has been right.*" We need only consider the Roman empire, the Aztec civilization in Mexico, the once-great British and French colonial empires, and many of the ancient Chinese and Japanese dynasties.

Clearly our present government methods are no longer working. To be effective leaders, we need to take our heads out of the sand and start seeing reality for what it really is, instead of what we'd like it to be.

Questions to Ponder...

- What kinds of government fragmentation and bureaucracy have you seen?
- How do you think these issues can be really resolved?
- Why have no lasting solutions to these issues been discovered?

Levels of Socio-Economic Fragmentation

In virtually every aspect of North American society, the pendulum of change is swinging wildly. Logic dictates that, with each swing of the pendulum, other related aspects of society are correspondingly impacted. Perhaps the bleakest result of this trend is the effects that rebound down through a nation's socio-economic structure.

While crime growth seems to have slowed overall, random crime is quite high; creating a sense of insecurity whenever you are out of your home.

Since the tragic day of September 11, 2001, metal detectors are now in every airport with the Government's TSA tight security, and concrete barriers surround capitol buildings and key vulnerable locations everywhere.

With one in every two marriages ending in divorce, we've given up expecting a two-parent childhood for all children. Nearly 40 % of today's children will sleep in a house without their biological father, as over 30% of all babies in this country are born illegitimate.

Since 1960, there has also been a 400% increase in illegitimate births, single-parent families have tripled, and births to unmarried teens have increased dramatically

The barbell-shaped society we have created is a society of the 'haves' and 'have nots.' It is a society with more than one in three families at the bottom, causing these families to have little or no stake in society. A low annual income is no stake at all—it's simply a survival treadmill. Contrast this with our previously 'bell-shaped' societal curve in which there were only a few rich and a few poor, with the rest of us in the middle. Looking at this, it's easy to understand why we've got more people with mental health, crime concerns, and stress-related problems and illness than ever before. Nor are Americans receiving the quality training needed to arm themselves for a more prosperous future. See Thomas Friedman's book (*The World is Flat*) mentioned earlier for lots of negative statistics on this, not to be repeated here.

American primary education is affected, too. Once viewed as a world standard, American students today are seriously lacking in reading, writing, math, and science skills. They consistently score only mid-level in international student comparisons.

It's not just academia suffering, either. The $500 billion hospital industry in the U.S. is undergoing tremendous transformation, as well. In just the last decade, well over 1,000 hospitals nationwide have either merged or shut down completely. Similar to education, this industry is caught in the middle of an ongoing tug-of-war between inefficient, fragmented policies and management and health care reform on a national level.

Our lives—and our nation—need renewal. Ian Mitroff, of the University of Southern California's graduate School of Business has an interesting term for what we are currently experiencing. He calls it 'the failure of success,' and further defines it as 'the erroneous belief that one can repeat blindly in all times and circumstances the assumptions that made one successful for one very special set of conditions'working. We're trying to administer a mere Band-Aid to what is really a gaping wound, but what happens in the long run is that the wound will just get larger. It affects all forms of communities and organizations.

Level of Community and Ethics Fragmentation

Also at stake today in our lives outside of our work is something far more fundamental than all the fragmentation and failure on the global, economical, political, or organizational levels. It is our inbred sense of ethics and values that is profoundly impacted by what is going on in each of these spheres. One very real result of the head-in-the-sand, leaderless approach seen in each of these venues is an almost isolationist, 'every person for themselves' ethic.

A possible explanation for this increasingly isolationist swing of the pendulum may be found in looking at our radically changing community. Once considered the world's melting pot, for instance, the U.S. has made quantum leaps in adding a veritable salad bowl of diverse cultures to its population. However, the United States' current fragmented climate of isolationism and separatism in our post 9/11 society only furthers our failures to create a true sense of community.

The U.S. Census Bureau predicted that, fifty years into the new millennium, current and new minority groups could collectively account for fully half of the nation's population. Asians, Hispanics, Native Americans, African-Americans, and other ethnic minorities are increasing rapidly while Caucasians numbers are stable. By the mid-nineties, African-Americans, Hispanics, Asians, and Native Americans already comprise more than half the population in many of the largest cities in the U.S. Currently, Asians and Latinos dominate immigration into the U.S., and this diversity continues to increase despite post 9/11 security. Now a "comprehensive" immigration solution seems to be escaping us into singular political points-making and finger pointing.

Accompanying this influx of diverse cultures is a corresponding diversity of religious faiths, as well. In a country where dialogues between Protestants and Roman Catholics were once considered avant-garde, religious organizations that now also include Hindus and Buddhists are constantly springing up. Over 300 Buddhist temples exist in the Los Angeles area alone. The U.S. National Conference of Christians and Jews changed its name to, simply, The National Conference, as it has included Muslims among its membership for over10 years.

However, it's not just the ethnic, cultural, and religious aspects of our community that are changing. Our workplace community mirrors the changes in national origin, adding gender, physical capability, and age to the mix. U.S. corporations employ more women and physically-challenged workers, from low-end clerical, to middle and upper-management positions, than ever before.

Also, the average life span in the 21st Century is far longer than in previous centuries, resulting in a community that contains multiple generations—each with its own unique set of values and standards. With such high diversity at every level, unity of values and unity of goals tends to be problematic at best. We are now, not the U.S.A. but the Red States vs. the Blue States.

Familiarity and respect for others' views and values does not spring forth fully formed; distrust is the more common norm. Given the fragmentation and change present in every facet of our lives today, this distrust is an understandable — if not entirely desirable—reaction.

In many respects, our ever-intrusive media aggravates this already glum scenario with its seemingly limitless regurgitation of dire news in the U.S. A., Iraq, and globally. The world described in newspapers and on television is tilled with dishonesty, deceit, manipulation, and all manners of misbehavior. Because news, by definition, isn't what's normal or ordinary, routine ethical conduct is seldom reported.

Another interesting twist on this 'live-for-yourself/don't-worry-about-the-rest' attitude was found in a Governing magazine article by writer Alan Ehrenhalt*. He cited a study that was done by the Chicago police department on cops that went bad:

Nearly all the cops who got fired had…a history of very small problems… they had missed court dates and shown up late to work, taken lots of sick leave, misplaced their badges and other official identification, gotten into a disproportionate number of traffic accidents, or engaged in more than their share of petty quarrels with other officers…"

What was really interesting is that "…the department concluded…that there is such a thing in the lives of its officers as character, and that it reveals itself in small ways as well as large ones." The article concluded, "When people who are routinely unreliable or duplicitous turn out later to be catastrophically abusive or corrupt, that is not a coincidence or a product of circumstance…it is a failure of character." We can see all around us today evidence that, in focusing solely on our own survival, the survival of the group as a whole weakens substantially.
*Alan Ehrenhalt, Governing, November 1994

'Doing the right thing'—most likely due to its scarce appearance just about everywhere these days—is a topic that keeps popping up. When asked about cheating on income taxes, a surprising 32% said they would; for those earning $50,000-plus, 45% admitted they would also consider cheating on their taxes.

Needless to say the corporate greed in the 21st Century and the hundreds of restructuring of annual economic statements of private sector firms is unprecedented. So are the convictions of the 200 Senior Executives for fraud excesses in their organizations. It is not just Enron and Tyco!

In short, we are experiencing a whole new redefining of our social norms for ethical behavior. Ethics, after all, are a set of rules that make social cooperation and cohesion possible. When powerful political and business parties begin to see ethics as something that applies to others, rather than themselves, that average citizen's natural reaction may be one of "all bets are now off"—they no longer see any inherent advantage in playing by the rules.

Levels of Organizational Fragmentation

Finally, no one would disagree that the structure of today's workplace is shifting and changing. The traditional, hierarchical command and control organization is often replaced by a differently structured, 'flatter' organization. New, highly sophisticated technology has placed intense focus on productivity— both in terms of quality and speed of production processes. Traditional manufacturing processes, designed to churn out standard products year in and year out, are giving way to extremely complex, but short-term, limited production processes and small niche markets. And, even these, are now usually moved offshore to China.

The huge, multi-corporate, 'dinosaur' firms that grew in the '80's and '90's have not fared well in the 21st Century—firms such as AT&T, General Motors, Westinghouse, and Sears. James R. Houghton, former CEO of Corning, Inc. put it this way a long time ago and it still holds true today…

"We cannot continue to rely on a management system that was designed for an era that is past; it was effective in the Industrial Age, but it is not compatible with [today's] demands"—and this was written in 1992! (*Planning Review September/October 1992*)

To fully comprehend how change has fundamentally altered the fabric of our organizations, all we really need to do is contrast the '70's and '80's vs. today. Throughout the 80's, most workers could reasonably expect stability, permanence, and predictability in their jobs. Most organizations had full-time, internal employees with fixed work patterns, who stayed with the organization until they retired. They put money and time into developing their employees, and provided health benefits. Organizations created value through slow growth then, job security and advancement opportunities for their workers existed.

In the 21st Century, however, less stable patterns are in place. Where there was once stability and consistency, now there is consistent fragmentation and change, temporariness, and uncertainty. A shifting workforce changed its shape; part-time or external employees, more flexible work patterns, graduated retirements, and specifically targeted turnovers are the norm. So are lack of benefits (see Wal-Mart) and lack of pensions (see United Airlines). Where organizations once developed their employees, valuing their loyalty and tenure, they now buy employees on an as-needed basis, and according to the performance of specific skills. This, in turn, has caused today's employees to feel alienated, burned out, and fragmented from the corporate world.

Job security is a thing of the past. In a climate previously abundant in advancement possibilities, job tentativeness and workers plateauing as a result of 'downsizing', 'right-sizing', and outsourcing jobs to India and elsewhere are the norm. Acquisition also is the byword as the organizations discover they do need to create value—they instead, simply purchase it.

Generation X is the first generation in more than a century-and-a-half that is not able to answer, 'Yes' to the question: 'Are you better off than your parents' generation?

Now, Generation Y is the Second Generation to be less well off!

America's now often turn to gambling, relying on good luck to assure their future. Lottery pots continue to grow as do the number of casinos (over 10 in San Diego County alone). More people now gamble as entertainment than go to professional sports.

Peter Drucker, in the Harvard Business Review, summed it up this way:

"... The [basic] assumptions on which the organization has built and is being run no longer fit reality.

The first reaction of any organization whose theory is becoming obsolete is almost always a defensive one. The tendency is to put one's head in the sand and pretend that nothing is happening

When a theory shows the first signs of becoming obsolete, it is time to start thinking again, to ask again which assumptions about the environment, mission, and core competencies reflect reality most accurately—with the clear premise that our historically transmitted assumptions, those with which all of us grew up, no longer suffice."

Yes, even the bureaucratic, mechanistic organizations of the past have a life cycle and many are declining. The failure of great size, bureaucracy, and its accompanying fragmentation has made many corporations unmanageable. Conglomerates, centralization and vertical integration are fast becoming a thing of the past. The places where we spend our working lives are also in radical need of rethinking and revamping.

Questions to Ponder...

- How have all the organizational failures and fragmentations affected your career? Your friends' and family's career?
- What management skill do you see lacking in today's executives as a result of all these changes?

Summary: A Fragmented and Broken Society and Organizations

It is clear to most of us that, on almost every level, our society and organizations are broken. They need serious, life-saving surgery. Yet, it's hard to see just how we can be leaders and bring our progress around to a community in which we feel a sense of stability, where our differences bring out the best in one another, make us stronger, and where everyone is an important part of the whole fabric of society.

Former Governor of Colorado Richard D. Lamm, in The Futurist, stated clearly how "America has entered into a cycle of decline. It is not irreversible, but, to some degree, it is inevitable. Our kids will live in a far different and more chaotic America—an America that doesn't have nearly the wealth or the opportunities that our generation had. Decline, like fog, creeps up on civilizations on little cats' feet, and America's decline began in the recent past. Tomorrow's futurist will wonder how we were so myopic."

Lamm went on to say, "We have seriously compromised our future. We have:
- over consumed and under invested,
- not adequately maintained our wealth-creating potential,
- spent more government money than we raised in taxes,
- consumed more than we produced,
- borrowed more than we saved,
- imported more than we exported (we are a society on its way to second-class status),
- students who are at the bottom of all international comparisons in education,
- cities which are battlefields,
- a disproportionate number of functional illiterates, [and]
- the world's highest crime rate..."

China and India are the growth countries of the first half of the 21st Century.

Despite these alarming declines in our moral statistics at all levels—governmental, societal and economical, and in organizational and community ethics—I believe there are ways to think and act at a higher level than the one on which we created these problems. A higher level called Systems Thinking—thinking at the holistic level, versus our fragmented levels of the past.

It doesn't matter which specific issue we look at...whatever it is, now is the time to let go of the fear, lethargy, bureaucracy, categorical funding, indifference, and the fragmented, reductionist thinking. This has us in imminent danger of becoming boiled alive much like those too-adaptable frogs in the chemistry lab. Clearly, however when we begin moving in a better, more productive direction, it won't happen quickly or easily. We've run out of free lunches; there are no more quick fixes, but it can happen; we owe it to ourselves, our children, and the society in which we coexist. We each have a responsibility to assist in leading toward our desired USA future—equally our own futures, and the future of our western society.

"The future strength of this country is not in a powerful air force, navy or defense, it is in our people once again being responsible citizens (and employees)."

—*Richard Riley, former U.S. Secretary of Education*

CHAPTER 2

Failures of Fragmented Fads...
Why complex organizations don't change

Overview

Let's look at organizations even more closely than in Chapter 1. What kinds of environmental changes are affecting firms of all types and industries today? The list is endless, but includes the following in our experiences as a Centre for Strategic Management:

- E-Business and E-Commerce are the main ways to do business and/or key distribution methods for all organizations.
- There are tremendous new opportunities for new firms of all types within this chaos and complexity. Technological changes (computers, software, telecommunications, Internet) that fundamentally change how we operate our businesses occur continuously. Genetics research and development, lasers, and high technology that combine to fundamentally change health care. Whole new industries are created by technology.
- China has become the world's manufacturing center.
- India is rapidly becoming the world's outsourcing center for IT, pharmaceuticals, and related industries and applications.
- Brand identities weakening, commodization trends everywhere as there is a strong, almost unquenchable customer demand for it all—quality, service, response, and choice. Customer loyalty has lessened—*what have you done for me lately?* Quality as a given and basic necessity for entrance into a market. Ethnic cultures and markets are raising their voices to be heard.
- Anything that will increase convenience and save time is a winning product or service.
- People now desire "experiences," not just products and service; thus squeezing profit margins further.
- With a strong global economy and marketplace, and there is increased competition everywhere. China's strategy seems to be to build numerous bi-lateral trade relationships around the globe.
- The Iron Curtain collapse is causing chaos in Russia and its Republics. Yet, we have growing democracies in the old Eastern European countries that are and have joined the European Union.
- Niche markets growing like wildfires. Substitutes for products are emerging as industries merge. Blurring of boundaries and elimination of the middleman in distribution continue.
- The cottage industry's growth is finally here. Outsourcing, partnerships, and strategic alliances rather than centralization and vertical integration are the key concepts of the 21st Century.

- There is scarcity of qualified workers in the U.S.A. The entire organization—employee social contract is changing.
- The need for raw materials of all types, not just high oil prices, has created a world-wide competition among nations, especially China and India.

Questions to Ponder...

- What kinds of changes do you see affecting your organization?
- What opportunities are these changing environment conditions creating for your organization?
- How do they affect you personally?

For the past 20 years there have been over 40 million jobs lost in America, while millions more are simultaneously being created here and abroad as the world changes. The dislocation caused by the economic effects of technology, internet, computers, robotics, etc. has been enormous. Today, there is no such thing as a career or lifetime job. Many of the companies that have been the leaders in the industrial revolution have fallen on very difficult times. They are trying extremely hard to make cuts in their human organizations in order to continue to maintain profitability. General Motors, Ford, and AT&T are three of the biggest companies in America and yet, have each laid off over 100,000 employees. This lead has been followed by many, many companies in the United States. The AT&T we knew is now actually gone (the name has been resurrected).

However, this downsizing of corporate America has not had its desired effect. The American Management Association's survey of member companies conducted each year has repeatedly found that downsizing fails to produce hoped for results. Less than half the companies that cut jobs reported even an immediate increase in operating profits and less than one-third reported an increase in productivity. At the same time, over one-third reported increases in turnover and almost three quarters of them reported decreases in employee morale.

Layoffs destroy employee trust. Downsizing results in the "survivor syndrome." In this syndrome, the actual winners are those who are let go, and the losers are those who must stay behind and pick up the slack of the departed workers.

Scott Adams as the creator of Dilbert, as most of you know, makes fun of true life examples of gross management incompetence. He points out the wrong ways we continue to manage and conduct organizational life that are terribly dehumanizing and ineffective as well. Scott Adams has been an extraordinary successful change agent in raising individual and organizational awareness of the failure of today's managers to manage change properly. A steady stream of poorly thought out and inept, true stories of management initiatives are the targets of his cartoons.

There is an emerging trend of strange bedfellows in environmentalists and libertarians who see corporate welfare as the new enemy. Ending corporate welfare, as we know it, has been their watchword. In the U.S. alone, it is estimated that there are hundreds of federal programs that support private business and cost tax payers more than hundreds of billions of dollars a year.

This reminds me of a story once told to me by a colleague in an executive search firm. He said that all companies tell him that they want him to find them the very best executive that he can. He nods his head in agreement. Then he goes and analyzes the organization to see what level of excellence the organization has in reality.

- He and others estimate that 10-20% of all corporations are incompetent and are in the *process of going out of business*.
- Another 33% or so are in the *dogged pursuit of mediocrity* and manage to survive in spite of themselves; having no particular skill or expertise.
- Another 33% or so are managing themselves well but *have no particular drive* for excellence. They are *present and accounted* for as they seem to have acquired a natural market share during this stage of their life cycle.
- Only 15-20% seem to be managers and leaders who are *making a serious effort and commitment to become excellent*. They invest significant resources in the pursuit of excellence and have a shared determination to make it happen.
- And of course only about 5-10% make it to where visionary leadership is an art form. These companies, such as General Electric, dominate their industry and are recognized as outstanding by their competitors. They have a very strong reputation in the marketplace.

Therefore, my search firm colleague calibrates which level of excellence the company is and matches them with an executive candidate at that same level.

If a company was in the dogged pursuit of mediocrity and he brought them the world's greatest executive for an open position, not only would the executive be insulted, but the company would say that was not the person they wanted.

So, if you believe your organization is pursuing a high level of excellence, check out these different percentages versus your own real level of excellence.

As you will also see in this chapter many, organizations talk a good game. However, the level of effort and hard intelligent work required to make the necessary changes to achieve excellence in today's complex and dynamic world usually fails to materialize.

Why 75% Change Fails

At the same time, most executives will tell you they are very busy, or even insanely busy, and that *time is the scarcest resource in their lives*. Into this void step management consultants and authors who are looking to install their own *"one as the best way"* to solve all of these corporate woes. Consultancy is over a $100 billion dollar a year business and is growing rapidly. Many of these corporate management gurus tout their way as the sole path to corporate salvation. This effort has beome so faddish and so broad that parody books have been written about **"Fad Surfing in the Board Room,"** etc. [Now new management gurus are even making fun of the other faddish management gurus (including me).] Systems thinking is not a fad!

Despite this huge management consulting field, most change efforts in corporations and public sector organizations still fail. The data on these failures is enormous and consistent. Estimates on failed major change projects are up to 75% or more based on research for our previous book published in 2005, on *Enterprise-Wide Change*. Those companies that reach full success in their major change efforts are usually estimated at 10% —20%. Thus, most major change efforts in organizations achieve mediocrity at best, and many fail miserably.

The data on why change fails is quite interesting. Gallup polls have shown that over 80% of business leaders often resist change. For very valid reasons #1, they have a vested interest in protecting the status quo. They also do not like to lose control of events and may not even know what to do about the change. The stock market, of course, helps publicly held companies to be quarterly rewarded and short term oriented. Further, most company executives are not rewarded for real change, but for maintaining a slightly consistent increase in earnings. Witness the fraud at Freddie Mac to achieve the moniker "Steady Freddie" each quarter.

Interviews with CEO's, however, have often reported a belief that workers could be much more productive if the CEO's could get them to change. Resistance to change in many ways blocks much change efforts. It is not easy to hire and retain competent people. Poor communications, poor employee attitudes and motivation block change. Failure to ensure employees know WIIFM (What's In It For Me) is a key missing ingredient in all change. The result is that employees often opt to not utilize their discretionary efforts in support of the organization's vision.

In our research at the Centre for Strategic Management we have pursued all of these and other research to find the top ten reasons why change efforts usually fail. Unfortunately our list of top 10 reasons why change fails (apologies to David Letterman) actually has 31 solid reasons and is still growing. Which of these might apply to your organization? Circle the numbers that apply.

Why Change Efforts Usually Fail

1. **Underestimate Systems Complexity.** Top level executives tend to underestimate what it will take. They have unrealistic expectations and fail to understand that the organization is a system of interdependent parts and different levels (individual, team, organization). Thus, knee-jerk simple and direct cause and effect solutions dealing with symptoms only are the result. Use of simple solutions versus the complexities of interdependent organizations as systems doesn't work.

2. **Details Lacking.** The failure to specify in sufficient detail the actual work required to implement the change; especially in larger organizations (content/process/structure).

3. **Change Knowledge Missing.** The failure to know, follow and use the "Rollercoaster of Change" as to how people go through change

psychologically change has three dimensions—cultural, political, and rational. Discounting the cost of the psychological effects of change or not investing in human assets.

4. **Reinforcers Lacking.** The lack of realignment of the business control systems such as performance measures, budgets, MIS, compensation, values. Absence of support and reinforcement/rewards for the new changes.

5. **Accountability Failure.** The lack of specific accountability, responsibility and consequences at every level of the organization. Inadequate executive accountability and leadership of change—failure to know their role as the active "champions" of the changes.

6. **Time Pressure.** Too many changes at once and a quick-fix mentality. Too short-term an orientation by senior executives. Even greed, obsession with short-term, fast buck, and super profits. Failure to budget adequate "lead" or "lag" time.

7. **Management Resistance.** Middle and first line management resistance, apathy, or abdication.

8. **Turf Battles.** Opposing and conflicting messages and turf battles in and from top management along with a split of executive views (as cancer) towards the change. Lack of focused and clear direction, teamwork, and consistency.

9. **Change Structures Missing.** Missing the formal structures, processes, and needed dedicated resources to lead and follow-up on the desired changes.

10. **Reactive Posture.** The failure to act in advance in a proactive fashion; allowing issues to fester and grow, or reacting in an eclectic fashion without a plan or organized framework and philosophy.

11. **Status Quo.** Vested interests and power in the status quo, the auto pilot mindset/complacency and the hierarchy can defeat most change efforts.

12. **Stubbornness.** Stupidity and stubbornness by senior management in not using proven research on what works. Instead, relying on their own inadequate models of change, mindless imitation of the latest fad, or using outmoded theories of motivation.

13. **Control Issues.** Senior executive desire to maintain control over people and events (vs. strategic consistency and operational flexibility) and their low tolerance for uncertainty and ambiguity.

14. **Participative Management Skills Lacking.** Inadequate senior management knowledge and skills on what to do and how to manage change; just plain poor execution—the routine blocking and tackling that great organizations do consistently well. Lack of skills by managers and executives in "participative management" techniques; including those of trainer, coach, and facilitator. This is where an organization's

greatest assets are; with management—so they will empower and utilize employees as their other greatest assets.

15. **Fatal Assumption Made.** Making the fatal assumption that everyone is for it, understands it, and that execution is only a matter of following your natural inclinations.

16. **Redistribution Failure.** Failure to redistribute financial resources based on future priorities/direction through lack of strategic budgeting. Denial and unwillingness to make the required "tough decisions."

17. **Politically Correct Desire.** The perception that it isn't politically correct to be a strong leader with convictions, expertise, and strong directions/opinions. Putting up with poor performance. This used to be the opposite; namely that megalomania—one man show is what works—the benevolent or not-too-benevolent dictator.

18. **Initial Bias Wrong.** A bias towards thinking that initially communicating direction, educating people, forming teams, and holding meetings will result in success. Bureaucracy and trivial activities will fill up the time allotted.

19. **Lack of Senior Management Modeling.** The unwillingness of senior management to model and gain credibility and trust towards the desired changes first, and to change their leadership and management practices and communications.

20. **Multiple Consultants and Philosophies.** Ineffective use of multiple consultants and/or philosophies on a piecemeal basis. Paradigms and belief in analytic approaches to a systems problem.

21. **Lack of Customer-Focus.** Failure to focus on customer wants and needs and satisfaction as your only reason for existence.

22. **Skeptics Not Involved.** Failure to value skeptics and to enroll a critical mass for change. The lack of use of high involvement methods, the Parallel Process, and opportunities for personal and group growth and development. People support what they help create.

23. **Poor Cross-Functional Teamwork.** Lack of horizontal, cross-functional communications, teamwork, collaboration, and task forces.

24. **Unsupportive Organizational Design.** Unsupportive organizational structure and design to the desired changes.

25. **Lack of Follow-Through.** The failure to follow-through and sustain the energy, momentum, buy-in and stay-in, effort and commitment as well as accountability over the long-term. Perseverance in the face of the first difficulty (vs. pulling the plug) is the key.

26. **Middle Manager Skills Lacking.** Failure to direct, train, empower, leverage, support, and build the skills of middle managers and first line supervisors.

27. **Poor Communications of Direction.** Poor communications and lack of clarity/stump speech about directions; the single most pressing problem in many organizations.

28. **Cherished Values Violated.** Violation of cherished values without clear understanding of why, and what replaces it.

29. **Debrief and Learn.** Failure to conduct postmortems, debriefs and distillation of learnings from previous change efforts.

30. **Cultural Diversity.** Failure to understand local, global, cultural or ethnic diversity—thus taking wrong, insensitive actions.

31. **Lack of a Game Plan.** Failure to have an "Implementation Game Plan" for the process of change—not just the content/tasks of the Strategic Plan.

32. **Political Environment.** The presence of a political and politicized environment and multiple agendas that block real progress.

33. **Powerlessness.** Inability to have decisions and change made in a timely manner (paralysis/bottlenecking)

There are so many reasons change fails that it is not surprising only about 20-30% of change is really successful. **Which ones are likely to fall prey to?**

This has been so frustrating to us in our work as management consultants that we have built into our work **48 checks and balances as fail safe mechanisms** to dramatically improve this probability of success. While this attached list is not comprehensive, it is at least illustrative of all of the things that can be used to help change occur successfully.

Change Management Fail Safe Mechanisms

1. Plan-to-Plan/Executive Briefing and "Engineer Success" (First)—clarify our three goals of a Strategic Management System
2. Parallel Involvement Process throughout the planning and implementation process (key stakeholder involvement)
   — buy in; stay in
   — build critical mass for change, especially middle management
3. Three-Part Strategic Management System and Systems Thinking—*a new way to run your business*; the basics; an ongoing process
4. Vision—mission—core values statements in usable formats; "customer-focused"
5. Cultural/values audit and the creation of a *culture change action plan—* strategic change project
6. Core values and core strategies placed on your performance appraisal form
7. Board of Directors involvement/ownership of the strategic plan
8. Desire to use Key Success Measures for accountability; executive leadership and regular status/communications to all stakeholders
9. A crisp and clear single driving force/positioning and associated *rallying*

cry that is the essence of your vision

10. It is the CEO's personal task to institutionalize this positioning/values ("monomaniac")
11. Key Success Measures (KSM) coordinator/cadre and reporting system
12. Key Success Measures (KSM) Continuous Improvement Matrix fully filled out with targets and measurements
13. Benchmarking vs. highly successful organizations (*best practices research*)
14. Establishment of an Environmental Scanning System (ESS) with specific accountability and feedback mechanisms
15. SWOT—staff involvement in its development as a reality check
16. Paradigm changes to strategies (listed from Ü to) and a focused number of strategies
17. Strategic Sponsorship Teams (SST) set up for each core strategy with their own team development established.
18. Annual department planning format using strategies as *organizing framework* (the "Glue")
19. Use of SBU *Proforma Matrix* to develop clear financial accountability for business units
20. Three-year business planning for all SBUs to ensure clear competitive strategies
21. Three-year business planning for Major Support Units (Functional Departments) also (by strategies)—WIIFM (especially a strategic HRM Plan for people management)
22. SBU definition to lead organization design philosophy and efforts, focused on the businesses we are in…the customers we serve…and the employees we empower to do their best
23. Development of a Priority Maintenance System to handle interruptions/ new ideas and lack of focus on strategies, business, and product development
24. Large group annual/department planning review meeting (critique/sharing)
25. Strategic Change Project Teams on big, cross-functional strategies/priorities
26. Personal Leadership Plans (PLP)/commitments developed by the CEO and top three executives of the organization; "monomaniacs with a personal mission"
27. *War Room* with all the changes and time-tables on the wall
28. Contingency planning; *what if* scenarios on key probable events
29. Annual planning and priority setting first to drive the budgeting process (top three actions per each core strategy); looking at alternative ways to gain funds
30. One day offsite: Plan-to-Implement/Executive Briefing on *The Smart Start to Change Management*
31. *Leading Strategic Change: Enterprise-Wide* Workshop; Taught to all management personnel; in-depth understanding of change management
32. Install needed key structures for change management, including

       Strategic Change Leadership Team to guide:
— Strategic Planning implementation
— All change of any nature
The goal is *System's Alignment and Integrity*

33. Yearly Comprehensive Map on the next 12 months' processes/structures of change management
34. Internal and external coordinator/facilitator and cadre for the change process —to support senior management
35. Create a Critical Mass Action Plan to support the vision, with ongoing$_{TM}$ communications planned throughout–use the Rollercoaster of Change^{TM}
36. A rollout/communications strategy plan with reinforcement materials (PR/HR led)
37. *Organization as a system* framework; Enterprise-Wide Assessment and diagnosis and a way to ensure *System's Alignment, Attunement and Integrity* to the Strategic Plan
38. Individual goal setting by all exempt employees tied to the Strategic Plan…then a true Performance Management System used and modeled by top management as a way to manage individual performance
39. Conduct HR Strategic Planning (The People Edge)
40. A *rewards diagnosis and improvement plan* to ensure your rewards/ recognition support the strategic direction (both financial and non-financial)
41. Set up an Executive/Employee Development Board (EDB) to manage promotions, executive hiring and succession plan, as well as development and training…all to support the vision, Strategic Plan, and core values/culture
42. Creating customer value through Business Process Re-engineering (BPR) action plan—Strategic Change Project linked to the customer
43. Professional Management and Leadership Practices (Strategic Leadership Development System/Centering Your Leadership) action plan—Strategic Change Project
44. Monthly/quarterly follow-up meetings to the Change Leadership Team by all departments for all employees; focus on vision, key strategies and rewards/celebrations
45. Strategic Business and job redesign and restructuring action plan to be more customer-focused—Strategic Change Project (Vital Few)
46. Creating customer value thru total quality/service action plan—Strategic Change Project (Vital Few)
47. Annual Strategic Review (and Update) (similar to an independent financial audit and update of the Strategic Plan/next year's Annual Plan and priorities
48. A Program Management Office (PMO) to manage all this on a Day-to-Day basis

Which fail-safe mechanisms above do you need to ensure success? Circle them!

Given these two lists it is no wonder that change usually fails to succeed in the way that it is planned.

The False Trails of Fragmented Fads

"The one best way" promulgated by the different leading management authors and gurus has led to fad after fad after fad. No one best way can solve all ills. The life cycle of fads proceeds from:

1. Early adoption of new ideas that are quite good to...

2. High acceptance of these solid concepts. Unfortunately, as maturity and widespread dissemination of these new change approaches occur it leads to...

3. Misuse or lip service in many cases.

4. Then the criticism and decline of that particular approach begins to be seen as a fad. It is repudiated by the research and then...

5. We start all over again as we search for the next sequential fad.

Unfortunately, this tendency for any change approach to go through a life cycle of growth, maturity and decline is a standard way that any life cycle occurs. Thus, the key is to reverse the decline of a change approach through better feedback and renewal mechanisms that bring the approach back to its initial roots and solid concepts. However, this is rarely done and abandonment is more likely.

Change Model Fragmentation:

In our research at the Centre, we kept finding these fads touted as the **one best way**. Thus, our research resulted in thirteen popular overall organizational change models for my book [*The Systems Thinking Approach® to Strategic Planning and Management.*] In the change models, we found many similar problems.

For example:

1. Only four of the thirteen dealt with the customer which is the key in any change process.

2. Very few of them had a focus on outputs and goals as opposed to processes alone.

3. Many of them did not focus on the need for cross-functional teams.

4. Less than one-third saw a need for any kind of strategic thinking or planning as a guide for the change effort.

5. Less than half dealt with the organization's culture as a key variable.

6. Most of them did not even look at the question of the values and beliefs system.

In general, these change models were much more technical, operational, economic-focused, or mechanistic in nature as opposed to also dealing with the issue of **people's hearts and minds being in tune with desired changes**. Only one out of the thirteen had a good feedback system and only one out of thirteen also had a system and processes to manage change in a strategic fashion.

Is it any wonder that most change efforts fail?

The most incredible consequences of too many consultants with too many **one best way efforts** occurring simultaneously in an organization were the improvements to Lindbergh Field, San Diego, California's airport in early 1997. It was reported in the *San Diego Union Tribune* that the tab for improving Lindbergh Field ballooned over 100% higher than expected to 232 million dollars. Ironically, a consultants report largely blames poor management by the San Diego Unified Port District as the reason for this overrun. Among other things, the firm concluded:

- (1) The Port District did not properly supervise the **138 consultants** on the project, leaving no one in charge to resolve disputes among them.
- (2) District officials did not sufficiently manage how much was being spent on this expansion or whether the consultants were keeping up with the building schedule!
- (3) The consultants had overlapping and confusing responsibilities, etc., etc.

The port administrators did not dispute the accuracy of the report which noted the lack of an individual with clear overall accountability for the project. Incredible isn't it!

Since then, the California Legislature removed the airport from the San Diego Unified Port District. They created an Airport Authority to find and recommend a location for a new airport which would be presented to the voters for approval.

Strategic Planning Fragmentation

Our research and extensive experience in the area of strategic planning (part of Strategic Management) reveals that about half of all companies have no formal process for gathering and producing future environmental intelligence to help with their planning efforts. *Old traditional, tried and true SWOT exercises which look at only current opportunities and threats, at best, are seriously inadequate in today's fast paced, dynamic, global environment.*

Over half of all planning processes do not even monitor future regulatory political climates or global economic conditions despite the fact that we are now in a global marketplace and economy. Is it any wonder that over half of all strategic alliances and partnerships with other organizations ultimately fail?

The Centre's research also compared fourteen different and popular Strategic Planning Models. We saw the same fragmentation. Less than 25% of all planning models had any form of pre-planning and organizing efforts to make sure that the effort was organized and tailored to each unique situation. Many of them had no *Ideal Future Vision* as the place to start. Only two out of fourteen had some kind of a measurement system like Key Success Measures beyond financials to define and track success. Over half of the models did not even link the strategic plan to the annual plan and budgets and **none of them** dealt with helping to organize implementation and change game plans.

No wonder many plans never get implemented and fall prey to the SPOTS syndrome, ("Strategic Plan on Top Shelf")...gathering dust. In addition, none of the models had any form of key stakeholder involvement in order to ensure plan ownership and plan acceptance. Less than one-quarter of the models discussed the longer term issue of Annual Strategic Reviews and updating of the strategic plan to keep it fresh and current in today's changing environment. The result is people like the well respected planning guru Henry Mintzberg wrote *The Rise and Fall of Strategic Planning* and *The Strategy Safari* in which he saw 10 different strategic planning models, none of which worked.

This led us to also research the many common mistakes organizations make when they do strategic planning. **See the list of sixteen common mistakes** and determine for yourself which ones you fall prey to. Fragmentation and failure of planning efforts are really running amuck in today's world.

16 Common Mistakes in Strategic Planning
1. Failing to integrate planning at all levels.
2. Keeping planning separate from day-to-day management.
3. Conducting long-range forecasting only.
4. Having a scattershot approach to strategic planning.
5. Developing vision, mission, and value statements as fluff.
6. Having yearly weekend retreats only.
7. Failing to complete an effective implementation process.
8. Violating the "people support what they help create" premise.
9. Conducting business as usual after strategic planning (SPOTS Syndrome).
10. Failing to make the "tough choices."
11. Lacking a scoreboard; measuring what's easy; not what's important.
12. Failing to define Strategic Business Units or Major Program Areas in an accurate and meaningful way—or having Strategic Plans for them either.
13. Neglecting to benchmark yourself against the competition.
14. Seeing the planning document as an end in itself.
15. Having confusing terminology and language/bureaucratic "make work" processes.
16. Trying to facilitate the process yourself instead of using a professional business facilitator.

Finally, a major study by Inc. Magazine found that 97% of all managers thought their companies had clear written mission statements, while only 77% of the front line employees did. However, when asked, "are all employees held accountable for daily performance and linked back to the mission statement," only 20% of **both** management and front line employees said yes. Is it any wonder **we have a crisis of accountability in today's world.** We do not hold people accountable despite the beautiful, sophisticated, doctoral thesis-type Strategic Plans and Vision/Mission Statements that abound in today's world.

Fragmented Failure in Achieving Customer Value:
Research conducted by the Technical Assistance Research Programs, Inc. (TARP) has consistently shown for years that customer loyalty, and thus customer profits, are maximized by **identifying customer needs and**

expectations and determining how effectively an organization can satisfy those needs and expectations. This was consistently reinforced through the Profit Improvement of Market Strategies (PIMs) Database in Cambridge, MA. It showed how customer-orientation, product quality, and innovative customer solutions are the keys to building a competitive business advantage.

Despite the clarity of research, far too few companies achieve a customer-orientation at the top of the evolutionary scale. Rather, companies are often driven by (1) regulatory decisions, (2) operational efficiencies and excellence, (3) anything to make a profit or (4) product orientation. While none of these are bad in themselves, they are not customer-oriented. Creating customer value must result from a total organizational effort and focus on the customer and their needs, wants, and demands.

Data consistently is reported that shows how we talk a good game about the customer being the king, but in reality we don't achieve it. Many executives know that their performance is driven more by internal operating measures than any kind of external customer ones. The author's own experience in giving CEO presentations has seen about 80-90% of all CEO's reporting both that customer measurements are lacking and that compensation and incentives are not tied to any measure of customer satisfaction. There is still a significant gap between the knowledge and awareness of customer satisfaction versus the customer-orientation and lack of actions that executives don'take.

In the same way, the Gallup organization has shown over and over again that there is a huge gap in the view of quality and customer service by customers versus management self-reports. This perception gap seems to hold a consistent difference in view of between 30% and 50%; a huge and disheartening gap. The rosy projections by management are not matched by the perception of the customer who is buying your products and services.

Fragmented Reengineering and Quality Fads:

In the same vain, the fad of business process reengineering made popular by Michael Hammer and James Champy in their 1990's best selling book, *Reengineering the Corporation* did not work well either. In a since lost *Quality* Digest article read by me over 70% of all quality/reengineering projects were reported as led by the CFO rather than by somebody with a customer and sales orientation. Thus, despite some successes, the reengineering to improve business processes to support the customer have usually turned into massive and radical cost reduction programs that also destroy company capabilities, competencies, and their human assets

Common complaints in process improvement, reengineering, and quality efforts for years included lack of measurable results, no strategic focus, and too much of a cost cutting focus. Leading to the survival syndrome, and great sounding programs that did not connect to improving the business of serving the customer. Six Sigma, in the 21st Century is a similar **one-best way** having mixed results today. **The one best way doesn't work: never has and never will, when dealing with complex organizations.**

Fragmented Approaches to Success:

In a massive four country study by the American Quality Foundation and Ernst & Young in the 90's they found some remarkable results. Despite the many different **one-best-way** fads of management gurus, there were only three universal beneficial practices with a combined significant impact on bottom line performance. This positive impact was regardless of the starting financial position of the organizations studied in the US, Japan, Canada and Germany. They found that the only three practices that contributed positively to the bottom line were:

(1) Strategic Planning and the deployment and implementation of change in a systematic way.

(2) Business process improvement methods **when** they were tied to customer needs, wants and expectations, much as the TARP research showed.

(3) Continuous broadening and deepening of the range of management and leadership practices.

The last finding is quite important as we often say that **people are our most important asset**. I don't believe that is true. **The most important asset in an organization is its collective management staff.** *Only* when they increase and broaden their range and depth of their leadership and management practices do they *allow* all employees to become your most important asset. Allowing peoples natural talents, abilities and motivation to flow in a focused direction is what leadership should be all about.

However, the research shows again and again that this is not the case. First off, management's roles are changing from command and control, to hands-on managers who direct and control. Today, managers need to be leaders who build shared visions and values and provide coaching and developmental support. Managers are not getting the training and development that they need to pull this off. It is widely known that top level executives get the short end of the stick when it comes to training and development.

Thus, top executives who bring the most leverage to an organization's entire staff receive the least amount of training and development. The author's personal research consistently shows that only two to three of the 15 top executives in a organization have any formal training or academic courses on how to lead and manage planning and change directly and effectively; their **primary job** in today's complex, dynamic global marketplace.

The obvious conclusion is that the major threats to companies are often seen as inadequate managerial skills, and inadequate succession planning and talent management for key posts within an organization.

Fundamental Management Misconduct:

As a by-product of all this, some kinds of morale mistakes that managers make often include (1) criticizing in front of other, (2) being dishonest, and (3) taking credit for others work. These are the three biggest ways that managers damage employee morale according to most studies.

While executives believe mentoring is an important part of a senior executive's job, the research on coaching skills is dismal. Development Dimensions, International of Pittsburgh, PA found that most management of performance usually occurs as nothing more than a poorly done performance appraisal that happens once a year. They found that managers' feedback and coaching was middling at best. Managers scored average overall in a lack-luster evaluation by their employees. In fact, performance appraisals were seen as very ineffective. Everyone knows we should provide feedback and coaching help to our staff. However, most managers do not do this despite the huge growth and popularity of a new industry, the coaching industry.

In the same study, the American Quality Foundation and Ernst & Young study just referred to found that empowerment only improved the effectiveness in one out of three companies. Those that were already high performers had the preconditions for effective empowerment to thrive.

In the bottom one-third of companies, they found empowerment actually had a negative bottom line impact due to the lack of the three practices on the previous page.

Failures of Communications:

Behind all of this, is the fact that poor communications and lack of involvement by managers has created a huge communications gap in many organizations. Every change effort the author has been involved with as a consultant over the past 16 years included managers and supervisors and employees believing poor communication skills are a major management problem. Close behind is rigid and inflexible management behavior as well as the failure to develop subordinates. This lack of good communications is a dire and fundamental leverage for all other kinds of changes to actually take place. In fact, major surveys have shown that only one-third of most employees believe that companies even listen to them, or act on their suggestions. Instead, most employees find out what is going on in organizations through the *grapevine* or e-mail (one-way communications at best). Very few employees typically believe that management communicates effectively about what changes are occurring in an organization. While management might make a good will effort to communicate, over half of all employees feel that the efforts leave employees more confused because it was a poor communications experience. Ever think why the typical U.S. company gets few suggestions per employee per year? In Japan, Toyota often gets forty to fifty implementable ideas from each employee every year. Toyota's remarkable record of implementing suggestions and ideas is a huge contrast to the poor communications and involvement of U.S. employees today.

The old *Ladder of Communication Effectiveness* indicated most organizational communications methods are **one way** and rarely produce what is needed. Repetition, repetition, repetition, and multiple face to face communications methods are crucial. Yet they are not performed well by most managers. In case you think that Internet access has improved management communications; most organizations see it as a major threat to productivity today. Employee time is now often too focused on accessing the Internet for overwhelming e-mails along with cell phones and text messaging for non-business purposes. This gets in the way of effective communications and productivity. Employees look (and are) busy, just not always productive and on company business.

As a result of all this management ineffectiveness and lack of communications, many employees say that they will not go the extra mile for the organization. They don't feel it is worth giving that extra effort. Is it any wonder that one in four workers today see themselves as angry? Younger workers are much more likely to report feeling angry than workers over age 50. This may help to explain why we have seen shootings of postal service supervisors by terminated employees over the past 10 plus years.

Fragmented Management and Leadership Development Practices:

Finally, our research into management and executive development led us to look at twenty-seven different authors for the *best practices* in leadership and management development. The results from this were quite dismal.

We have identified **Six Natural Levels of Leadership Competencies** needed today from the research on Systems Thinking, the natural way the world works. Yet no one author or expert provides all of these in his/her framework except the Haines Centre for Strategic Management.

The Six Natural Levels of Leadership Competencies are:
1. Self-Mastery Competence
2. Interpersonal Competence
3. Intact Team Competence
4. Cross-Functional Competence
5. Organization-Wide Competence
6. Strategic Competence

Here are the results of our research above

- All authors and leading practitioners who dealt with helping managers enhanced their **self-mastery**.
- However, only half dealt with improving **interpersonal relationships**.
- Only six out of twenty-seven dealt with how to help managers facilitate and empower **teams**.
- Even worse was the lack of focus on assisting managers to collaborate and deal with conflicts **across functions** and across departments. Cross-functional teamwork is the key to improving processes in support of customer satisfaction. Only three out of twenty-seven authors dealt with this item in their leadership and management development.
- Half of them dealt with the strategic side of integrating **organizational** outcomes.
- However, only one-third dealt with how to help managers create **external strategic alliances** and partnerships; a key variable in success today.

Summary:

In summary, what we have found in our continuing research is that no leadership and management development authors, and their consulting and training firms, teach and assist using all six competencies listed above.

In fact, only three of those twenty-seven authors dealt with four of the competencies and only three of them dealt with even three of the competencies.

All of the others **focused mainly on one or two leadership competencies rather than the full-range and depth of leadership and management development that is needed** according to the landmark American Quality Foundation and Ernst & Young study.

Questions to Ponder…

- What management misconduct have you seen the most?
- Which fragmented approaches to change fads have you experienced?
- What should have been done differently in those change efforts?

The really sad commentary on this failure of fragmented **one-best-way** management fads is that the search for the holy grail of fads continues unabated. From The Learning Organization

- To Six Sigma
- To Strategic conversations
- To coaching and mentoring
- To Appreciative Inquiry

Yet we predict that it too will go through the fad cycle and frustrate many of us within the next three years.

We believe that these accumulating failures of one-best way organizational change can be traced to a fundamental but mistaken assumption that organizations and people are machines. We want our organizations and people to behave as living systems but we **only** know how to treat them as machines, robots and mechanical people. Needless to say, this mechanistic view and its resultant one-best-way solution creates fads and low probability of successful organizational change. Yet fundamental organizational change is required by almost every company in today's dynamic and wide changing global economy.

This chapter is not meant to be a doom and gloom one alone. The truth is that the human spirit always manages to survive in spite of overwhelming odds and all obstacles. The march of human progress is a powerful, long-standing trend over the past three hundred years in the U.S. A. Organizations and the world have innumerable and chronic problems, yet we humans have this amazing capacity to find solutions. **We believe this book is one of these solutions.**

Chapter 2

Failures of Fragmented Fads
Summary of Key Concepts

> If you are doing buiness now
> the same way you did five years ago,
> it is probably obsolete.
> —*Jack Welch*

1. World Trade is growing rapidly and we now have a global economy with enormous competition and consumer pressures.

2. Tremendous business opportunities are being created at the same time as massive dislocation of employees as we move from the Industrial to the Information Age.

3. The sad story of employee mismanagement has caused the rise in popularity of cartoonist Scott Adams and his **Dilbert** cartoons.

4. Corporate Welfare is one new enemy along with Corporate/Executive greed.

5. Despite all the so-called management gurus and numerous "one best way solutions," about 75% of most large scale changes fail to achieve their objectives.

6. The causes of this change failure are numerous; 31 in our research; including the piecemeal models themselves that are used for change.

7. The kinds of Fragmented Change efforts that often fail include:
    - Strategic Planning
    - Customer Value/Focus
    - Enterprise-Wide Change
    - Cultural Change

8. Some of these change efforts miss some common-sense needs such as:
    - Effective Communications
    - Executive and Leadership Development
    - Focus on the Customer

9. Sadly the next cure-all is usually viewed by many as another "one best way".

10. Many of the fads still function under the mistaken belief that organizations and people are machines; not living systems. The good news is that this real truth is becoming a *conscious* reality in some organizations today; with enormous positive implications.

CHAPTER 3

Looking Beyond the Information Age...
Rhetoric or reality?

Why are such drastic changes occurring?

Thus far, we've looked at many aspects of our organizational, global, political, and individual lives which seem to be changing before our very eyes. Among these changes, some have been good, some inevitable, and far too many not so good. **It's clear that change introduces some measure of chaos and uncertainty into every level and aspect of our modern organizations and society.** It's the Rubik's Cube effect in action with all its unintended consequences.

The 20th century certainly had its share of enormous and profound events. It brought us such milestones as World War I and II with the aftermath–long-term global growth outside the Eastern bloc, as well as the creation of a war-time atomic bomb, with its subsequent peace-time energy uses in power and healing. Some changes–such as inventing the computer, putting men on the moon, and the fall of the Berlin Wall–were not only profound; they were also exciting and hopeful.

Now in the 21st Century, a veritable explosion in technology over the past ten-plus years has brought our world closer together at every level [Friedman's *The World is Flat*]. Where technical information previously doubled every 5 years, it now seems to double every 12-18 months. Each new day we see significant change happening everywhere–technological breakthroughs in our work, our communications, and our lives–leading to breakthroughs even in our planetary awareness.

Much of today's current change is a result of technological advances of a positive nature in numerous scientific disciplines. The recognizable boundaries of state and nation are becoming increasingly blurred by Internet connectedness and communities. Now "Web 2.0" even has a life of its own (*The Economist,* May 13, 2006, page 80).

On every continent, countries are joining a single global economy with China and India (not just the European Union or U.S.A.) starting to lead the way.

Telecommunications around the globe and into space have become instantaneous through such continuously changing innovations as NAVSTAR, TIROS, and SKYNET satellites; SKYPE, VOIP and the like. Enormous advances in fiber-optic cable continue—now literally connecting every major continent on earth, through the Internet and satellites.

Technology is also responsible for new directions in world-wide business and industry. Internet–the world-wide web originally created so scientists could talk to each other instantaneously–has expanded dramatically to billions of users around the globe, and is increasing daily with no end in sight. Once called the Information Superhighway—it has taken on a life of its own. With the Internet, what we once viewed as a broad global marketplace it has shrunk down to the size of an individual laptop computer, "razor" cell phone, iPods, or Blackberry, many with the same complex audio, video, and connectivity features.

Innovations such as robotics, "mechatronics" - micro-processing capabilities built into manufactured products—sophisticated machine tools, automation, lasers, miniaturization and nanotechnology have completely re-created our working processes. "MPP"(Massive Parallel Processing) and mass customization have fundamentally changed the production and services side of the business and E-Commercial communities.

In addition, the marriage of computers with biotechnology has created an avalanche of progress within the genetics/biotech industry. The decoding and exploration of human genes are having such profound impact in worldwide industry and commerce that veteran venture capitalists have compared it to the Oklahoma land rush of the last century. Genetics engineering is already commonplace in areas such as seeds, food production, and animal husbandry.

Obviously, our work lives, and every aspect of our personal lives are profoundly affected on a daily basis—with more and more electronic innovations. It's also changing the ways in which we work–witness today's burgeoning cottage industry (see Free Agent Nation by Daniel Pink).

Substantial gains in the development of advanced materials such as advanced ceramics components—the stronger-than-steel and lighter-than-aluminum materials used to house computer processors, computer disk drives, and many more uses currently only guessed at—promise even more changes in our computer hardware. Advanced materials find their uses in a wider and wider variety of applications from golf clubs to going into space.

Questions to Ponder…

- What other positive technological changes do you see?
- What is causing such incredible change?
- What do you think is coming next?

Technology is changing our organizations and home lives in obvious ways. Mutually-enhancing, interactive cable, direct broadcast satellite, and mobile and Internet phone systems have brought us new viewing, learning, and communicating capabilities. Called multi-media or the 'infotainment' industry, it is actually a confluence of a number of formerly separate industries. Where we once had to leave home to work, shop or bank, we now have home shopping and banking networks; where we once took our cars to rent movie videos, we have video-on-demand, TIVO, and the like available through our cable and phone lines. Intra and Internets allow us to work wherever we want; not just at the office. Mobility and wireless WiFi are now king.

Technology is having a beneficial impact on individual human health. People are living longer due to enormous improvements in prevention and in the treatment of illness, surgical technologies, general lifestyle and wellness, fitness advances. Many diseases which used to cut people's life spans in half have been obliterated.

What's causing these multi-dimensional changes, both positive and negative in this book? Is it terrorism? Is it China and India? Is it technology alone? Is it the decline and fall of western society as we know?

Or is it that what we're experiencing is actually a completely new age requiring a new approach to life and work?

Let's get into our helicopter for a better view.

A Common View of the Earth's Ages

To better answer these questions; let's study, for a moment, the history of our various ages. For the purpose of clarity, let's first examine the definition of an "Age":

Definition of an "Age":
That which is defined by our concept and singular shared view of the nature of reality.
—*Webster's Dictionary*

With the dawning of the era, which, in our shared view, we called the **Agricultural Age**, we replaced hunting and gathering (the **Hunting and Gathering Age**) with planting, harvesting, and livestock breeding. Where our cycles were once tuned to animal migration, we now looked toward seasonal growth cycles.

The **Industrial—or Machine—Age** came when we developed the skills to create mechanical tools, then standardized and produced them on a massive scale. Farming and food supplies grew immensely, but the need for a corresponding growth in farmers did not. Productivity skyrocketed and factories, rather than farms, became the order of the day. People moved to towns and cities to work in manufacturing, further breaking our ties to the land. The Industrial Age had arrived.

Today, however, our manufacturing job base has *decreased* and much of it has moved to China. We have experienced a shift to a knowledge-based society—a society in which, for most people, knowledge replaces capital and labor as the determinant for success. As it did in the Agricultural Age, productivity has also skyrocketed in manufacturing.

In the 1990's Canadian futurist, Cliff McIntosh, stated it this way to me:

"[Many] management and supervision [jobs] are made redundant by infomated technologies. Dumb machines are replaced by intelligent equipment. Factory and office space are replaced by cyberspace. Cash is replaced by electronic blips.

But, governance and most corporate structures stay locked in a blend of the agricultural and industrial eras."

Searching for our 'new age' or 'right answer'

Accompanying McIntosh's summation have been numerous and varied contemplations by leading theorists on our status today and in the future. As most everyone knows by now, acclaimed futurists Alvin and Heidi Toffler claimed that "we are living through the birth pangs of a new civilization whose institutions are not yet in place."* Authors of the book, *The Third Wave*, the Toffler's see the changes in our society as three historic waves. The First Wave occurred when agriculture began spreading across the globe, as many as 8-10,000 years ago. The Second Wave came in the middle of the seventeenth century, and was created by mechanical innovations, and established a strong, long-lived urban-industrial economy. The Third Wave emerged in the U.S. in the mid-fifties, when white-collar and service workers first began to outnumber blue-collar workers in the industrial world.

* *'Getting Set for the Coming Millennium,' Alvin* & Heidi Toffler, *The Futurist*, March-April, 1995

The Tofflers' view of the Third Wave has now been eclipsed with today's common view of us in the **Information Age** (a Fourth Wave). Since this Information Age is our reality today, is it responsible for such a severely negative decline in so many areas of our society for the past 10 years? And is it responsible for our management failures—and the failure of companies to change? It seems unlikely that the Information Age could be the cause behind *all* this negative change in our global, organizational, political, socio-economic, and personal lives.

Well, then...what about the rapidly expanding telecommunications advances mentioned, that promise to advance as yet unheard-of new technologies well into the next three or four decades; i.e., well beyond the Internet, digital broadcast satellites, fiber optics, cellular phones, etc.? Does that mean we're really in a new **Telecommunications Age**...and that *it is* actually the root cause of all our societal changes?

And, if that's true...what about the Genetics Age we're supposedly in next? After all, way back in its May 28, 1990, issue, *Business Week* officially proclaimed that the **Genetics Age** had begun. Is that the cause for our problems? And, if it is true, will the Genetics Age cause even more negative change as a by-product that will impact us for decades to come?

There may be other reasons for all the change, turmoil, complexity and chaos we are experiencing today. One answer might be found in the astounding diversity and mass migration around the world...more than ever before. It's estimated that an unprecedented 100+ million people world-wide currently live outside their homelands, usually for economic betterment. Could this movement and diversity be what is causing all this disruption and chaos?

In any case, what we're currently facing in this Information Age is a situation in which we have a tremendous negative decline in many aspects of American society and in organizational and managerial effectiveness. Yet at the same time, we have unprecedented technological advances and new successful start ups as major corporations...witness Google, e-Bay, Amazon, Microsoft, My Space, etc. We simultaneously have old societal and organizational questions and issues which are still unresolved and festering, along with many new technological advances and issues. Yet, at best, we only have singular and simplistic answers. We don't even know really what key questions we should be asking—and we certainly have no real map of the terrain to help us find our way out of the chaotic maze of change, despair, and decline.

How can we resolve this dilemma? We can no longer stick our heads in the sand and try to ignore it as an inevitable part of the Information Age. Do we just accept that, as in other past civilizations, there will be an insurmountable decline in our societal and organizational life cycles? Do we simply continue to adapt until we become boiled alive, like the unfortunate frog in the chemistry lab?

How can we know what path to choose–both individually and collectively— in order to create a positive, long-term future for ourselves and our organizations? What does our ideal vision of the future even look like? Can we even share a common vision—or are we just stuck with continuing confusion, accompanied by a negative decline in hope for renewal, and a long-term war on terrorism just like the Cold War?

Most importantly, how do we know what methods to use that will actually make our work, our lives, our organizations, and our society better?

We've gone as far as we can

The fact is each of these singular fads and answers are 'right' in some ways. Yes, we are in the Information Age, yet each answer, when taken individually, is a bit simplistic and one-sided. None of them are comprehensive enough to explain or help us understand such an extensive range of change that is impacting every level of modern life.

None of these labels, such as the "Information Age," the "Telecommunications Age," the "Genetic Age," nor any of these other concepts—such as diversity, the media, etc.—gives us a means to understand the full magnitude and implications of the change occurring all around us. Nor do they offer any real insight on how we can weather such change and go on to create a healthy, positive future.

One thing is certain, even when we do know the right questions to ask, it doesn't guarantee that we'll find the right answers. Most of the practical answers we need and long-term solutions to the rampant changes we face today are not forthcoming from the media, scientists, politicians, corporate management consultants gurus or any other distinct, visible leadership in our society. If there were, we'd have already implemented them.

It's becoming more and more obvious that **wanting quick answers and quick fixes** and getting them to work are two very different things.

For real answers that can guide us through this maze of change and tough, intractable problems, we must instead look at the world in an honest, reality-based manner. As Russ Ackoff so accurately points out in his book *The Second Industrial Revolution*:

"...since World War II, we have entered into a period which will be to the future what the Renaissance was to the past. We have moved into a new age that is fundamentally different from the age from which we have come–an age that began with the Renaissance and ended essentially with World War II, but like other ages it doesn't end on a date, they fade away...

...*[and] we are attempting to deal with problems generated by a new age with techniques and tools that we inherit from an old one.*"

This is an important point about the "inherited tools" that bears further examination. If we look at the Industrial Age, for instance, we recognize that the prevailing standard was economy of scale—greater volume, lesser costs. It applied to physical structures and organizations across the board. To get a safe, reliable car, steel was added. To get more work production, more people were brought in. Governments became increasingly complex, with greater and greater staffing numbers, until progress became strangled by the vast amounts of red tape and bureaucracy.

In this manner, we analyzed issues, breaking them down into their component parts, then problem-solved them. We got so good at this across the globe that we engineered and built a thoroughly industrialized and man-made world on top of our planet. We converted and black-topped natural lands until the natural, physical nature of the world became invisible. We also created–both inside and outside our organizations–numerous disciplines and specialists in every aspect of our lives, from health care, to law, engineering, education, social services, finance, information systems, and more.

Despite all the great monuments to the industrialization, technologies, and creation of modern organizations and society—as well as domination over our natural environment—*something is wrong!* Why else are we experiencing such alarming, long-term statistics in such fundamental problems as terrorism, greed, crime, illegitimacy, dependency, drug addiction, lack of civility, and illiteracy not to mention survivor syndrome, Dilbert examples, stressed-out workers, etc.– 'Moral Statistics,' as the Victorian English dubbed them.*

'Queen Victoria was right,' March 13, 1995, *USA Today*

No matter where we look these days, it's clear that the Industrial Age thinking we've employed in the past has taken us as far as it can. Yes, we've created the planet's most industrialized society. It has long lost its "most civilized" title, however, and its current state of fragmentation and failure is indicative of deeper, more fundamental problems. Breaking down whole concepts, systems, and even disciplines into their smallest parts and then dealing with each part separately has taken us where it can–but it can go no further. To continue in our leadership in this way and view of the world will only guarantee further fragmentation...a vicious cycle if ever we've seen one.

Despite all our Technological and Information Age advances so far, the undesirable outcome is that we're still looking at only parts or fragments of the whole picture. Our lenses and filters are too restricted, while the perspective we need is so much broader; the solutions we need don't yet even exist in our "radar scope". Too frequently we continue to be tied to the ongoing Industrial Age mentality and thinking, perpetuating the error of applying simplistic *'cause-and-effect'* and *'one right answer'* thinking from a prior age to the age in which we presently exist—whatever you may want to call it.

Questions to Ponder...

- Do you agree we have gone as far as we can in our current societal direction? Why? Why not?
- Why do we have the two opposing curves occurring at the same time in the chart? What is wrong with this picture?
- What characteristics are changing in our world today that might indicate our " Information Age" is still changing?

Why analytic thinking no longer works

"From an early age, we're taught to break apart problems in order to make complex tasks and subjects easier to deal with.
But this creates a bigger problem...we lose the ability to see the consequences of our actions, and we lose a sense of connection to a larger whole."
-Peter Senge, The Fifth Discipline

Make no mistake, breaking away from our outdated and tired linear analytic, and mechanistic thinking won't be easy; it's been an integral part of our modern society for a long time. In fact, we rarely differentiate analytic thinking from other thinking; we tend to see them as one and the same.

Some believe that our problems today stem from the Agricultural Age, when humans found ways to dominate nature and make it subservient to our immediate needs. The Industrial Revolution furthered that, as it was a 'revolution' which took over and conquered Mother Nature...or so we though, others disagree.

Russell Ackoff , the senior-most renaissance guru of Systems Thinking believes that these old techniques and tools came about as the Agricultural Age came to a close, and the Machine/Industrial Age came into being. He felt that the three fundamental ideas shown below evolved during the Machine Age. He further argued that these must now change, if we truly want to move forward, with a unified front, into a new age.

Machine/Industrial Age Fundamental Ideas

1) Reductionism

Reductionism followed the premise that if you take anything and start to take it apart—or reduce it to its lowest common denominator—you will ultimately reach indivisible elements; for instance, in reductionism, the cell would be the ultimate component of life.

2) Analysis

A powerful mode of thinking, analysis takes the entity/issue/problem apart, breaking it up into its components. It is at this point in analysis where you would solve the problem, then aggregate the solutions into an explanation as a whole. **Analysis tends to explain things by the behavior of their parts–*not* the whole!**

Even today, analysis is probably the most common technique used in corporations. Managers 'cut their problems down to size'–reducing them into a set of solvable problems/components–and then assembling them into a solution as a whole. It is still *so* much the norm that many continue to equate 'analyzing' as synonymous with 'thinking,' as I mentioned earlier.

3) Linear and Sequential Mechanization

Mechanization seeks to explain virtually every phenomenon by resorting to a single relationship–**cause and effect**. Mechanization has a key consequence, however–when we find the cause, we don't need anything else, **so the environment is irrelevant**. Indeed, the whole effort of scientific study is about only two relationships that can be studied in isolation and in laboratories.

Thus, the Machine/Industrial Age was how we perceived the world as a whole, i.e., assembly lines, mass production, man-made machines, school classrooms, and a mechanistic (versus organic) world/earth, as well. We have evolved from mechanical machines for mass production to **thinking of the whole world as a man-made machine**; not as 'Mother Nature,' with a will and mind of her own.

While the analytic, reductionist, and linear, sequential mechanistic approaches may *appear* to resolve ongoing problems, they usually fail to provide long-term, permanent solutions. Perhaps the most crucial thing to remember about analytic thinking is that its central, linear approach is to problem-solve one issue at a time...and only *then* move on to the next issue in the hierarchy.

Simple linear analytic thinking is about cause-and-effect—one cause for every one effec, it is the common 'either-or' question. Its weakest link–and the reason it's not working in today's world—is that it doesn't take into consideration the environment, other organizations, other systems, and the circular multiple/delayed causality that surrounds each cause and effect. Nor does it often consider its interrelationships and interdependencies with other parts and externalities until later.

Analytical thinking run amuck

In case you're not convinced our current approach is on its last legs, consider the following dramatically visible examples of how mechanistic thinking simply isn't working to our benefit anymore:

1) IRS rules and regulations—over 5,000 pages that continue to cost American taxpayers hundreds of billion dollars each year in compliance activities—not to mention "corporate welfare" costing another hundreds of billion dollars (if not trillions) in tax breaks every year.

2) Educational code in California—over 7,000 pages that often restrict school districts from innovative or creative, holistic ideas for learning.

3) The U.S. Naval Academy rules & regulations— over 1,000 pages...as compared to 10 pages when it opened 160 years ago. Both rule books cover the same topic areas, but where one assumes readers are mature and possess common sense, today's 1,000 pages spell out each and every probability.

4) Health care—thousands of small, specialized entities and programs, often based on categorical grants created for singular, simplistic problems and solutions.

5) Social services—similar to today's health care situation, U.S. social services is famous for dealing with simplistic cause/effect symptoms, versus the root causes.

6) Thousands of virtually unaccountable, specialized government districts—water districts, assessment districts, school districts, etc., etc., etc.

7) Separate, autonomous city, county, state, and federal government levels—endless divisions within endless levels, with little or no common governing techniques or coordination. Why, for example, are taxes collected at the federal level and merely passed down all the way to cities with categorical strings attached? This generates more bureaucracies, all without any **direct** purpose of serving citizens.

8) Federal intelligence agencies—we have sixteen (yes, that's right...*16*!) agencies of the federal government concerned with intelligence. They sound like alphabet soup, too–CIA, NSA, DIA, NIS, NSC, etc. and yet they did not prevent 9/11! Now, in response, we created a 17th and super agency (Homeland Security), too!

9) Congressional subcommittee—every time a new issue comes along it seems Congress establishes a new subcommittee. There are now too many committees and subcommittees to enumerate; attempts to eliminate some are usually met with restrictions as each Congressional member buttresses their own fiefdom. Bills going through Congress face review by many, many subcommittees; this creates delays and serves as a detriment to good government, which, unfortunately, becomes the lowest common denominator. Yet over 15,000 special favor "earmarks" worth hundreds of billions for special Congressional deals were in the FY 2006 Budget (and never reviewed—just automatically approved).

10) Union work rules and job descriptions—which creates hundreds and hundreds of job titles, pay ranges and micro-specialization creating the jokes on "How many 'X' does it take to change a light bulb."

11) Layer after layer of management in organizations—banking being the worst. How many layers of vice presidents (and third assistant vice presidents) are there?

12) One-best way management fads—those that we have already mentioned as the one-best way to the holy grail—they have included Six Sigma, TQM, Customer Service, Courageous Conversations, Mentoring, Coaching, The Learning Organization—on and on they go.

13) Red tape—and if you're still not convinced, get the Heritage Foundation study, called *Red Tape America*. It cites literally hundreds of regulatory horror stories and anecdotes that graphically illustrate the unwanted, even destructive, results of red tape federal regulations.

Gradually, people and organizations of all types *are* attempting to move beyond looking for the one simplistic cause-and-effect or one right answer to our diverse and complex set of problems. We are starting to become more sophisticated and apply multiple solutions to patterns of events or issues.

In particular, the organizational world has begun to recognize that correcting one isolated problem at a time doesn't work...perhaps it never did. We are moving beyond solving isolated events, to trying to resolve the pattern of events mentioned in these early chapters.

This is the primary reason behind the plethora of fads and business application methods that have sprung up in the past decade—they are all well-intentioned attempts to deal effectively with multiple, complex, and interrelated problems. We're at least beginning to search for integrated solutions that work—hence, the constant presence of these popular new business terms such as collaboration, cooperation, integration, alliances, partnerships, cross-functional teams, teamwork, and the like.

> "If you always do what you've always done,
> you won't always get what you've always gotten...
> because the world has changed!"
> —*Stephen Haines*

So, what we are facing now in our uncivilized society, moral statistics, and failures in management and organizational change isn't very pretty. Some of our approaches have met with a measure of success, many with none at all. Many have even made things worse, such as some of our management techniques (see Dilbert) over the past thirty years. None, however, are taking us where we need to go as modern organizations and as a society in today's global 21st Century.

Thus, the common-sense next step is to look elsewhere, or deeper, or to a higher helicopter level, or in radically different ways, seeking successful experiments, common elements, concepts, and leadership frameworks that we can apply more broadly to our many diverse and complex issues.

A global paradigm shift

To step back and make sense of what's going on today, we must in effect play the same role the astronauts played starting in the '60's and '70's—introducing us to a fragile Earth floating in a vast universe, forcing us to see our planet in ways we'd never dreamed of.

We, too, must now begin to pull ourselves above all this tumultuous change and chaos, and shape our own version of the astronauts' 164-mile perspective on the world in which we exist. It is clearly to our own advantage to reshape how we think. Probably the worst thing we could do at this point would be to *avoid* thinking about our world in different ways. In his book, *Liberation Management*, Tom Peters puts it this way:

"Perplexed is what we should be. The times are perplexing, confusing; not to be perplexed and confused is dangerous."

Bostonian Jim Ansara, CEO of Shawmut Design & Construction, agreed. "These days growing my company feels like what happens when you play one of my kid's video games. You work like crazy to get to the next level, only to have the game become infinitely more complicated as a result," he says.

To make sense out of the chaos, we must first get a clearer, more holistic view of *all* the changes and shifts that are occurring, rather than blindly analyzing and attacking one crisis at a time...one after another. As the old saying goes, we must begin to see the forest, not just the trees. When we look at our world in this more broad way, it becomes even easier to see that what we've been doing no longer works. We've used up all our energies—and all our resources—in putting out brush fires which occur in more and more circular and destructive patterns.

Like it or not, we're in the middle of what must become a global paradigm shift. In our current state of fragmentation and mechanistic, Machine/Industrial Age thinking, we are beginning to recognize the boundaries and limitations we have placed on ourselves. Our maps, tools, techniques, and solutions are bankrupt–we may as well admit it. We still are not seeing, however, a shift to something else that *does* work, a more holistic frame of reference; a new paradigm.

Paradigms are a set of rules and regulations that establish boundaries and tells us how to behave appropriately within those boundaries. If that paradigm has changed—*whether or not we recognize it*—its boundaries and rules (and our corresponding behaviors within those boundaries) no longer apply.

Paradigm is an over-used term but it is still a useful term. Paradigms show us what's important–as well as what's not—and they help us focus our attention. The danger, what Barker termed the 'paradigm effect,' comes when our existing paradigms ignore new data or facts that don't agree with it. The paradigm effect also blinds us to effective, even necessary strategies for future success; they are outside our radar scope and field of vision. We are not up in our helicopter.

No Final Answers—Just Paradigm Changes:

There are no final answers, just solutions that work for today and in today's situation **and every solution has within it the seeds of its own destruction**. That's because every solution creates new issues/problems; hopefully of a higher order. Anticipate the problems and decide they are the ones you want to deal with. Then, be flexible and adapt to continual changes in the environment.

For Example—Some examples of paradigm shifts include:

- Environmental importance
- Swiss watches/quartz
- Hybrid cars
- Solar/ethanol
- PCs and Blackberry
- Xerox
- E-mail/Blogs
- Videos/DVDs
- Microwave
- Electronic shopping
- Mass customization/ robotics

- Global Village
- Flexible work hours/ electronic cottages
- Fiber Optics—WiFi
- NAFTA/ MERCUSAR
- Hong Kong 1997
- Cellular/airfones/ satellites
- Nanotechnology
- CDs to iPods to iPhones
- Bio-manufacturing
- Sickness/Wellness

- 24 hour work day
- Tubes— transistors—chips— nanos
- Transportation: walk, boats, animals, train, cars, bus, mass transit, airplane
- Flight: balloon, Wright Brothers, bi-planes, single wing propeller planes, jet planes, Concorde, satellites/rockets, space shuttle, space industrialization

One of the best ways we all know to make this paradigm shift clear is an exercise called 'The Nine Dots.' In our exercise you are aske to connect all nine dots with a single line.

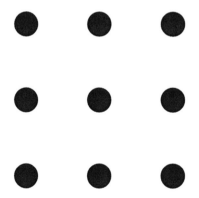

Figure 3-1: Nine Dots Puzzle

While it is old, this is an excellent example of the limits and boundaries most of us place on our own abilities to imagine beyond that which we already know. Once you've been shown the answer—which is that there is no rule or boundary that says you can't go outside of the dots to complete the puzzle—it seems ridiculously obvious. All of us are so good at conforming to everyday rules and boundaries (i.e., paradigms), though, that it's almost impossible for us to *see* this—much less figure out how to ***get outside the nine dots or get outside the box***.

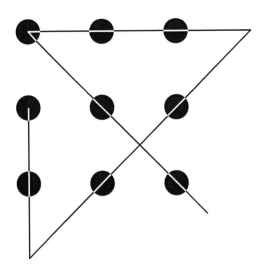

Figure 3-2: Nine Dots Solution

Further Outside the Box for the 21ˢᵗ Century

If you can solve this puzzle with four straight lines, try it with **three straight** lines, still connected end to end. And further still "outside the box", solve it with **only one straight line** (over 10 ways if you are creative). See the author for the answers if you don't know them—they are easy if you get *outside the box*.

Where is our *"out of the nine dots"* thinking as applied to our humanness?

Look at the current explosion in technology we're experiencing. We've seen, accepted, and integrated the technological systems advances that are such an inherent part of the Information Age. Yet we resist consciously applying the concepts and systems thinking process behind it. My basic premise is that we are rapidly moving from the Information Age towards the **Systems Age**, we just don't yet "see it."

We often hear the phrase "high tech/high touch," which presumed that as technology began its high-velocity advances it would be accompanied by similar growth, and change on the human side. But here we are, right in the middle of enormous, "high tech" growth, yet the "high touch" concept is not fulfilled.

Summary: Identifying the changes in all our systems

People are still searching for meaning and for solutions to our organizational and societal problems in today's world, yet we too often continue to resist getting outside the dots–i.e., our current rules and boundaries–to find the solutions that work. As the graph below illustrates, we have traveled from the Agricultural Age, through the Industrial Age, and on into the Information Age. At the end of each age, we have had to make the difficult paradigm shifts; stopping and letting go of old obsolete rules and boundaries and taking on new unproven methods on faith alone.

> *Insanity*
> *is doing the same things in the same way*
> *and*
> *expecting different results*
> *—Attributed to various sources including this Author*

Today, we see the explosion of information availability caused by technological advances, hence the common view of the "Information Age." While I agree with this view, I think we must look deeper at what is really happening; we must go beyond the mere accessibility of information. The irony is that, while our technological systems–computer networking, satellites, Internet, telecommunications—grow more powerful and provide more information (even to the extent of an information overload for many of us), our *human* systems— i.e., our society and its moral statistics—grow weaker and weaker. It is insanity to me for this to go on and one like boiled frogs.

Yet, as leaders, we seem to be hanging onto the old fragmented, reductionist, and simple cause-and-effect Machine and Industrial Age thinking, rather than shifting to a more holistic view of thinking as our frame of reference and orientation to life in a new Systems Age. We are still, as Russ Ackoff reminds us, **"attempting to deal with problems generated by a new [systems] age with techniques and tools that we inherit from an old [mechanistic] one."**

Now isn't this just insanity?

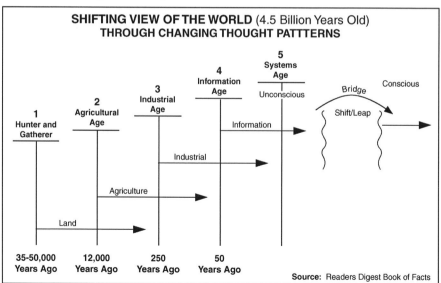

Figure 3-3: Shifting View of the World

Whether or not we are fully aware of it, we are now unconsciously moving quickly into the Systems Age. To become fully aware, however, we will first need to make a complete mental leap and shift of faith from our previously unconscious and casual use of the buzzword 'systems' into conscious and disciplined 'Systems Thinking.'

I have used this "insanity" quote for years, as I kept seeing organization after organization, and leader after leader, follow this same disruptive path. They continued their resistance to shifting their view from old paradigms to new ones. While it's instructive to think back to others who have tried to remain entrenched in old thinking, leaders of all types today have got to learn and apply the lessons of the past to improve our human condition in the present. To wit:

"Everything that can be invented has been invented."
—Charles H. Duell, Director of U.S. Patent Office, 1899

"There is no likelihood that man can ever tap the power of the atom."
—Robert Millikan, Nobel Prize winner, Physics, 1923

"I think there is a world market for about five computers."
—Thomas Watson, CEO, IBM, 1943

Questions to Ponder...

- Where else have you seen analytical thinking run amuck?
- What paradigm shifts of any kind do you see occurring now in our society?
- Does all of this add up to a "shifting view of the world?" Why? Why not?

It's a basic truth of human nature that we resist new thinking...and we resist change...just as you may be resisting this Systems Age concept right now. The anecdote below, borrowed from an *Executive Speechwriter* newsletter, shows that this resistance to new things goes as far back as Aristotle's time:

"For centuries, people believed that Aristotle was right when he said that the heavier an object, the faster it would fall to earth. Aristotle was regarded as the greatest thinker of all times...surely he could not be wrong. All it would have taken was for one brave person to take two objects, one heavy...one light, and drop them from a great height to see whether or not the heavier object landed first.

No one stepped forward until nearly 2000 years after Aristotle's death, In 1589, Galileo summoned learned professors to the base of the leaning Tower of Pisa. Then he went to the top and pushed off a ten-pound and a one-pound weight. Both landed at the same time. But the power of belief in the conventional wisdom was so strong that the professors denied what they had seen...they continued to say Aristotle was right."

This failed and fragmented approach to success is another clear example of how isolating and treating each element alone (even in a package deal) can upset a whole system or society. As Ludwig Von Bertalanffy, a 1920's biologist who helped create the field of General Systems Theory put it:

*"In one way or another, we are forced to deal with complexities, with 'wholes'
or 'systems' in **all** fields of knowledge.*
This implies a basic reorientation in scientific thinking."

I believe that—though there may not be a clearly-marked yellow brick road
for us to follow out of Oz—there *are* strong, sure ways that we can apply toward
building that road. WE just have to be willing to suspend our disbelief and
resistance, **"get outside the nine dots," and shift the way we look at our world
to a systems view for the coming Systems Age.** In the appendix, the author has
identified over 25 scientific disciplines that are doing just that!

As French author Marcel Proust put it one hundred years ago:

> "Our real voyage of discovery consists not in seeking new land-
> scape but in having new eyes."

So...if you are willing to "have new eyes" and see today's reality for what
it really is—however tentative I and others are—I invite you to travel with me
as I explore how the Systems Age is rapidly becoming the successor to the
Information Age.

For Systems Thinking is a way to get up to the astronaut's 164 miles above
earth, or at least at a helicopter level viewing it in a more holistic way and find
Strategic and Systems Thinking: *The Winning Formula.*

Chapter 3
Looking Beyond the Information Age
Summary of Key Concepts

- Our world has experienced a number of truly profound changes—invention of the computer, putting men on the moon, the fall of the Berlin Wall, the dot.com bubble.

- Technological advances now seem to double technological information every 12–18 months, causing dramatic changes in the way we work, communicate, and operate our lives.

- After many, many years, the Uruguay round of GATT talks were successfully closed. So have global telephone rate tariffs been dramatically reduced.

- China has become the manufacturing center of the world.

- Common markets are proliferating around the globe as countries are privatizing, slashing tariffs, and opening their doors to foreign investment.

- Every continent and most countries are becoming part of our global economy.

- India and China are rapidly growing, challenging North America as economic heavyweights in the 21st Century.

- Innovations such as NAVSTAR, TIROS, and SKYNET satellites, as well as advances in fiber-optic cable, now connect literally every major continent on earth instantaneously.

- The Internet has expanded to more than a billion users around the globe.

- The marriage of computers with biotechnology has created an avalanche of progress within the genetics/biotech industry.

- Human gene-mapping capabilities have spurred a tremendous worldwide industry and commerce comparable to the Okalahoma land rush.

- Advanced technology is positively affecting not only where we work, but what we do and how we do it with such innovations as Blackberries, WiFi, complex cell phones, text messaging, e-mail, and iPods.

- Our home lives have also been positively changed by new opportunities provided by the Internet, interactive cable, direct broadcast satellite, and WiFi phone systems which bring new viewing, learning, and communicating capabilities.

- Technology has improved both prevention and treatment of illness, eliminating many diseases which used to cut people's life spans in half.

- Our massive changes introduce chaos, complexity, and uncertainty into every level and aspect of modern organizations and societies around the globe.

- So, how does all this positive technological change square with the chronic societal and organizational issues of this book? What is going on?

- The author believes we have gone as far as we can in our current way of solving problems in our social/human systems. A new higher helicopter view is needed.

- Analytic thinking no longer works—reductionism and mechanistic views of the world are countered by our view of each of us on earth as interdependent living systems. Analytic thinking has run amuck over and over again in all aspects of our lives.

- The author believes we are moving quickly into our nest "Age"; from hunting and gathering, to agricultural, to industrial, to information, and now to some new Age.

- This global paradigm shift is to a new "Systems Age"— and is occurring in over 25 scientific disciplines the author has identified so far.

- Fortunately. The old/new field of General Systems Theory (from biology) has already given us a conceptual start with its definitions, characteristics, and meanings—which is Part II, next.

What's Wrong With This Picture?

We have a tremendous negative decline in most aspects of American Societal trends and employee alienation during a time when we are benefiting from unprecedented technological advances.

How we think…

Is how we Plan…

Is how we act…

And that

Determines the results we get in life and work

PART TWO

Systems Thinking for 21st Century Success

"The empires of the future are the empires of the mind."

—*Winston Churchill*

SIMPLICITY AND COMPLEXITY

"I wouldn't give a fig for the simplicity this side of complexity.

But,

I'd give my life for the simplicity on the far side of complexity."

—Justice Oliver Wendell Holmes

SIMPLICITY AND GENIUS

"Any idiot can simplify by ignoring the complications.

But,

It takes real genius to simplify by including the complications."

—John E. Johnson, TEC Chairman
(The Executive Committee)

Part Two Introduction

Strategic and Systems Thinking: The Winning Formula

We cannot deny that there is chaos and complexity all around us in today's globally, interdependent world. It is here and it isn't going away. There is a thin line of order around it all that enables us to function effectively in our jobs and in our lives. To understand this thin edge of order in our lives, just reflect on how much catastrophic effects we have had on people's lives in the past decade due to natural causes such as tsunamis, hurricanes, earthquakes, fires, swollen rivers, mud slides...or thought man-made disasters such as power outages, terrorism, wars, stock market tumbles, crime, cancer, organizational fraud and greed, management incompetence, savings and loans scandals, Watergate and old the other "_____gate" political scandals.

So how does one come close to this simplicity that doesn't ignore complexity? To answer this, contrast simplicity and simple.

We see simple as this mechanistic age view of (1) one-best way, (2) direct environmental free cause-effect, (3) singular change efforts, (4) independent solutions, and (5) knee-jerk almost naive solutions such as training or better communications alone.

We see simplicity as embodying three criteria:

1) It must provide us with a **better view** of the complex solution, i.e. a more holistic and complete helicopter view such as the astronauts had 164 miles above earth.

2) It must provide us with a **model or framework** to see all the complexity and its Rubik's Cube web of interrelationships and some how **make sense of it**. In other words, see the whole as primary and the parts as secondary— but see and understand it all...and be able to use it for decision-making in a practical way.

3) It must provide **ease of remembrance** if it is to be used daily in practical ways. The **"Rule of Three"** is key here as people are generally able to remember three items easily. However, when the list gets to four items, our memories seem to fall off dramatically.

Interesting, only Systems Thinking meets all three of these criteria.

First, of all **Systems Thinking** views the world as one globally interdependent system and all the levels of systems within it in holistic terms, i.e., the basic premise of Systems Thinking is "the whole is primary and the parts are secondary. Looking first at the whole and its purposes in its environment gives us a better view.

System (sis'tem) n.: A set of components that work together for the overall objectives of the whole.

Secondly, the basic concepts of Systems Thinking deal with this web of relationships and their interdependence versus looking at each part separately and alone. Since living systems are the basic and natural unit of life on earth, these concepts are natural and normal to us. They make common sense; even if we don't use them, giving rise to the phrase "uncommon, common sense."

Thirdly, the rule of three is generally how life operates. It is why four-leaf clovers are so unique and good luck. Three-leaf clovers are the norm. So is our air—land—water, sun—moon—stars, ABC's, and on and on.

Holism is embodied by the use of the use of three's:

Topics	A	B	C
1. Person (and Teams)	Body	Mind	Spirit
2. Change Management (all human interactions)	Structure	Content	Process
3. Learning	Skills	Knowledge	Attitudes

A Lack of Systems Thinking:
- The focus in education and industry is often Column B (Mind—Content—Knowledge).
- Column A is often taken for granted or a given (Body—Structure—Skills).
- Column C is often seen as "not appropriate" to discuss or get into at all… thus ignored (Spirit—Process—Attitudes).

The Reality of System is that all are important!

Any of columns A—B—C that are missing or poorly aligned with the total system will cause problems in learning, change, and teams or people.

A Work in Progress:

However, don't take our word for how Systems Thinking fits this "Simplicity" view, read on in the rest of this book. While this book is a **work in progress** and we will always struggle to explain clearly what's in our hearts and minds on this new paradigm, we have felt sufficiently clear that Systems Thinking provides this in order to write this book.

CHAPTER 4

Systems...the basic unit of life

Seeking out the Systems Age

> *"Problems that are created by our current level of thinking can't be solved by that same level of thinking."—Albert Einstein*

There are concrete ways for us as leaders to create a map that will personally guide us toward a successful future. To create that map, however, it's clear that we will need to rise above today's traditionally accepted linear, mechanistic thinking. We must, in Einstein's terms, go to a higher level of thinking than analytic thinking. Rather than deal with isolated sets of problems as the issue, we must learn to look at and deal with *whole systems—in their environments*—removing ourselves from analytic thinking in which the parts, rather than the system, are primary.

Already, as organizations and as a society we are applying such 'Systems Thinking' to assist our technological advances as we work with our information systems and their networks. Think about it—so much of our current technological advances are based on:

1) **The system as the basic unit of operation**—i.e., our personal computer system or our cell phones.
2) **The system being very powerful**—i.e., the latest Intel chip and its predecessors/successors
3) **The system networking and communicating**—i.e., after all, their real effectiveness comes when they're working together, i.e., Internet, the infotainment industry, etc.

However, we have not yet learned how to begin applying the same Systems Thinking concepts we are using in our technology to our human society and our organizations. Despite the Information Age, human and societal systems are not progressing well–primarily because we do not see what is standing before us—i.e., systems and systems dynamics of all types.

> *"Everything is simple you see—but you just have to see it"*

Systems are the most fundamental unit or building block of both our natural and technological environments. We just need to learn to see them and work with them. While it may be only human to miss this point, we can ill afford to continue in this fragmented vein if we want to move forward in a positive direction. For even knowledge and information—the basic tenets of the Information Age—are useless without the attitude and skills to use that knowledge and be leaders in improving ourselves, our teams, our organizations, and our society.

In his 1972 article, *The Systems Age: The Second Industrial Revolution*, Russ Ackoff concurred with the biologist, Ludwig Von Bertalanffy, that systems are the new/old and natural/organic organizing concept of science, and said, *"It is for this reason that I am going to refer to the new period as the Systems Age."*

The bad news for Russ Ackoff was that he was 30 years ahead of his time. As the Author views him as a personal mentor, the good news is he made a strong comeback in the 21st Century.

In his article, *System Dynamics as an Artifact for a Systems Age*, Peter Senge agrees with Ackoff, portraying our world as moving towards a 'systems age,' an era in which we see ourselves as integral to the overall, holistic web of life.

Until we raise our level of awareness and see the ongoing, holistic living systems in which we live, work, and exist, we won't be able to make the mental paradigm shift that will enable us to fully integrate into the Systems Age. As Drucker said, "we need to shift our assumptions"...**and shift them to a systems view as a new orientation to our whole lives**.

Developing a Systems Thinking mindset

This shift to systems thinking involves us moving away from seeing single or isolated elements, structures, functions, and events to seeing the processes by which they interrelate to one another. We begin to recognize that what is key to systems thinking are the *patterns* which develop from what we previously may have looked at as a series of isolated events. **It is this process of diagnosis and discovery** that will ultimately give us a practical guide toward **finding systems solutions to our systems problems**. As leaders, we really don't deal with problems today; **we deal with messes of problems which require more holistic or systems solutions**.

As we discussed earlier, our archaic, linear approach to solving our problems has not prepared us to consciously recognize the systems that form the basic unit of our lives. In *Models of Man*, author Herbert Simon states that:

"The capacity of the human mind for formulating and solving complex problems is very small compared with the complexity of the systems we seek to understand.
...we can create...complex and realistic maps of our systems, but our intuition is then insufficient to provide guidance into their dynamics or help us find high-leverage policies."

Though systems can be complex, this does not by any means restrict our abilities for Systems Thinking—we simply need to develop those few concepts on the far side of complexity and develop our abilities to use this simplicity. To do so, we must consciously recognize that *everything we do has affected and does affect everything else we have done or will do*. The following is a great example of how every event, no matter how seemingly small, affects everything else in the chain of events:

EVERYTHING EVERYWHERE NOW TRULY AFFECTS EVERYTHING ELSE
by Ian Mitroff

March 4, 1984 ESM (small Florida securities dealer) collapsed.
↓
Home State Savings Bank, Cincinnati (small savings and loan) closed its door (1/2 of loan portfolio in ESM securities).
↓
Run on savings and loans in Ohio - taken over by the Bank Board
↓
Jitters on deficit-ridden financial system and market.
↓
March 18-20, 1994   U.S. dollar fell 6% against British Pound (one of the biggest drops ever recorded).
↓
British oil assets measured/traded in U.S. dollars.
↓
British oil assets took a severe beating.

A more recent example is how a prominent builder in San Diego (one of the my clients) could not get the raw building materials he needed to build the new development he had planned. It seems that the great "sucking sound" taking away his needed raw materials was coming from China and India's vociferous growth appetite.

Even on a subconscious level, the tired, outdated mental models on which we shape our daily lives can hold us back or propel us forward as leaders. These mental models, or concepts—call them what you like—are our way of understanding (or misunderstanding) the world in which we live. Other words used to describe this mindset are 'world view' or 'Weltanschauung' (German for "view of the world")—or paradigms, as discussed in the last chapter and as popularized by Joel Barker. Since these are the prevailing beliefs on which we base all activity, putting ourselves in touch with them and holding them up to the light is crucial. **Our mindsets need to change folks!**

Knowing the biases that make up our mental models will be the key to our present and future successes. As detailed here, our paradigm shift to Systems Thinking is a shift away from seeing *elements, structures, functions, and separate events* (analytical thinking) to seeing *processes and their interrelated patterns* (relational thinking). From there, we must graduate toward developing *mental models around these patterns* (partial Systems Thinking), and, finally—through a process of diagnosis and discovery—developing a fully integrated, *holistic, Systems Thinking model and approach* as our prevailing belief and mindset.

As we begin to shift toward seeing the interrelationships that connect all our living systems, we will soon begin to see just how broad the practical applications from the field of Systems Thinking already are. In recent years there has been an avalanche of reengineering and restructuring methods that we've attempted to apply, not only to our organizations, but in virtually every aspect of our lives. There have been attempts—we'll get to them later—at integrating solutions on multiple systems levels, such as collaborating, cooperation, cross-functional teamwork, partnering, alliances, and more.

In analyzing these many and varied trends, a couple of distinct patterns appear. **The first thing we see is that change itself**—with all its inherent complexity and chaos—**is constant**. This chaos could be attributed to our aborted attempts to solve the problems of our current complex and interdependent systems with an Industrial Age mentality and tools that have become obsolete over time. On the other hand, chaos and turmoil are a natural part of any systemic change—it certainly isn't surprising when one considers the enormous, multi-level amount of disruptive change happening today in all our societal systems.

The second pattern that emerges is that most of our systems are indeed changing in relationship to each other...most of them simultaneously. We've looked at the speed with which our global, governmental, socio-economic, political, and community systems are changing. We've also looked at how our technological systems are growing and changing—which in turn affects every other system in our lives.

Looking at how one system's change affects every other system also introduces a level of complexity to our evaluation. In *Complexity: The Emerging Science at the Edge of Order & Chaos*, M. Mitchell Waldrop offers some insight into this:

> *"Why did the stock market crash more than 500 points in a single Monday in 1987? Why do ancient species remain stable for thousands of years, then suddenly disappear? In a world where nice guys finish last, why do humans value trust and cooperation? At first glance, these questions don't appear to have anything in common...but in fact, every one of these statements refers to a complex system."*

Waldrop observes that "these complex, self-organizing systems are adaptive, in that they don't just passively respond to events the way a rock might roll around in an earthquake...instead, all these complex systems...have the potential to bring order and chaos into a special kind of balance."

Waldrop, together with many other leading-edge authors, approaches to dealing with systemic change, all touch on something key. Change, with its inherent complexity and chaos, is not something to be feared or avoided. Rather, we need to see it as a natural and constant element in the life of all living systems.

> *"Change is the law of life. And those who look only to the past or present are certain to miss the future."*
> —John F. Kennedy

When one life element changes, it simultaneously changes and affects many other elements, and on and on, in a circular pattern. Why? Because life itself is made up of complex and interdependent systems. Just think of any ecosystem—such as a low-land marsh, for instance—and the many types of biological and living systems that are dependent on it.

Think of any major change you want to make in an organization, how many other parts of the organization are affected as well? That is whey we coined the *Rubik's Cube* Effect of all the *unintended consequences* we face. We face them because we do not *"understand the consequences"*.

Much as it is not possible to change one element of any marsh or technological system, without having an affect on that entire system, it is equally impossible for one system to change without affecting other systems. We all live on one planet that has a fragile ozone layer preserving life as we know it (the edge of "chaos"). The fact is, whether we believe it or not, at this and every other level of life, we exist as part of many interdependent systems.

For us as human beings, our growth and maturity over our life cycle proceeds from:

1)   Childhood dependency, to...
      ↓

2)   Teen-age independence, to...ultimately...
      ↓

3)   If we do mature (in some instances, a big 'if'!) interdependence

Unfortunately, it is only at this *inter*dependent stage that we begin to understand and appreciate the interdependency of life and its systems in organizations and on earth.

With this in mind, we as leaders can serve ourselves far better by treating our sets of societal and organizational problems as systems problems, and seek answers that will integrate systematically within each key interdependent system. As implied earlier, we're not off-base with this belief—even now, collaborative, team, and systems-oriented efforts are becoming more and more common in our organizations and communities today.

Systems Thinking is natural for dealing with our current realities, because it accommodates multiple goals as well as multiple causes. This is a primary reason that Systems Thinking works...after all, in reality, can you think of *anything* that has only one goal or desired outcome? Usually, it's just the opposite— we commonly have layers of goals within goals—and expectations within expectations.

Systems Thinking is about thinking "synergistically," wherein 2+2 = 5. What this points out is that, in analytic/reductionist thinking, we're **'micro smart'**–that is, good at thinking through individual projects and elements—but **'macro dumb'** about not considering and planning for the whole portfolio (2+2=3).

Systems...the natural order of the universe

"Systems Thinking helps you see patterns in the world and spot the leverage points that, acted upon, lead to lasting beneficial changes."
—Steve Haines

As we've said repeatedly, *we are already beginning the Systems Age...we're just not yet fully aware of it.* To emphasize this, let's take another look at all the issues and sets of problems and challenges covered in the first few chapters. Whatever we looked at—whether it was global fragmentation or fragmentation within governments, organizations, communities, teams, families, societies or individuals—the problem is that 'the system' is broken and ineffective. A closer look at organizations saw frequent failures of organizational and all the numerous management fads within it.

Most of the technological changes and advances we noted are advances in the use of mechanical and electronic systems (particularly the latter), or in improvements of systems linking and working with other systems (telecommunications, satellites, Internet, etc.). The common thread is that they all fall within the definition of systems.

As we begin to see more clearly and consciously that systems make up our world, it becomes important to explore the basic structure and elements of systems. As you can see here, there are several different *types* of systems:

- *Mechanical/electrical systems*— i.e., cars, clocks, assembly lines
- *Human (living) systems (including social & organizational)*— i.e., individuals, teams, families, organizations, communities, nations
- *Electronic/telecommunications systems*— i.e., personal computers, local area networks (LANS), wide area networks (WANS), supercomputers, Internet
- *Ecological systems*— i.e., the 21 eco-regions of North America, the Continents, Earth
- *Biological systems*—i.e., birds, fish, animals, insects, plants

In addition to these basic, fundamental types of systems, there are many other kinds of man-made systems, as well as innumerable combinations of the five types above. Also, there are *open* and *closed* systems.

A **closed system** is one that is isolated from its environment—such as an experimental, sterile chemistry lab.

An **open system** is one that accepts inputs from the environment around it, and acts on those various inputs to create new outputs into the environment.

Closed systems are the exception; every living system in which humans operate is an open system—some, more so than others.

Questions to Ponder

- What other kinds of systems can you think of?
- Do you believe that living systems are the natural order of life on earth? Why or why not?
- Can you think of any truly "closed" systems on earth?

In looking at our world with a Systems Thinking perspective, it's helpful to use the agricultural world as a familiar analogy. Farmers recognize, for instance, that the living systems in which they work have natural cycles of cause and effect within the natural environment. They make the connection between the cow's milk and the grass it eats, as well as the manure that fertilizes that grass and their fields. They connect the sun, rain, and temperature as the key environment context for their farm.

There are other natural and universal laws that can help steer us toward this systems perspective.

- There is the life cycle—birth, growth, maturity, decline, death–of all living things.
- There is the twelve-month calendar year–along with the 365-plus days, four seasons, and 24-hour days that it consists of.
- There are both the male and female roles in procreation.
- Everywhere we look, we can see living, breathing examples of systems in our world.

We may not necessarily know *why* these natural cycles work, but through the mechanisms of our life within them, we absolutely know that they *do* work. We also know that—just like farmers—when we ignore them, we experience the consequences.

Natural laws (or principles) are unchanging and consistent on our planet. The natural law of gravity, for instance, exists on this planet. Should we attempt to build a plane without regard for gravitational law, the plane will neither get up in the air nor stay there—regardless of how many other things we do correctly.

In recognizing the infinite presence of natural laws (or principles) in our lives, we see the roots of Systems Thinking. It's about looking around our physical and natural environment, and acknowledging that there are constant principles that will always be there, unchanging. In Systems Thinking, once we've identified these principles, we learn to work *with* them–much like working with the natural laws of the universe. *Systems thinking is not about trying to change, defeat, or coerce the natural laws and patterns that exist in our world. It's about working in accord with them so that we may achieve our desired outcomes.*

In order to survive, we human beings need the physical, social, mental, and spiritual systems that stimulate and nourish us. We need the very environment within which we exist, which contains all *its* own systems (land, water, air, wind, fire, sun, moon)—well, you get the picture.

Even our physical bodies display a wide range of systems within systems. Take, for example, our **organs as systems**:

- The brain and spinal cord make up our *nervous system*
- Our hearts, arteries, lungs, and trachea make up the *cardio respiratory system*
- The mouth, stomach, liver, gall bladder, pancreas, and intestines make up the *digestive system*
- Abdomen, pelvis, genitals, prostate, uterus, vagina, and ovaries make up the *reproductive system*

- Head, neck, back, abdomen, limbs, gluteus maximus make up the *muscular and nervous system*
- Skull, ribs, vertebrae, pelvis, and limbs make up the *skeletal system*

Carrying this even further— from the whole to the microscopic— makes it easy to understand the systems-within-systems and subsystems concept. Each of the 100 trillion cells that make up our bodies contains a nucleus (except for the red blood cells), and each nucleus contains:

- *46 chromosomes*—humans have 23 pair, one each from our mother and father
- *DNA*—the blueprint for producing the proteins and chemicals essential for life
- *Genes*—the piece of DNA that contains the instructions for making proteins

When you think about the complexity of these systems and subsystems—as well as the innumerable ways in which they must interconnect in order to complete their functions—it boggles the mind. The way to remember it all easier is through General Systems Theory and our three Systems Thinking concepts (and a fourth one on changing systems) coming up soon in this book.

Systems in general...General Systems Theory

To better understand systems as the natural order of our planet we must look at the nature of the global system itself.

As mentioned earlier, in the 1920's, Ludwig von Bertalanffy and other biologists proposed research into the idea of a general theory of systems that would embrace *all* levels of science, from the study of a single cell to the study of society and the planet as a whole. They were seeking generalizations in order to create a recognizable standard of scientific principles that could then be applied to virtually any body of work. Out of this proposal came years of rigorous scientific research and a new field/theory called the 'General Systems Theory.'

In 1970, Geoffrey Vickers in his book, *A Classification of Systems,* put it more in layman's terms:

"The words 'general systems theory' imply that some things can usefully be said about systems in general, despite the immense diversity of their specific forms. One of these things should be a scheme of classification.
Every science begins by classifying its subject matter, if only descriptively, and learns a lot about it in the process...systems especially need this attention, because an adequate classification cuts across familiar boundaries and at the same time draws valid and important distinctions which have previously been sensed but not defined.

In short, the task of General Systems Theory is to find the most general conceptual framework in which a scientific theory or a technological problem can be placed without losing the essential features of the theory or the problem."

In Chapter 5, we will review this General Systems Theory and the four concepts that make up its architecture or framework.

The Systems Thinking Approach®

In Summary:
- We are governed by the natural laws of life and living as open/living systems on earth
  —so—
- A successful participant must learn the rules
- Analytical thinking is old Industrial Revolution Thinking.

Chapter 4
Systems...the basic unit of life
Summary of Key Concepts

1. Simplicity comes from:

    *   a better, more holistic view of the situation

    *   a mental model or framework to make sense of it

    *   an ease of remembrance (rule of three)

    Only Systems Thinking meets all three of these criteria—hence the book title.

2. Systems are defined as "a set of components that work together for the overall objective of the whole".

3. The system is the basic unit of life.

4. This shift of thinking is from seeing events to seeing relationships and trends. We do not deal with problems but with "messes of problems".

5. Knowing our biases that make up our mental models is the key to future success.

6. To understand these **inter**dependencies, we need to personally mature from dependence to independence to the maturity of interdependence.

7. Systems are either more open or more closed—depending on how much it interacts with and gets feedback from its environment.

8. Living systems are based on the natural laws (or principles) that are unchanging and consistent on our planet. Success will come in the future by working in accord with these natural laws.

9. General Systems Thinking is based on the scientific research and work of biologists from the 1920's through the 1970's. Ludwig von Bertalanffy was their most visible leader. So, Systems Thinking is actually the Science of Systems Thinking, *the natural way the world works*!

CHAPTER 5

The Science of Systems Thinking
The architecture and organizing framework for 21st Century thinking

Overview

In accepting the General Systems Theory definition that a system is a set of components that work together for the overall objective of the whole, we begin to see the 'whole systems architecture' at work in our world and in our lives. If we truly want to be leaders and have power over our future, we must view Systems Thinking as our most basic foundation and organizing framework for success and growth in the 21st century.

To successfully integrate Systems Thinking as a foundation for success and growth, we need to begin to understand what I call the architecture of systems–their structure, characteristics, dynamics, and logic. Indeed, there is a great deal of natural logic and dynamics basic to systems, which is probably the primary reason we're hearing the term so much more regularly today–and not solely in the context of business.

The SCANS report (Secretary of Labor's Commission on Achieving Necessary Skills) outlined five learning factors that are considered crucial to the future job performance of today's students. You guessed it, 'systems' figured prominently in the report's wording. As shown here, it's one of the five SCAN competencies:

"Systems: Understanding social, organizational, and technological systems, monitoring performance, and designing and improving systems."

Whatever problem we look at within our socio-economic system—in the welfare, health care, and tax reforms struggling within our governmental systems—in the rapid decline of our moral statistics in our community/family systems—or the failure of organizations and managers to change— it is clear that none of our systems exist in a vacuum; they all impact each other in an infinite number of ways.

In order to completely assimilate the Science of Systems Thinking and systems solutions into our daily lives in a holistic manner, it is imperative that we fully understand and internalize what a system is, as well as its architecture and dynamics. This chapter will cover the four main Systems Thinking concepts from this science—it is a science about living systems vs. the natural way the world works!

Systems Thinking Concept #1   *Seven Levels of Living Systems*

We now know there are many different *types* of systems, as well as more *open* than more *closed* systems. We also understand that we must factor in not only the system we are examining, but also the *components* of that system—including how those components (or subsystems) *interrelate* to each other and with the system's *environment*, as well.

In addition to these considerations, we need also to be aware of the **Seven Levels Of Living Systems**. In his classic book, *Living Systems*, James G. Miller contributed this key concept on systems levels that is so key in and between our organizations and people today.

The **Seven Levels Of Living Systems** include:

1. Cells—the basic unit of life
2. Organs—the organic systems within our bodies
3. Organism—single organisms such as humans, animals, fish, birds
4. Group—teams, departments, racial/gender groups, families, etc.
5. Organizations—firm, community, city, private, public, not-for-profit
6. Societies—states, provinces, countries, nations, regions within countries
7. Supranational Systems—global, continents, regions, Earth, galaxies

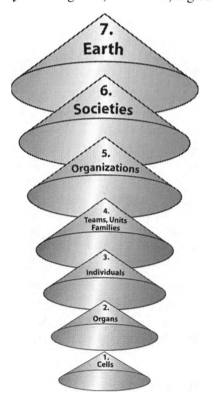

Figure 5-1: The Seven Levels of Living Systems

These levels of systems clearly illustrate how every system impacts upon every other system in this hierarchy. These levels demonstrate the hierarchy of 'systems within systems.' We really start seeing the characteristics of systems when looking at the **Seven Levels Of Living Systems**—for if the definition of a single system is 'a set of components that work together for the overall objective of the whole'—then that is surely carried through to *groups* of systems interacting together to ideally achieve the objective of the larger system in which they all co-exist.

In this way, when we look at any of our human organizations—social, political, commercial—as *levels* of systems within other systems, we further cement the systems concept. Once we begin thinking in terms of systems connected to systems, it becomes easier to see how problems are connected to *other* problems—and it forces us to look at solving those problems in a new light. (Usually, in fact, the solution to a systems problem is found in the next highest system—a helicopter concept Einstein knew when he used his famous quote earlier about problems not being solved at the same level [of systems] that created them.) We will discuss this in detail in the next chapter.

Systems Thinking Concept #2   *Twelve Standard Systems Characteristics and Dynamics*

This section will cover the Twelve Characteristics inherent in every living system (as researched by the members of the General Systems Theory Society.*) It will also present some principles of Systems Thinking derived from these Twelve Characteristics.

* Adapted from *Academy of Management Journal*, December, 1972

Twelve characteristics of living systems

The following twelve characteristics and their dynamics are always present in living systems. They have been adapted, with my own comments, from the *Academy of Management Journal*. For ease of retention, I have characterized them in three conceptual groups:

    I)   The whole system
    II)   Internal workings
    III)   The long-term consequences

However, keep in mind that it is the *interactions, relationships* and *fit* of all these *parts* and *characteristics* into one *whole system* that is key... rather than each characteristic alone.

I. The Whole System

Characteristic #1.   *Holism, Synergism, Organicism, and Gestalt*

The first and perhaps most obvious characteristic of systems is that the whole is not just the sum of the parts—the system itself can be explained only as a totality. In Systems Thinking, holism is the opposite of elementarism, which views the total as the sum of its individual parts.

For example, as human beings, we write letters, but our hands cannot write alone as separate parts; they can only do so as part of our overall human system. This is the basic definition of a system—a holistic unit that forms 'the natural way of life.'

Example:

Many executives believe a corporate strategic plan is just a 'roll-up' of lower level plans. This is an excellent example of elementarism that usually results in poor implementation and lots of turf battles/'silos' being perpetuated—with no holistic strategic plan to serve as an overall framework in which they can work and cooperate. Remember in Systems Thinking, *the whole system is primary and the parts are secondary.*

Characteristic #2.   Open System View

In Systems Thinking, we look at systems in one of two ways: (1) a closed system or (2) an open system. As implied earlier, one of the best examples of a closed system is that of an experimental lab, in which the entire environment around the experiment is strictly controlled. Open systems, on the other hand, are noted by an ongoing exchange of information, energy, or material with their environment. Most of the systems that we humans deal with are considered open systems.

Biological and social systems are inherently open living systems; mechanical systems may be open or closed. The concepts of open and closed systems are difficult to defend in the absolute. We prefer to think of open-closed as a dimension; that is, systems are relatively open or relatively closed.

For example, as human beings we survive by adapting to our physical environment through the necessary processes of food, clothing, and shelter. This is a good example of natural law at work—a basic, unalterable fact of life (and Maslow's first level in his hierarchy of needs).

The three keys to success for a system are 1) its ability to be interactive, 2) to fit, and 3) be connected with its environment. A crucial task in systems is the scanning of—and adapting to—it in some form.

Example:

Excellent organizations are known for their intense desire for being open to the feedback process, and constantly searching for other information they can receive from their environment in order to thrive and be number #1.

Characteristic #3.   Input—Transformation—Output Model

The open system can be viewed as a transformation model. In a dynamic, processing relationship with its environment. An open system will always receive various environmental inputs, transform these inputs in some way, and then export the outputs back into the environment. *This is THE Systems Thinking model and our Core Systems Technology. It is THE framework and/structure to internalize for each of us who wants to be more successful in the 21st Century.*

Example:

In order to survive over the long-term, we as human beings must take inputs, i.e., eat, drink water, breathe, sun, and sleep, and then transform these into the vital nutrients we need to be active and accomplish tasks in our own world.

Example:

Though many prominent authors think they already understand the input/output systems model, they often fail to remember the transformation step of Characteristic #4—the feedback loop—thus failing to fully understand how the transformation occurs. The feedback loop makes the system model a complete, holistic, and circular framework, with infinite practical applications.

Characteristic #4.   Feedback

The concept of feedback is important in understanding how systems both maintain a steady state and can improve if desired. Information concerning the outputs or the process of the system is fed back as new inputs into the system, perhaps leading to changes in the transformation process leading to improved future outputs.

Feedback can be both positive and negative, although the related field of cybernetics is based on negative feedback. *Negative feedback* is information and input which indicates that the system is deviating from a prescribed course and should readjust.

Feedback is a key issue to stimulate learning and change, and is essential to hear and understand, even (and, in many instances, *especially*) the bad news we don't like to hear. For this reason, we have devoted the last chapter in this book to "Feedback: The Breakfast of Champions."

Example:

When you boil all the rhetoric about 'learning organizations' down to its essence, what the term really implies is about gathering as much feedback as possible...even negative feedback...and acting on it to create new learning. Only through feedback can organizations hope to learn and grow at all systems levels–individual, team, organization, and in alliances/partnerships. World class, Olympic and professional athletes seek daily feedback on their performance. Why don't organizations have this same intense zeal for feedback?

Characteristic #5.   System Boundaries

All systems have boundaries which separate them from their environments. The concept of boundaries helps us understand the distinction between open and closed systems. The relatively closed system has rigid, impenetrable boundaries; whereas the open system has permeable boundaries between itself and the broader environment.

Boundaries are relatively easily defined in physical and biological systems, but are very difficult to delineate in social systems, such as organizations. For example, this may be why U.S. society provides so much protection for individual rights, and less so for 'the common good' of a community.

In organizations, the boundaries are relatively open with their environment, making it somewhat vague in terms of knowing and fully understanding its boundaries. In society today, with world-wide, instantaneous communications, our global environment has become more and more open (*Flat* to Friedman).

Example:

A key to shifting from analytic to Systems Thinking is to be able to mentally recognize the system and its boundaries. Only then can you work with and hope to change the system.

Many governmental organizations are very unclear where their boundaries end, and where the boundaries of the individual citizen begins. This is part of how our current 'big government' got started, ultimately making us more and more dependent on it, while simultaneously robbing us of our vitality, spirit, and self-initiative that created the U.S.

Environmental scanning is key to long term organizational success and growth. For example, what did Toyota know about the environment that GM didn't know or care about that led to Toyota becoming a leader in Hybrid Cars?

Characteristic #6.   Multiple Goal-Seeking

Biological and social systems generally have multiple goals or purposes. Social organizations also seek multiple goals, if for no other reason than that they are composed of individuals and subunits with different values and objectives. Today's multi-cultural and diverse society is making it more and more difficult for us to resolve the differing goals we bring with us.

Since multiple goal-seeking is a characteristic of all systems, it follows that a shared, common goals and vision for any organization or society is crucial to coordinated and focused actions by its members. Clarity begins with clear desired outcomes. Failure to answer and get agreement on this characteristic first is what creates chaos and complexity instead of clarity. This is where clarity and simplicity start.

Example:

When organizational leaders fail to anticipate or plan for multiple goal-seeking, the clash of individual versus organizational goals causes much conflict and lost productivity for all concerned, ultimately creating a lose-lose situation. Thus, the dehumanization, delayering, and mechanization of work have resulted in alienating many of today's workers.

II. The Internal Workings

Characteristic #7.   Equifinality of Open Systems

In mechanistic or closed systems there is a **direct** cause and effect relationship between the initial conditions and the final state. Biological and social systems operate differently. Equifinality suggests that certain final results may be achieved with equal and different initial conditions and in different ways.

As an example, how many different kinds of educational institutions are there from which one can get a college degree?

This view suggests that social organizations can accomplish their objectives with diverse inputs and with varying internal activities (conversation processes). For this reason, there is usually not one 'best' way to solve most problems. It is also the origin behind the old cliché, 'there are many ways in which to skin a cat!'

Example:

The lack of one best way to solve today's problems in organizations and in society in general is why *'strategic consistency'* to commonly agreed-upon, multiple goals (see Systems Thinking Characteristic #6) yet *'operational flexibility'*—or empowerment—to achieve them is so crucial. It encourages us all to challenge our minds and use our mental skills to determine *how* to achieve goals, as long as those goals are clear and agreed upon—in other words, a shared vision. **Clarity and Simplicity!**

Characteristic #8.   Hierarchy

A basic concept in Systems Thinking is that of hierarchical relationships between and within systems. A system is composed of subsystems of a lower order and is also part of a suprasystem of a higher order. Thus, there is a hierarchy of the components of any living system in our world. In today's politically correct environment, the concept of hierarchy is not popular, but it is a permanent fact of life in any living system.

As an example of this, look at the concept of nature's food chain—it is an inescapable hierarchy. The question we must always ask ourselves is how each element will fit into the holistic system so that it can assist in accomplishing its multiple goals.

Example:

Since systems are hierarchical, the organizational system is higher than the department/unit/team as a system, which is higher than individual employee as a system (whether we like it or not). If we don't like the hierarchy or fit, we need to either work to change how the hierarchy works or lessen it —but it can't be eliminated, as some would naively propose— *it's simply a fact of life within systems.*

For instance in today's flat world, the individual consumer, or blogger has tremendous interaction and communications due to the Internet, among other tools. Hierarchical leaders of all types seem often to have missed this fundamental change.

Characteristic #9.   Subsystems or Components

The whole idea of a system is to optimize—*not* maximize—the fit of its elements/parts in order to *maximize the whole*. If we merely maximize the elements of systems, we actually sub-optimize the whole (i.e., 2 + 2 = 3). For example, the two best basketball teams in the National Basketball Association

(NBA) in 2005—2006 were the San Antonio Spurs and Detroit Pistons. They embody the *team* concept of $2 + 2 = 5$. The Los Angeles Lakers lost it a few years before when Kobe Bryant and Shaq O'Neill, two of the very best players did not get along.

Example:

In organizations it is often the norm for individual departments to attempt to maximize their budgets and influence in the organization, ultimately to the detriment of other departments and, ultimately, the organization as a whole. *Balancing the demands of each department is difficult and should be a key role of senior organizational leaders.* Unfortunately, this leads to conflict resolution issues that many leaders in both private and public institutions would rather ignore.

Characteristic #10.   Entropy (disorder)

Closed physical systems are subject to the force of entropy or disorder, which increases until eventually the entire system fails. The tendency toward maximum entropy is a movement to disorder, complete lack of resource transformation, and death. For example, people with the anorexia disorder fail to eat sufficiently to maintain their physical bodies, and eventually wither away and die.

In a closed system, the change in entropy is always towards running down and death. However, in open biological or social systems, entropy can be arrested and may even be transformed into *negative entropy*—a process of more complete organization and enhanced ability to transform resources—because the system imports resources from its environment that proactively transforms it. This is why education and learning is so important, as it provides new and stimulating inputs (termed 'neg-entropy' above) that have the power to transform each of us.

The old cliché on entropy goes something like this: *'From the time we're born, we begin to die'*— is an apt one here. Our cells completely regenerate every seven years, and, in a sense, we become completely a new/older person.

Example:

Most change efforts fail because they aren't given enough follow-up, reinforcement, booster shots, and new energy. Though many managers want to get everything up and running on auto-pilot, this is the antithesis of what actually makes change happen. In systems terms, it takes negative entropy—what we call new energy in normal terms—to make change occur.

In fact, the concern most executives have is for 'buy-in' from their employees, when 'stay-in' is usually even more important, and certainly more difficult to retain over time (*Sustaining High Performance* is the title of my first book on this topic). The #1 key to successful major change is a monthly meeting of a Change Leadership Team, led by the CEO, to provide continual "stay-in" and booster shots.

Characteristic #11.   Steady State, Dynamic Equilibrium

The concept of 'steady state' is closely related to that of entropy. A closed system eventually must attain an equilibrium state with maximum entropy—death or disorganization. However, an open system may attain a state where the system remains in 'dynamic equilibrium' through the continuous inflow of materials, energy, information, and feedback.

Our tendency to resist change in our lives and in our organizations, and go back into balance in this dynamic equilibrium, is normal and natural. However, in today's rapidly changing environment, the desire for the predictability of habit—accompanied by the desire for stability—can only come to us through our becoming adaptable and flexible to change in a very personal way. **Death, taxes, and change are today's three certainties of life!**

Example:

Unfortunately, this is why 'cultural change' is so difficult to achieve—even more so than isolated change. It requires changing *all* aspects of the internal workings of an organization so it is in a fundamentally new 'steady state.' It means changing both peoples' values and changing the organizational processes. It means reinforcing/rewarding the new desired culture so strongly it overcomes the desire for stability and familiar habits. However, it is well known that when strategy and culture collide, strategy usually wins out.

Characteristic #12.   Internal Elaboration

Closed systems move toward entropy and disorganization. In contrast, open systems appear to move in the direction of greater differentiation, elaboration, and a higher level of organization. As humans, we grow and develop physically, emotionally, and intellectually.

This can also lead to organizational complexity and bureaucracy in its worst form. Complexity must be continuously resisted as it occurs naturally—it is a part of the natural process of ossification, rigidity, and death, as well. This is the Rubik's Cube Effect rather than a search for clarity and simplicity to combat this.

Questions to Ponder...

- Which of the Seven Levels of Living Systems are key to organizational life? Why?
- Which of the Standard Systems Dynamics are not clear to you? Review them again.
- Which two or three Standard Systems Dynamics do you see as key and leverage for successful change in your life, job, or organization?

Systems Thinking Concept #3   The A-B-C Systems Model

As a systemic, practical framework for describing universal relationships, Systems Thinking is a marvelous vehicle. Systems Thinking principles state that all the parts in any system can only perform in light of the purpose for which the whole exists—*no* part can be affected without affecting all other parts. So, when studying any system—be it organizational, organic, or scientific in nature:

The place to start is with the whole—all parts of the whole, and their relationships to one another—evolve from this.

In Systems Thinking, just as parts must be looked at only in light of how they perform toward the goal, so must each system be looked at in terms of its interaction with other systems. Much as it is not possible to change one element of any technological system without having an affect on that entire system, it is equally impossible for one system to change without affecting other systems.

All systems have the following general properties that characterize them as systems:

1. The performance of the whole is affected by every one of its parts.
2. The way that any part affects the whole depends on what at least one other part is doing; i.e., no part of the system has an independent effect on the whole.
3. If you take these parts and group them in any way, they form subgroups... which are then subject to the same 1st and 2nd conditions above...i.e., *a system is an indivisible whole!*

To truly comprehend the systems concept, it is critical to understand that a system goes beyond simply being an entity as a whole—**it is also a living, breathing, ongoing process, requiring inputs, outputs, and feedback from its environment**. These are Characteristics #1—#6 just stated. The following conceptual model of a system provides a clear visual image of these six characteristics that together define every living system:

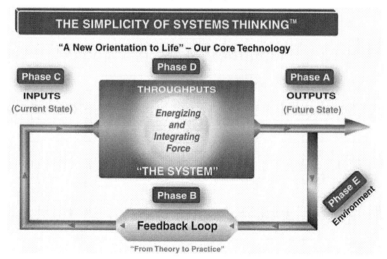

Figure 5-2: The Simplicity of Systems Thinking

As we've alluded to previously, there are five primary, A-B-C-D-E phases in every system—the *input, throughput* (or action), *output*, and *feedback* phases all within the *environment*. The sixth characteristic of living systems is their multiple outputs in every case

Phase A—Outputs

The defining Phase in the Systems Thinking model is Phase A, the output that results from that system's activity. Phase A asks the question: **"Where do we want to be (within the environment)?"** This is **THE** question to clarify the results we want. This, in part, is why we refer to Systems Thinking as *'Backwards Thinking'* – you begin with the desired outcomes and work backwards to achieve these results. This is the #1 systems question *always* asked in any situation in life—and it must be asked in the context of its environment and the other levels of systems around it.

Phase B—Feedback

The next part of the systems model is Phase B, the feedback loop. It is at this step in Systems Thinking that we start Thinking Backwards to determine what must take place for our desired outcomes to occur. This phase asks the #2 systems question, **"How will we know when we achieve our desired outcome?"** It concerns itself with how we know when we have achieved that outcome—what means we will use to measure that achievement. Phase B is where you actually determine how successful Phase A is on an ongoing basis, and *feed it back* to the system from the environment. 'Feedback is the Breakfast of Champions' is the theme of a later Chapter, and a key to learning and the popular 'learning organization' concept.

Phase C—Inputs

This Phase, with its question, **"Where are we right now?"** is the input Phase—the Phase in which the system begins to understand where it is and how to create strategies and specific actions for closing the gap between what's happening right now (Phase C), versus what should happen ultimately (Phase D). This Phase C is why linear thinking is so prevalent as it is where analytic thinking begins. It is how we think and read: *left-to-right*. It is what differentiates the two thinking concepts: 1) linear/analytic and reductionist thinking, versus 2) Systems Thinking. Analytic thinking starts with today and problem-solves isolated events versus seeing inputs, and today, only in light of the desired future outcomes (Phase A).

Phase D—Throughputs

This Phase—the throughput Phase—asks, **"How do we get there from here?"** It's all about the system's inner workings itself with each component interdependently implementing the necessary, ongoing processes, activities, people, relationships, and changes to create the desired outcomes (Phase A). This strategic and action phase is where most of us live—in the day-to-day. It is where we often are most comfortable.

Phase E—The Environment

The boundaries of each system define its environment as well. All living systems are open to their environment, part of the systems within systems, and Seven Levels of Living Systems. All systems constantly interact with the many facets of their environment

As long as we consistently apply these A-B-C-D-E Phases, Systems Thinking provides a generic and practical, universal framework to literally any set of system issues can be successfully solved. Whether we're looking at the physical systems that make up our environment or at the family, team, organizational, and social systems that make up our communities and globe, **the systems framework clarifies and simplifies** *how* we define/approach and evaluate/solve all of our problems and issues.

In this way, we are free to begin using this Systems Thinking A-B-C framework as our new *"orientation to life"*. It offers a clear and simple way to look at all our issues and problems as *systems*—a set of components that work together for the overall objectives of the whole system.

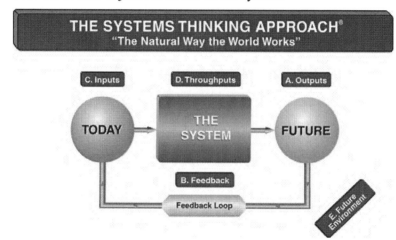

Figure 5-3: The Systems Thinking Approach

Indeed, Systems Thinking's A-B-C-D-E Phases offer five clear-cut and simple questions to pose in literally any system you evaluate (i.e. all **Seven Levels of Living Systems**):

Phase A) **Where do we want to be?** (i.e., our ends, outcomes, purposes, goals, holistic vision)

Phase B) **How will we know when we get there?** (i.e., needs and wants, connected to a measurable feedback system)

Phase C) **Where are we now?** (i.e., today's issues and problems)

Phase D) **How do we get there?** (i.e., close the gap from Question C to Question A in a complete, holistic way)

Phase E) *(Ongoing)* **What is changing in our future environment that will affect us?**

Versus *Analytical Thinking* which
1. Starts with today and the current stae, issues, and problems
2. Breaks the issues and/or problems into their smallest components
3. Solves each component separately
4. Has no far-reaching vision or goal.

The good news about Systems Thinking is that it gives us the clear, needed leverage for addressing *all* of these problems. Jay Forrestor, at M.I.T., believed that our traditional analytic or reductionist thinking was problematic based on the limited understandings and fallacies of the past, and that, in solving problems, it actually created more problems than it solved (the Rubik's Cube Effect).

A terrific support for this core systems technology came when we at the Haines Centre were applying these five phases in developing our Reinventing Strategic Planning to Strategic Management Model (Planning—People—Leadership—Change to deliver Customer Value). In doing background research, we looked at 27 other strategic planning and strategic change models. Of the 27 we mentioned earlier, none incorporated the five, A-B-C-D-E Systems Phases or took the system's environment and feedback loop into consideration...only our Reinventing Strategic Planning Model was based on the fundamental, full systems framework. See our later Chapter for details.

Figure 5-4: Reinventing Strategic Planning into Strategic Management.

When all is said and done, the *real* beauty of full Systems Thinking is that by using its clear and simple, five-phased systems framework, literally anyone can consciously develop systems solutions for their systems problems. In a later Chapter, we will show where the parts and elements of TQM, re-engineering, and many other organizational development and change concepts fit in the systems model. By doing this, you can find the flaws in these change strategies and successfully correct them, thereby increasing simplicity and dramatically increasing your chances for success.

How Systems Change

"We have not succeeded in answering all our questions. Indeed, we sometimes feel we have not completely answered any of them. The answers we have found only serve to raise a whole new set of questions. In some ways we are as confused as ever. But we think we are confused on a higher level and about more important things."
—Anonymous

As the quote above implies, the further I delve into the study of systems, the more I understand that, like this book, it will perpetually be a work in progress. Though I believe strongly in everything said thus far in this book—and most especially in the fundamental truths of Systems Thinking—I agree with others mentioned in this book that seeking solutions for the multi-level problems facing us today is a journey in which the *process* is as important as the *structure* of the five questions we raise.

Systems Thinking Concept #4:   The Rollercoaster of Change™

While it is true that Systems Thinking by its very nature creates more questions than we presently have answers, complexity and chaos are a natural and constant element in all of life. This is why, throughout our lives, we often feel like we're on a rollercoaster. It's important to remember, though, that the ups and downs are a normal, regular aspect of change in our lives—and it's perfectly natural. In fact it is **THE** key concept of Systems Thinking regarding "how Systems Change." There is a regular and consistent process of change. We even have coined a term for it; the **"Rollercoaster of Change™"**.

This Rollercoaster of Change is an extremely important concept underlying all change. Without understanding, anticipating, and planning for the Rollercoaster (shown here), an organization cannot complete successful change efforts or become a learning environment that continually renews and creates its own desired outcome.

The Rollercoaster of Change is natural, normal, and highly predictable!

...And it is the only "theory" of the process of change you need to know.

Time is a major factor that the Rollercoaster of Change makes us take into consideration. In even the best of cases in which someone wants to change, understands it fully, and even has the skills to do so, it still requires a minimum of 12-18 months for that individual to change the desired habit. With this in mind, how long might it take for others to change, especially if they may not have the same knowledge, skills, and attitude you do?

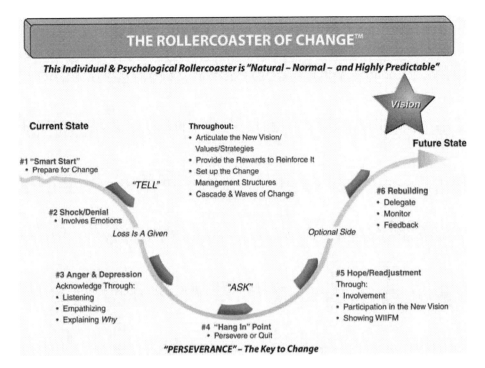

Figure 5-5: The Rollercoaster of Change

The Rollercoaster of Change helps people, teams, and organizations know better what to expect—even, in some instances, when to *not* trust intuition. Leaders (including parents) plan and lead change, for example. Thus, they usually experience the various stages of change before employees or children do. Since executives are usually ahead on the Rollercoaster of Change, their intuition or how they are feeling about specific change is often the opposite of their employees—i.e., "If I'm at a point where I'm feeling good or reassured, they may still be angry or upset in their stage of the cycle."

The fact of the matter is that all change is a loss experience. As Harry Levinson, in *Psychological Man*, puts it:

- Loss creates a feeling of depression for most people. One loses preferred modes of attaining and giving affection, handling aggression, dependency needs all those familiar routines which we have evolved and usually taken for granted.
- Loss is a difficult experience to handle, particularly what one leaves behind is psychologically important.
- All loss must be mourned and the attendant feelings disgorged if a restitution process is to operate effectively.
- Most organization change flounders because the experience of loss is not taken into account. To undertake successful organizational change, [a leader] must anticipate and provide the means of working through that loss.

The key to successfully riding the Rollercoaster of Change—no matter how many times you do it (and we *all* experience it multiple times a week, if not daily)— is to accept even the negative emotions that accompany it as natural and expected. The Catch-22 feature of the Rollercoaster is that once you start through it, you cannot go back and erase what you started. Instead, attempting to reverse changes already begun will just set another Rollercoaster into motion—only this time from the lower spot at which you tried to reverse it.

The only way up the right side of the Rollercoaster is through self initiative/ mastery and/or through supportive leadership. In fact, those elements that help people through it the most are parallel with needed leadership skills:

1. *Active listening*
2. *Asking questions*
3. *Empathizing*
4. *Only then, explaining the changes, and why they are necessary.*
5. *Ask each person to figure out WIIFM*

As a leader, make sure that team, or organizational members understand that depression and/or resistance to change is natural, normal, and highly predictable. The worst thing you can do is to push someone or tell them they "shouldn't feel that way." The importance of people's "buy-in" and "stay-in" are so critical, leaders will need to mimic Peter Drucker's "monomaniac with a mission" in implementing, correcting, and improving the organization's desired changes in order to help each person ride the Rollercoaster successfully.

"Nothing in the world can take the place of persistence. Talent will not; nothing is more common than unsuccessful men with talent. Genius will not; unrewarded genius is almost a proverb. Education will not; the world is full of educated idiots. Persistence and determination alone are omnipotent."
—Calvin Coolidge

Regardless of the complexities and difficulties of change, be assured that they are an unavoidable aspect of all change—*they* **will** *happen, whether you plan for them or not*. By employing the Rollercoaster of Change in planning for change, however, people, families, teams, and organizations can find themselves better prepared for both the expected and unexpected realities of change. The biggest risk of all is to stay the same, and *not* change. Today's predominant reality for all of us wanting to survive *and* thrive is that short-term chaos and emotion are part of the keys to long-term advances.

As a result, when one person changes, it simultaneously changes and affects many other people...this is normal and to be expected. Why? Because life itself is made up of complex and interdependent systems.

Questions to Ponder...

- Are you clear on the five A-B-C-D-E Systems Phases?
- What does the "E" or fifth part of this System's Concept stand for? Why is it key?
- Is the Rollercoaster clear to you? Can you apply it in your own life right now?

"If you don't know where you're going, any road will get you there."
—*Yogi Berra*

The road we follow in Systems Thinking, then, takes us from initially seeing events to beginning to see patterns by developing new, conscious mental models of change. When we arrive, finally, at Systems Thinking, we realize that—not only have we been engaged in a process of diagnosis and discovery— we will *always* be on this Systems Thinking roller coaster of diagnosis and discovery.

In Systems Thinking, we recognize that **it is what we do with change that creates the outcomes we desire**. Systems Thinking teaches us that the only thing *we* can change is our own behavior, and that we must assume responsibility for our own destiny. Rather than ask, 'What are the problems?', we first ask instead a new question, *'What are we doing that's causing the problem?'* Once we know, it is easier to ride the roller coaster of change successfully.

Why do we keep saying "Change is natural, normal, and highly predictable?" We researched and looked at over 20 different theories of change and found that they are all the same, just with different terms and visuals.

Also, look at these examples:

"Historical and Natural Cycles of Change"

1. **The Environment**
   - Santa Anas
   - El Ninos
   - Volcanoes
   - Earthquakes
   - Seasons
   - Moon
   - Day/Night
2. **Economics**
   - Bull/Bear Markets
   - K-wave (Nikolai Kondratieff, 1926)
   - Recessions, Depressions
   - Profit taking
   - Inflation
3. **Civilizations**
   - Inca/Aztec Empires
   - British Empire
   - French Empire
   - Spanish Empire
   - Japanese Empire
   - Chinese Empire
   - Roman Empire
   - Greek Empire
   - Current Western Civilization

4. **Ages**
   - Hunting, gathering
   - Agriculture
   - Industrial
   - Information
5. **Industries**
   - Start up
   - High growth
   - Maturity
   - Decline
   - Renewal or Death
6. **Travel**
   - Walk
   - Use animals
   - Row boats, canoes
   - Use cars, wheels
   - Bus/Mass Transit
   - Airplanes
7. **Flight**
   - Balloons
   - Wright Brothers- biplanes
   - Single wing propeller
   - Jet planes
   - Concorde Plane/Space Shuttle
   - Satellites, Rockets

Summary of these Four Concepts

To date, there is only one theory or body of thought that offers a fully integrated systems solution to our systems problems. That solution is General Systems Theory and these four concepts. To put it succinctly, consider Joel Barker's fundamental paradigm shift question:

We must ask ourselves this question repeatedly. In order to reverse our failures, and, instead, successfully evolve through the Rollercoaster of Change, we need radical and positive change.

The view we need is this: **"If I could change only one person in this world it would be myself."** We must look not only at our individual rights that are the foundation of a democratic society; we must also consider the responsibilities we have as citizens for the common good of society as a whole. We must stop looking at our Supervisors and others in organizations to change. Look at ourselves instead and where we are on these four concepts.

In short, we must stop attempting the impossible—solving systems problems with fragmented, reductionistic, and isolated efforts that are geared toward singular goals. Rather, we must *fundamentally change and adopt Systems Thinking, with its focus on societal, community, and organizational outcomes, as our new basic orientation to life— if we want any chance of changing direction toward a more positive long-term future!*

The chaos, change, and fragmentation our organizations and society are facing today are within our power to change. If we are willing to face the responsibility of doing all the hard work that comes with it, it is entirely possible that we can learn not only to welcome and embrace change...but to use it to our best advantage, as well. Systems Thinking is not a panacea, but it does offer leaders real hope and new helicopter vistas from which to view and solve life's Rubik's Cube of problems. As Cliff McIntosh said in *Keeping Current:*

> *"To shape governance for the future, we must think in [these] terms: how to control social systems without the weight and cost of Industrial era bureaucracies. The central 21st century issue is invention and mastery of systems that provide the good life and ensure the survival of life on Earth."*

Partial Systems Thinking...some progress
> *"Thinking across boundaries, or integrative thinking, is the ultimate entrepreneurial act. Call it business creativity. Call it holistic thinking. To see problems and opportunities integratively is to see them as wholes related to larger wholes, rather than dividing information and experience into discrete bits assigned to distinct, separate categories that never touch one another."*
> *—Harvard Business Review*

There are already many, many fields of thought (over 25 scientific disciplines in all) that deal with the interrelationship of processes and patterns—Systems Thinking in its broadest sense. This includes the fields of Cybernetics, Chaos Theory, Gestalt Therapy, General Systems Theory, Complexity Theory, Socio-Technical Systems Theory (Eric Trist) and systems change—as well as project management, information systems, operations research, telecommunications, and more. See Chapter 10 (Epilogue) for a full list identified by me. It has been approached, at least in relative terms, by many diverse theorists: Von Bertalanffy, McIntosh, Ackoff, Senge, Forrester, the physicist Fritjof Capra, Gregory Bateson, Meg Wheatley, M. Mitchell Waldrop, Peter Drucker, and many others.

Many of these fields and concepts approach problem-solving from more of an integrated view. However, some of them—such as Six Sigma, Total Quality Management, re-engineering, process redesign, The Balanced Scorecard, benchmarking, work empowerment—are struggling in today's organizational environment, some even dying the slow death of fads.

In our view—though they are well-intentioned efforts—they would more correctly be called **"partial systems" solutions**, rather than fully-integrated systems solutions. While they are indeed efforts to concentrate and focus on patterns (and known relationships) rather than just isolated events and activities, they tend to focus more on surface issues rather than in-depth attempts to develop organizations systematically. They do not yet look at their strategies and their problem-solving from a fully integrated, holistic or systems methodology. This Systems Science begins with defining their Ideal Future Vision or ultimate purposes first.

As you will see, none of these concepts meet the fundamental Systems Thinking test below. Therefore, they are really partial systems views, integrated checklists, and the like. As we have stated, Systems Thinking includes:

1. Starting from the helicopter point of view of understanding what a complete, holistic, A-B-C-D-E system looks like in its environment
2. Starting in the right place with defining your vision and desired outcomes first (*begin with the end in mind*)
3. A feedback loop to track, measure, and report back system results within its dynamic environment
4. Lastly, utilizing the entire system and its web of relationships, concepts and the likes so as not to fall victim to the Rubik's Cube Effect.

Partial systems rarely meet all three of these tests—rather, they are usually checklists of integrated and related points important primarily to their authors. That's why these concepts fall into a *partial* systems approach—i.e., they are related components—but usually miss the full, holistic systems focus. Ultimately, they become fads whose time has past. Though we have benefited from their presence, they somehow still weren't enough. In the end, each concept failed to make the fundamental, full-system changes that were required...and needed to achieve the desired outcomes.

Partial Systems Thinking Example #1:

Total Quality Management (TQM), in particular, has been strongly in evidence; there are many examples of it even today. At its outset, it was an innovative concept around the idea of delivering consistent and continuous quality to the customer. There was a tendency, however, to look only at the general process and overall end of improved quality, and not to focus particularly on the customer.

Even Deming, with his 14 points of TQM, didn't mention the customer specifically by name. What was frequently neglected, in addition to customer satisfaction, was an often unspoken expectation of a bottom-line profit for shareholders – an outcome or dimension that was indirectly anticipated as a result of the process, but rarely achieved.

"The greatest obstacle to achieving my goals is that I don't know what my goals are."
—Ashleigh Brilliant

Partial Systems Thinking Example #2:

There are others today that are identifying this problem and making concerted efforts to 'look at the whole.' In his book, *Total Improvement Management*, Dr. James Harrington identified five main approaches to improvement: 1) total cost management, 2) total resource management, 3) total productivity management, 4) total technology management, and 5) total quality management.

In developing his model, Harrington even went so far as to cite the best elements from each program and point out areas in which they overlap, finally blending them into an overall program of 'total improvement management.' Note that Harrington had an underlying base of 'value to stakeholders'—he is definitely getting closer to true, holistic Systems Thinking. However, similar to other engineering-trained, analytic thinking scientific disciplines, Harrington still doesn't employ the complete A-B-C-D-E process phases within a systems framework.

Partial Systems Thinking Example #3:

The Workbook for Implementing the Five Tracks, by Calvin Brown, presents a program for managing organization-wide improvement on a more holistic level. Described in *Managing Beyond the Quick Fix*, by Dr. Ralph Kilman, it uses a five-track model that includes many of our organizational factors—culture, management skills, team-building, strategy-structure, and reward system. Still no systems framework of interdependencies, processes, outcomes, and feedback loop, however.

Partial Systems Thinking Example #4:

Though there have been many improvements in productivity and processes, as well as increased efficiency and effectiveness, information technology is still a long way from fulfilling its tremendous potential. What many experts are finally realizing today is that the technology cannot stand alone. It cannot be treated as an isolated entity – it must be developed within the scope of the systems that make up its total environment.*

* *TQM & Information Technology: Partners for Profit*, James B. Ayers, *Information Strategy: The Executive's Journal*

"I am wary of the word 'system' because... 'system' is a highly cathected term, loaded with prestige; hence, we are all strongly tempted to employ it even when

we have nothing definite in mind and its only service is to indicate that we subscribe to the general premise respecting the interdependence of things."
—Kast & Rosenzweig, quoting the psychologist, Murray, Systems Thinking

Some further progress in scientific disciplines

There also exists today an on slaught of books that, like the examples just discussed, begin to look at our modern society from an outlook that more closely aligns itself with Systems Thinking. Though they are too numerous to discuss in detail, here is a brief list of those that are clearly striving to incorporate a systems approach:

- *The New Paradigm in Business*, **edited by Michael Ray & Alan Rinzler**—*Defines the new business paradigm as "doing business from our most profound inner awareness and in connection with the consciousness of others...and as physicists, systems theorists, ecologists, biologists, chemists, and virtually all scientists...tell us, there is a wholeness and connectedness between all living things."*

- *Nature's Imagination*, **edited by John Cornwell**—*A collection of scientific essays from mathematicians, astronomers, neuroscientists, and philosophers that negate the idea that the whole can be explained by examining each of its parts...and "shows that scientists in every discipline are reaching for a new paradigm that accounts for the whole–from the individual...to the universe itself."*

- *Bionomics: Economy as Ecosystem*, **Michael Rothschild**—*Discusses the economy as a living ecosystem..."Key phenomena observed in nature–competition, specialization, cooperation, exploitation, learning, growth...are also central to business life."*

- *Reviving the American Dream*, **Alice Rivlin**—*Deals with the log-jam between state and federal politics through a systems viewpoint.*

- *Leadership & the New Science and a Simpler Way*, **Margaret Wheatley**—*Postulates that chaos is how things work in natural systems, that order develops naturally within chaos, and that chaos is a natural step in achieving a higher order.*

- *Complexity: The Emerging Science at the Edge of Order & Chaos*, **M. Mitchell Waldrop**—*Describes all of our systems as complex...with "the potential to bring order and chaos into a special kind of balance."*

- *The Collapse of Chaos: Discovering Simplicity in a Complex World*, **Jack Cohen & Ian Stewart**—*Looks at the chaos and complexity of our world's natural and living systems, and derives simplicity from the interaction of the two.*

As you can see, today's leading thinkers and scientists from many disciplines are collectively coming together more and more from a systems perspective. More and more, they're seeing the general interdependence of our natural systems, while still searching for a complete framework.

The abundant partial Systems Thinking out there today has definitely had a hand in moving us *toward* full Systems Thinking, but it doesn't get us there all the way. The dilemma in partial Systems Thinking on one hand is that it provides us with better, more clear ways to focus on those things that trouble us today, in the immediate present. On the other hand, it leaves us out in the cold on any elements that haven't been incorporated or anticipated...therefore creating suboptimal results, and even new disturbances, as by-products.

What von Bertalanffy, Waldrop, Cliff McIntosh, Ackoff, Senge, Trist, and all the others in these diverse approaches have in common is that they recognize that **the behavior of all living systems follows certain common and 'natural' principles of systems and systems' change.** They all bring some increased understanding of our complex world, so we need to learn, understand, and appreciate them, even though they are still being discovered and articulated. These systems apply to every living system at every level–individual, team/family, organization/county, organization/society. They understand that what we see changing on one system level will also affect another system level, which in turn affects yet another level, and so on. Therefore, they attempt to make the best use of this change by applying systems solutions.

In Summary—The Benefits

Systems Thinking has six primary, far-reaching benefits which give us:

1. A framework and way to make sense out of life's complexities, since all living things *are* systems.
2. A way to learn new things more easily – its basic rules are simple and consistent—they stay the same from system to system.
3. A better way to integrate new ideas together within the systems context.
4. A clearer way to see and understand what is going on in any organization or any system and its environment. Complex problems become easier to understand, as do the interrelationships of parts and multiple cause-and-effect cycles.
5. A new and better way to create strategies, problem-solve, and find leverage points—keeping the outcome/vision/goal in mind at all time
6. The key #1 Systems Thinking question with which to begin any discovery—problem-solving or otherwise.

Lastly, Systems Thinking gives us a better language, a more complete and holistic way of thinking and being. Its principles are much like a wide-angle lens on a camera; they give us a better helicopter view on our 'radar scope'—thus, a more effective way of thinking, communicating, problem-solving, and acting. Without Systems Thinking, we face a situation in which:

"Today's thinking (and problem-solving) is the source of tomorrow's problems."
—Stephen Haines

If we truly want to move forward toward a better, stronger future – and if we agree with futurist Cliff McIntosh when he says, 'the central 21st Century issue is [the] invention and mastery of systems that provide the good life and ensure the survival of life on Earth' – we know we must begin now to make substantial inroads in changing how we look at our organizations and world.

Questions to Ponder...

- What other partial Systems Thinking examples can you think of?
- What other scientific disciplines do you know that are also leaning towards Systems Thinking?
- What benefits do you personally see with Systems Thinking?

This is why the KISS method and the concepts of 'clarify" and 'simplify' are so crucial to success in our lives and organizations. It is why **Strategic and Systems Thinking**: *The Winning Formula* is our search and the title of this book.

Success or failure in this Systems Age will depend, ultimately, on what we adopt as our primary mental model/frameworks and guiding principles. In von Bertalanffy's words, remember, the macro principle is that *"in one way or another, we are forced to deal with complexities, with 'wholes' or 'systems' in all fields of knowledge."*

Recognizing and understanding these four General Systems Theory concepts, frameworks, and principles will aid us immeasurably in our efforts to identify, diagnose, and work with systems that need changing in order to achieve their desired outcomes.

> **BFO**
> **(Blinding Flash of the Obvious)**
> It's the system, stupid!
> but
> We are blind to the system—it's too obvious.

Following in Part III (Chapters 6—10) are some implications of these four concepts and dynamics that we at the Haines Centre *for* Strategic Management have developed over the years. They can go a long way toward helping us identify *what* needs to be changed, and clarify *how* it can be changed. However, it is important to remember that the applications of these four concepts are growing and changing; thus, the term **'some'**. Like everything else in systems, I—as well as all of us at the Haines Centre—am still learning, shaping, and evolving. Read on to examine the applications of these concepts in the following chapters as we try to "bridge this gap."

Chapter 5
The Science of Systems Thinking
Summary of Key Concepts

1. While these four concepts are broken down into apparently separate concepts for purposes of this chapter and book, nothing could be further from the truth. They are also closely interrelated to each other. This is in keeping with Systems Thinking's key principles that "the whole is primary and the parts are secondary."

2. It is also why these concepts are uncommon, common sense in the management literature. They were developed by biologists; not management theorists!

3. So, the holistic view of all these four concepts together is primary and their separate concepts is secondary. The overall holistic purpose of these concepts is a new orientation to life and a new way to think—to act and to achieve better results in your lives. Both at work in organizations and in your life in communities.

3. However, to better understand these four concepts, here are their relationships:

Concept #1: Seven Levels of Living Systems shows the different levels of systems that exist naturally. To accomplish good Systems Thinking, you first need to know what system you are discussing. Since theses seven levels each exist interdependently within all those higher level systems, one of the standard systems dynamics is revealed.

Concept#2: Standard Systems Dynamics show the 12 characteristics that are the same for each of these seven levels of living systems. They describe the standard dynamics one could expect in each living system.

A key note here: Did you ever wonder why consultants/executives can work effectively across different firms and industries? Or why books, training, and university courses/degrees apply generally to all organizations? It might be obvious by now that there are standard dynamics of every organization because they are all composed of human beings and operate at the same level of living systems. While executives think their situation is always unique, it is not usually totally true.

Concept #3: The A-B-C Systems Model is constructed by combining six of the twelve standard dynamics. It describes how each of the seven levels of living systems actually functions. Whether you are an individual, a team, or organization, it functions in the same basic circular way within the environment.

Concept #4: Changing Systems through the Rollercoaster of Change™ describes how each system (all seven levels) undergoes change. The basic sequence and cycle of change is the same for each level. The words and details may be different but the cycle is the same. It is within this cycle that the standard systems dynamics occur.

PART THREE

Bridging the Gap...
Systems Solutions to Systems Problems are Everywhere

Systems—The Natural Order of Life on Earth

The Synergy of Systems Solutions
Vs.
The Failure of Fragemented Functions

The dominant paradigm in our lives is "Analytical Thinking."

However,

The Natural Order of Life in the World is a Systems one.

Problems that are created by our current level of thinking
can't be solved by that same level of thinking

—Albert Einstein

So…if we generally use analytical thinking,
we now need real "Systems Thinking" to resolve our issues.

—Stephen Haines

CHAPTER 6

The Seven Levels of Living Systems (Concept #1)
"Awake, the Systems Age is here
...for each of us"

Overview-Applications of the Seven Levels

We've looked at why Systems Thinking and the oncoming Systems Age gives us more simplicity and a better, more centered framework for addressing our current issues. Now, these next chapters will devote themselves to exploring how we can bridge the gap and provide systems solutions through each of the four systems concepts...and how each of the four concepts together form a web of systems.

This first Systems Concept, Seven Levels of Living Systems was introduced in the last Chapter. Of most interest to this book is Levels 3—6:

Level #3—Individuals
Level #4—Groups/Teams
Level #5—Organizations
Level #6—Society/Community (the environment around organizations)

Levels #1 (Cells) and #2 (Organs) are often the purview of biotech researchers, health care professionals and their organizations. As consumers and people concerned with our bodies and our health, we all should be vitally concerned with these as well. They are just not the focus of this book.

Level #7 is also of vital concern to all of us on "Spaceship Earth". It is the topic of many other books, debates, and professions. Thus, this book makes no attempt to apply Systems Thinking to those Levels we are applying on an individual or business level (#1, #2, and #7).

Regarding Levels #3—# 6, it is a common sense notion (i.e. simplicity, again) that organizations are composed of individuals, teams and the organization as a whole interacting in its environment. However, to fully appreciate these Seven Levels, realize that there are also interactions, collaborations with, and "collisions" of these systems with other systems as well.

In other words:

- **Our interpersonal relationships** are the result of collisions of two separate yet interdependent individuals as systems (Level #3 interacting with another Level #3).
- **Our inter-department/group relationships** at work are also the result of the collisions of two distinct and separate (yet interdependent) teams/departments

as systems (Level #4 interacting often as cross-functional project or process teams).

- **All organizations** definitely collide with many **other systems in our environment**; including societies, competitors, suppliers, Special Interest Groups (SIGs), the community and most importantly, our customers and potential customers.

We use the word **"collision"** here specifically to call attention to the way in which many of these systems interact. The mechanistic view of the world lead many of us to see these systems as separate and independent rather than valuing and appreciating the interdependencies within organizations and the interdependencies of all life on earth.

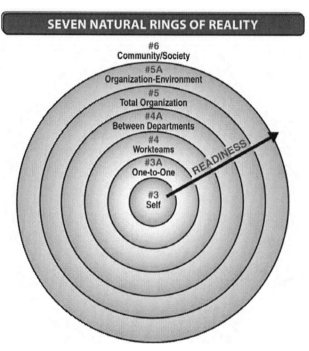

Figure 6-1: Seven Natural Rings of Reality

As a result of these levels and collisions/interactions of these levels, we developed a model to apply these levels as our **Six Rings of Reality** and readiness as the reality of life. Note the different purposes of each of these different levels in organizations.

The general purposes of working at each ring are:

Ring #3: **Individuals ("Self-Mastery")**

- Improve personal competency and effectiveness

- Trustworthiness issues

Ring #3A: **One-to-One Relationships ("Interpersonal Skills/Effectiveness")**

- Improve the interpersonal and working relationships and effectiveness of each individual

- Trust issues

Ring 4: Workteams/Groups ("Team Empowerment/Effectiveness")

- Improve the effectiveness of the workteam as well as its members

- Empowement issues

Ring #4A: Intergroups ("Conflict/Horizontal Collaboration")

- Improve the working relationships and business processes between teams and departments horizontally to serve the customer better.

- Horizontal collaboration and integration issues

Ring #5: Total Organization ("Fit"/Strategic Plan)

- Improve the organization's systems, structures, and processes to better achieve its business results and portential; and develop its capacity to provide an adaptive system of change and response to a changing environment while pursuing your vision and strategic plan.

- Alignment issues

Ring #5A: Organizaton-Environment (Alliances)

- Improve the organization's sense of direction, response to its' customers and proactive management of its environments/stakeholders by Reinventing Strategic Planning to Deliver Customer Value.

- Adaptation to the environment issues

We use the word **Reality** here to help us locate (i.e. Reality) where we are in our daily lives and work tasks. It helps to be clearer on our purposes once we know what Level of system or collision/interaction of systems we are dealing with.

We also use the word **readiness** to show how much more complex and difficult it is to deal with the higher and higher Systems Levels. The readiness and willingness as well as the skills growth need to be greater as leaders in order for effective work to be accomplished. It is also why organization-wide **culture change** is so difficult as it requires changes at all the other levels and collision of levels within the organization (i.e. #3, #3a, #4, #4a, #5, and #5a).

Thus, when attempting organization-wide change, the chaos and complexity are so great as to render successful change as **unusual**, rather than the norm just as Chapter 2 detailed. However, as managers and leaders we need to be aware of these Levels and develop the unique knowledge and skills required to be successful in working at each of these **"Seven Rings of Reality"** (go back to the purposes of each).

These **Seven Rings of Reality** are an application of the Seven Levels of Living Systems. We will use them throughout this book as we weave these four Systems Thinking Concepts together. It will be applied to us as leaders.

Q uestions to Ponder...

- Do these collisions of systems make sense to you as areas of reality on organizational change?
- Are you clear on the purpose of each?
- Which of the Six Rings of Reality are key to organizational success?

Visionary leadership...for each of us
"The truth is that we are all leaders just as we are all followers."

At the Haines Centre for Strategic Management, we concentrate much of our focus on leadership. The reason for this is a fundamental but important discovery we have made in our collective years of studies of organizational change and leadership. It is, simply, that *"an increased understanding of the skills of individual leaders enables us to better develop ways for improving our own (and others') capabilities."* Knowledge isn't enough; it's putting it to productive use through our skills and capabilities that is key.

This point of view comes when we look at something as basic as knowledge and learning, key essentials to real leadership. Most consider knowledge and learning to be simple, straightforward, and even synonymous. Yet, while knowledge is indeed necessary to learning, leaders recognize that, in the Information and Systems Age, skills and attitudes are even more crucial than knowledge alone. Learning is actual knowledge, skills, *and* attitudes. Knowledge is the easiest to come by, especially in today's Internet World. The result of all three kinds of learning is competency; the ability to perform competently in a certain area.

Thus, as a Centre, we looked at these Seven Rings of Reality to see what the focus of leadership development was. We researched 27 different and popular authors, researchers, and training and development companies. The results were startling as the attached shows:

Leadership Development Competencies
Best Practices Research

Centering Your Leadership	27 Other Authors
1. Enhancing Self-Mastery	1. 27 out of 27 had a similar item
2. Building Interpersonal Relationships	2. 17 out of 27 had a similar item
3. Facilitating Empowered Teams	3. 6 out of 27 had a similar item
4. Collaborating Across Functions	4. 3 out of 27 had a similar item
5. Integrating Organizational Outcomes	5. 13 out of 27 had a similar item
6. Creating Strategic Alliances	6. 9 out of 27 had a similar item

Note none had all six competencies. Only three had four competencies and only four had three competencies.

As a result of this research, we at the Centre spent two years trying to make sense of this data for use with our clients and the leadership competencies they needed to compete successfully. We finally realized that these Six Rings of Reality were also the **Six Natural Levels of Leadership Competencies** that are needed in all organizations. While every leader doesn't need all six, many do. The more senior you are, the more likely it is that you will need all six competencies.

The successful organization will be the one that centers its leadership with a firm grounding in each ring of the *Systems Thinking Approach®* to leadership competencies. When put together, these six competencies can be depicted, along with their outcomes, as follows:

In the years of Centre research, we also developed the five key skills underlying each competency. While this is not a comprehensive list, it is one that gives organizations, individuals and teams the ability to tailor their own needed skills within these six competencies and 30 skills. Then, each leader can use a survey to determine where you stand in your current leadership competencies in all six rings:

When all is said and done, an effective strategic leadership development system is what gives an organization its only true competitive advantage over the long term. Also remember, when establishing your organization's leadership development system, be sure to incorporate all six of these systems levels. Only if your collective management members become leaders and develop a competitive edge can all your people be empowered as a strong "people edge."

Leadership Competency #1: Enhancing self-mastery

Leadership is a contemplative art, requiring life-long learning, committed application, feedback, and more learning. This is especially true for the middle and senior executives of the organization, who must have an individual goal of self-mastery, including:
- Having a clear vision and plan for yourself
- Creating balance in your body, mind, and spirit
- Gaining control over your own behavior
- Pursuing lifelong learning

There's no question that the pursuit of self-mastery develops a heightened awareness, and thus is crucial to effective leadership. It not only improves personal competencies, it also develops competence in maintaining individual integrity and achieving individual balance—thus building an organization-wide faith in its leaders.

Leadership Competency #2: Building interpersonal relationships

Just as critical to effective organizational leadership is competency and strength in building interpersonal working relationships. This creates the outcome of focusing our emotions and our minds, furthering the presence of organization-wide trust in the integrity of its leaders.

As we saw in Chapter 5, self-mastery is the primary building block in becoming skilled in interpersonal relationship competency. Without self-mastery, it is virtually impossible to develop skills in interpersonal relationships—the skills which are paramount in generating trust in organizational leadership. Most importantly, trust of leaders has a direct impact on the interpersonal relationships, productivity, and effectiveness of *all* organizational members.

Leadership Competency #3: Facilitating empowered teams

In Chapter 5, we saw how mastery over interpersonal relationships directly impacts the effectiveness of teamwork. Effective teamwork is an especially crucial element in the total organizational system effectiveness. Facilitating empowered teams results in achieving the purpose for which the team was formed. An organization's health and success relies heavily on the competence of unit/department leaders facilitating empowered teams.

Effective teamwork is needed at all organizational levels and in all departments, and all organizational systems and processes. The key to leadership competency in this area lies in cooperation and collaboration to serve the customer, not an outdated vertical hierarchy and bureaucracy. Leadership in facilitating empowered teams, integrating department-wide cooperation, and team conflict resolution can vastly improve both working relationships and effectiveness—thus achieving their desired outcomes and mission. This is, quite simply, *the* primary building block of organizations as systems.

Leadership Competency #4: Collaborating across functions

As teamwork becomes more and more integral in today's organization, a growing skill leaders need is effective collaboration across functions. Collaborating across functions puts workers at all levels more closely in touch with what services their customer values—which in turn teaches the organization as a whole how and where more efficient business processes need to be developed.

Organizations will need more and more to develop senior and middle management leadership that is competent in keeping all functions focused together on consistently serving the customer's needs and wants. *Quite simply, cross-functional teamwork, business processes and project management is how most work gets done in organizations.*

Thus, cross functional teamwork is the biggest weakness in most organizations.

Leadership Competency #5: Integrating organizational outcomes

Overall management of change and cultural transformation in order to create customer value on an organization-wide basis is, obviously, a sorely needed leadership competency for today's organizations. However, if the desired outcomes are: 1) an organization-wide shared vision and values, 2) integrated organizational outcomes/results, and 3) organizational synergy, then this Level of Competency is crucial to organizational success.

Today's more senior organizational leader will be required to wear many hats in order to integrate total organizational "fit," including: 1) improving organizational systems, structures, and processes to better achieve its business results and potential, 2) developing its capacity to provide an adaptive system of change and flexible response to a changing environment while pursuing their overall vision and strategic plan.

Leadership Competency #6: Creating strategic positioning

The Ph.D. of all senior leaders involves a clear understanding and close management of their organization's positioning in the marketplace in order to be globally competitive. If your organization's positioning is clear, you'll need to stick to your knitting and your core competencies establishing and sustaining strategic positioning in today's intensely competitive world.

Questions to Ponder…

- Are all Six Levels of Leadership Competencies clear? Do they make sense to you? Review them again.
- Which ones are your own strengths…and your weaknesses?
- Which ones are the strengths and weaknesses of your organization overall?

Details on Leadership Competency #1: Self-Mastery

This next section will provide tips and practical applications for utilizing Systems Thinking at the first and most personal of these levels—as individual leaders, managers and supervisors. We'll explore self-mastery, both what it is and how it can be achieved through developing our own vision, balancing our body, mind, and spirit, gaining control over our behavior, and life-long learning. We will illustrate how using Systems Thinking as a framework for thinking, acting, and growing as individuals can better prepare us to become the leaders that the 21st Century so clearly needs. Lastly, we will look at where self-mastery is already happening in today's world...and where else it needs to happen.

In other words, understanding and incorporating the fundamentals of vision and leadership in all aspects of our lives—both professional and personal—better equips us to face, benefit, and contribute positively to solving life's challenges. Secondly, we believe that the corollary to developing leadership skills is knowing what goes into being a follower—i.e., *"it is not possible to lead effectively unless you first know how to follow."*

Think about it for a moment—in our day-to-day lives, we are continually called upon to be both a follower and leader. In our organizational lives, we plan and lead meetings and change efforts. We also support the change efforts of other leaders. In order to maximize our effectiveness, we not only need leadership skills, we must also anticipate and integrate the cooperative actions and capabilities of ourselves with others that are necessary for moving forward toward an overall organization vision.

Maturity is also an important component in leadership. In our own life cycle, we go from the dependence of childhood, toward gradual independence as an adolescent and young adult, and ultimately to the most mature adult level of interdependence. In developing leadership skills, we learnl that only at the interdependent level can true Systems Thinking take place—as opposed to the independent/silo level of maturity. This independence is primarily concerned with seeing ourselves as separate and distinct from others and society. (Sound familiar? Analytic, independent, silo thinking and problem solving?)

The essence of what individual development and leadership are all about then is this—*taking the lead in making work and life better and in serving the common good together with others*. In Systems Thinking terms, it creates the strength that makes the whole greater than the sum of our individual parts. In order to achieve this "greater whole," however, we must as leaders understand that we only progress when we look first at what *we* are doing, comparing ourselves against ourselves, rather than against others. To truly become the leaders we want (and need) to be, we must personally seek continual progress, not perfection—i.e., **we must first develop mastery over ourselves and our own actions!**

Self-Mastery: What is it?
"What are we here for…what are the goals of life?"

In our individual lives, self-mastery creates the foundation we need to be a positive contributor to society. At the base of self-mastery is gaining clarity in determining what it is that we are here to accomplish or to "master." All of us ask ourselves at one time or another, "Why am I here? What purposes am I supposed to serve? What responsibility do I have to a common good—or am I here just for self-aggrandizement and hedonistic purposes?" In the final analysis, we are human beings; our search for meaning in our lives is crucial to our own success and failure.

The truth is, to achieve self-mastery, each of us as humans needs some higher sense of purpose—something which shows us that human society is enhanced by our presence—something we can reach for outside ourselves.

> *"The greatest good is what we do for one another."*
> *—Mother Teresa*

In his timeless book, *Man's Search for Meaning*, World War II concentration-camp survivor Victor Frankl showed us that, out of all camp prisoners, those that survived to make productive post-war lives were not necessarily the most physically strong. It was those individuals who found something meaningful left to do in their life, outside of their internment, that was greater than the torture and starvation they were experiencing on a daily basis. Frankl himself survived by concentrating on an image of himself giving a speech to a packed concert hall on the universal search for meaning.

Unfortunately, we exist in a time obsessed with individual rights—and self-serving words such as "me" and "I" reign supreme in our language today. This is one of the primary reasons our own maturity is so important a consideration for self-mastery and leadership. It requires us to look beyond merely a self-oriented purpose, and seek a higher, external purpose outside (yet connected to) ourselves.

For each of us, analytic and independent thinking is a stage (however necessary) on the road to self-mastery. In and of itself, self-mastery is about learning how to best manage and "master" ourselves, so that we may then better serve others. Our search for purpose and meaning should not be just about acquiring the most toys, money, and possessions—but about using our talents and gifts to make a positive difference in organizations and society.

Self-Mastery is also about knowing and being aware of ourselves intimately, both our strengths and our weaknesses. It is this self-awareness that helps us build another key factor in self-mastery—self-esteem. High self-esteem—which simultaneously motivates us to reach for self-mastery and makes it easier to do so—is the primary tool that gives us the patience, resilience, and perseverance we need for continually reaching for and striving toward self-mastery.

Virtually all the pioneers in self-concept research associate improved personal competence and achievement with high self-esteem. When combined with self-efficacy—i.e., our image of ourselves based on personal competency through achieving and doing—high self-esteem brings us a strong sense of self-worth; thus furthering our desire to strive for increased self-mastery.

Only through consciously and intentionally gathering and strengthening our self-esteem and self-efficacy can we begin to develop the skills, attitudes, and self-worth needed to pursue a higher sense of purpose outside ourselves, so that we may better serve others.

When we are successful in finding our individual sense of purpose and following it, as well as, combining it with a path of continuous learning and self-development—self-mastery begins to occur. The word, "mastery," itself, implies a lifelong process aimed at continuously understanding and integrating the natural principles and systems upon which human life is based.

> *"I believe the true road to preeminent success in any line of work is to make yourself master of that line."*
> —Andrew Carnegie

In whatever work we attempt to master—or path we choose to follow to a level of a fully functioning human and interdependent being with others on our planet—we traverse four stages of growth toward interdependency and self-mastery:

Four stages of self-mastery

1. *The "rookie," trainee, or novice stage* in which we are just becoming aware of ourselves, our behaviors and their impact, and those things we will need and want to learn.
2. *The "apprentice" or technique-seeking stage*, in which we begin to develop a few of our "bag of tricks"—those techniques, activities, and specific solutions we will use over and over, often times regardless of their appropriateness—"a *solution* in search of a problem."
3. *The "professional" stage,* in which we develop frameworks, models, and relational perspectives around which we frame our issues and discussions.

4. The master, mentor, sponsor or "jazz musician" stage, wherein we have mastered the natural order of life and Systems Thinking, as well as those strategies, and wisdom that represent the highest skills and competencies in any area of learning we choose—self-mastery being first and foremost.

True self-mastery is ultimately about becoming a jazz musician, with the ability to improvise brilliantly as necessary to any given situation, yet never misusing the "melody" or the natural way the world works (a systems framework). It is about mastering our own self, our knowledge, skills, abilities, attitudes, and capacity for change on a conscious level.

Have you ever heard that old saying, "The more I learn, the more I realize I have yet to learn"? Well, it's never been more true than on our road to self-mastery. Over and over on that road, we learn and gain experience in different things at varying times. It's even normal for us to be in all four stages at once, depending on what different kinds of learnings we're experiencing at any time (even simultaneously), on many different levels—both in our personal and professional lives.

It's entirely possible, for instance, for me to be achieving self-mastery within the realm of my profession, but not within my role as, say, a father. Throughout my life, I am performing as a jazz musician in some area, while still on a rookie or novice level in a different area. This is why it is so critical for us to fully integrate Systems Thinking into our lives, so that we can accept that on an interdependent level, we expect a constant exchange of information and feedback at all the levels and all the roles in which we simultaneously exist. This continuous state of flux is perfectly natural; it means our systems are at work. *Let go of defending yourself and all your ideas and actions; be a naive learner—it's a wonderful place to be.*

Even (or perhaps *especially*) at the jazz musician stage, there is a certain *humbleness.* We are aware—not of how much we've already learned—but how much there is still to learn in so many other areas of life. Remain open to feedback of all kinds, both positive and negative, from every aspect of our environment, and interactions. In the final analysis, every piece of information that comes to us can help us learn (remember Characteristic #4 of Living Systems—feedback?).We don't reach a Systems Thinking, interdependent level of mastery overnight; neither do we gain experience in each individual life role or skill overnight. This is a perfect example of why consistent, strong self-esteem is such an inherent characteristic for achieving self-mastery. It is about a life-long learning and continual self-improvement *attitude.* Do you have this attitude or not?

Successful self-mastery is about creating a balance in our life so that we become more centered and "*on*-purpose," as psychologist Wayne Dyer phrases it in *Your Sacred Self.* It's about pursuing a consistent balance and integrity within ourselves—to our attitudes, values, emotions, and self-esteem—those things by which we shape our underlying character. I believe the ultimate goal of self-mastery is living life on an intentional and *conscious* level, pursuing our greater purpose of a life of service to others with integrity and consistency.

The concept of being "consciously intentional" is crucial to achieving self-mastery. Most of us, when we hear the term "self-mastery," assume that it has something to do with getting so good at what we do "out there" that we don't even have to think about it, we just do it. Ultimately, this is exactly what self-mastery becomes, but we won't reach it without a whole lot of conscious, intentional, self-control "in here" in our hearts and in our minds.

The truth is, full self-mastery is never completely attainable; but it *is* an ongoing process and pursuit of *a state of being and living* in today's complex society. To become consciously intentional of continuously striving toward self-mastery, we need to intentionally control how we behave and control how we think and perceive all of the dimensions in our world—we must become proactive and *act* as though we were enroute to our higher purpose, rather than simply act and *re*act to what goes on around us. To better understand these concepts and how they can be reached, we can look at the specific strategies, or primary *how's* of achieving self-mastery.

Self-Mastery: How to achieve it

There are some distinct areas of progressive activity that can help us achieve self-mastery as a competence: 1) having a vision and a plan, 2) creating balance in body, mind, and spirit, 3) gaining control over our own behavior, and 4) pursuing life-long learning. Within each area, we'll examine the 'how's' for achieving self-mastery, then describe the actions that make them possible.

Skill #1 Vision and plan

As in any systems framework, we begin with two key systems questions. First, there's the question, "Where do I want to be?", followed by, "How do I get there?" To fully answer these questions, you need to first decide what specific results and life purposes you stand for. Then make the key behaviors necessary to accomplish your purposes a focus and priority in your life. These questions are extremely important to achieving self-mastery because they deal with developing your life vision and then committing and aligning yourself to pursuing it.

A clear Ideal Future Vision on the individual level is just as significant in your personal life as it is in the workplace...without it, we stumble, falter, even lose our way or sense of purpose. Your own personal Ideal Future Vision gives you a framework that summarizes where you want to go in life, your career, and what you want to accomplish. Speaking metaphorically, it's your own personal atlas, with your own personal destinations, and it contains specific maps of all the places you want to reach during your life. As in any undertaking, it's a sure thing you won't reach all those places unless you first sit down and create the overall plan, then back it up with the action plans—i.e., those steps (or maps) necessary to achieve it.

How do we create this vision and the game plan for achieving it? Self-mastery isn't possible without the self-direction that results from developing and committing to clear goals. It is, in systems terms, our critical Phase A from which all the basic A-B-C systems processes flow. This is what we mean by the power of using the Systems Thinking Concepts together. The A-B-C model is useful in working at any of the Seven Levels of Living Systems.

There's no question that goal-setting is the #1 criteria for success in any aspect of life—all the research on this is quite clear and specific. So are *you* clear on your vision or purpose (Phase A) for your life, and all the roles you'll play in it? See if you can answer this question for these and other categories:

My Personal Vision
Personally:
1.   Physical/Health
2.   Mental/Learning
3.   Emotional/Spiritual
Mother/Father
Son/Daughter
Family Member
Extended Family
Professional/Job—Career/Business
Lifestyle/Wealth
Friends/Colleagues
Community/Society
What/Where Else?

Obviously, clear goals and vision are imperative; if left alone to stand on their own merit, however, they will not be sufficient for attaining self-mastery. As in any situation, your goals or multiple outcomes must be formally set into a plan of action if you are truly committed to achieving them. The reason for this is two-fold: 1) it helps you clarify your ongoing short-term priorities and areas of focus, and 2) it provides a simple, highly-visible framework that helps keep you on track towards your *multiple goals or vision.*

Goal-setting works because it directs your attention and focuses your highest priority on performance. It also mobilizes effort, increases persistence and discipline, and promotes learning. Setting goals without framing them in some sort of action plan changes nothing, however. The most effective goals are usually those that are mapped out in a specific progression. That's where strategic life planning comes in.

Strategic Life Planning, as practiced by us at the Haines Centre for Strategic Management, encourages self-mastery because it gives us a visible framework for balancing the essentials that feed us, both in our professional lives and our personal lives. To truly achieve our higher purpose in life, all of the integral components of our individual life must work together for the overall objective of our being (Characteristic #1 of Living Systems). To that end, we need to envision our lives at the individual (and/or family) level in much the same A-B-C phases as in any other system.

Strategic Life Planning is essential because it gives us a structure by which we can measure whether or not we're hitting our desired goals. Creating your own individual (or family) strategic life plan using Systems Thinking is as useful and rewarding as strategically planning for a business—provided you religiously include all five A-B-C phases, checking and re-checking against the following questions:

A) Where do I really want to be in the future? (i.e., What are my ends, outcomes, purposes, goals, holistic vision?)

B) How will I know when I get there? (i.e., Are my specific needs and wants connected to a measurable feedback system?)

C) Where am I starting from, right now? (i.e., What are my issues and problems, and my strengths and weaknesses today?) [SWOT Analysis].

D) How will I get there? (i.e., What are the primary strategies and actions for my Ideal Future Vision that I need to take today in a complete, holistic way?)

E) What will or may change in the environment that will effect? (i.e. Helicopter view of life.)

My wife Jayne and I have had a Strategic Life Plan for the past 16 years, and it has made a significant difference in focusing and living our lives the way we want. In fact, all our Partners in the Haines Centre for Strategic Management have life plans, as well. A summary of our plan is shown here:

STRATEGIC LIFE PLAN
OF
STEVE AND JAYNE HAINES
2007—2010

OUR VISION

Our vision is to be more physically healthy and lead an intimate and happy life together. We are financially secure long term and chose when and how much to work.

We will make a positive difference in our own lives...the lives of each other, our family including our grandson, Sebastian...and the lives of the primary people with whom we come in contact.

"Make a Difference"

OUR MISSION

Our purpose or reason for being is to "*make a difference*" through our existence, in the following ways:

1. Caring for each other and with ourselves love, sharing, intimacy, fitness, learning, and balance in all aspects of our lives (e.g. body, mind, emotions, spirit, and time freedom).

2. Sharing with our family and close friends our love, caring, support, time, and celebration of life in mutually enjoyable ways.

3. Assisting clients and Centre Members in the definition and achievement of their Visions.

OUR CORE VALUES
As the way we live our lives while "making a Difference"

1. Integrity

2. Sharing

3. Learning

4. Service

5. Environmental Awareness

6. Spirituality

7. Simplicity

8. Fitness

B

OUR KEY SUCCESS MEASURES

The quantifiable measurements of our vision, mission, and values on a year-by-year basis to ensure continual improvement towards achieving our Ideal Future Vision are:

1. Healthy
2. Prosperous
3. Honesty/Integrity
4. Sharing our abundance
5. High quality professionalism and service
6. Proactive strategic life management
7. Travel and celebrate life
8. Simplicity

C

CORE STRATEGIES

STRATEGY #1:   HEALTHY
BECOME FIT AND HEALTHY IN BODY, MIND, SPIRIT AND TIME
(e.g. CHANGE TO A HEALTHY LIFESTYLE).

STRATEGY #2:   FINANCES
DEVELOP A PROFITABLE BUSINESS MODEL AND BECOME
FINANCIALLY SECURE.

STRATEGY #3:   PROFESSIONAL SERVICES
BE OF SERVICE TO OTHERS WITH HIGH QUALITY PROFESSIONAL
SERVICES AND CUSTOMER SERVICE.

STRATEGY #4:   SHARING ABUNDANCE
MAKE A DIFFERENCE THROUGH SHARING OUR ABUNDANCE.

STRATEGY #5:   INTEGRITY
CONTINUALLY LIVE WITH INTEGRITY AND HONESTY (e.g. ALL
VALUES)

STRATEGY #6:   PROACTIVE
PROACTIVELY PLAN AND MANAGE OUR LIVES AND STRATEGIC
LIFE PLAN (i.e. A STRATEGIC MANAGEMENT SYSTEM) TO ENSURE
OUR VISION IS LIVED ON AN ONGOING BASIS.

STRATEGY #7:   CELEBRATE LIFE
TRAVEL, VACATION, AND CELEBRATE LIFE WITH EACH OTHER,
FAMILY, AND FRIENDS.

D

IMPLEMENTATION

1. Check plan during summer and big vacations.
2. Update and Year End review cycle in November/December.

Hopefully, this personal style can be used as one example you can use to develop your own strategic life plan. Once you've developed your plan, you'll need to go forth and act on it in a focused and responsible way.

Skill #2 Balance in body, mind, spirit

The place to start with is the whole.
All parts of the whole and their relationships to one another evolve from this.

When we look at the intricate balance of the parts and the whole in Systems Thinking, it's clear why balance is an essential ingredient for optimizing ourselves. There are three primary parts to us as humans: 1) our physical body, 2) our minds, and 3) our spirit or inner soul—all of which make me uniquely me, and which makes you the only you there is.

I've developed a simple mental equation that helps us keep on track in understanding the concept behind body-mind-spirit balance, and it goes like this: BMS = KSA = Learning (or *Body-Mind-Spirit* equals *Knowledge-Skills-Attitude* equals *Learning*).

1. When we think of our physical body, we're actually thinking about developing and balancing those physical muscles, fitness, and *skills* we require to thrive—work, play, build, shelter, protect, grow, and so on.
2. The realm of our minds has to do with gaining mastery over the way we think—the *knowledge* and awareness of what's going on around and within us, and how we need to control and focus our thoughts to thrive on a moment-to-moment and day-to-day basis.
3. Our spirit, on the other hand, concerns those *attitudes*, values, and character we develop as we better connect ourselves to a supreme being and sense of purpose outside ourselves.

Each of our body—mind—spirit elements need to be in balance (like functioning on all cylinders) as humans. As in anything else that's fundamental to our lives, keeping our body—mind—spirit in balance is not an easy task. It is, in fact, quite difficult and a life-long challenge, but it is crucial to a life of purpose and value. The more we can sustain an ongoing balance within ourselves, the better we "fit" and perform within our world, and the better we can serve the world in which we live. I've said it before—starve any of these three essential parts of ourselves and we starve as human beings.

Let's look at what we need as human beings to maintain our body—mind—spirit balance and to be healthy and flourish. The widely-accepted needs without which we do not feel complete as individuals include:

(1) *Physical body needs:*

First, we have the obvious need for protecting our *physical* body from harm, so that it may allow us to pursue the best quality of life possible. In order to survive, we must have fuel (food/water), protection from the elements (housing, clothing), and, in our modern world, money. In addition, because we are physical beings, we must exercise and condition our body so it maintains the strength and agility necessary for us to accomplish our purpose in life. Lastly, we need the skills necessary to the achievement of our unique life's purpose. Ask yourself, regularly : *How effective am I in my skills and my physical being/health?*

> ## Why Thinking Matters
> The way you think creates the results you get.
> The most powerful way to impact the quality of your results.
> is to improve the ways you think.

(2) *Mind or mental needs:*
"Thoughts lead to purposes...
purposes go forth in actions...
actions form habits...
habits decide character...
and character fixes our destiny."
—*Tyron Edwards, Forbes Scrapbook of Thoughts on the Business of Life*

All the physical strength in the world means nothing unless it is accompanied by *mental* health and fitness. Our capabilities in complex thought processes must be continually stimulated and challenged in order to remain healthy and grow.

One thing the Information Age has surely accomplished is showing us how important mental fitness is after all, information is merely a bundle of data and statistics without the intellectual ability to sense patterns and string it all together.

Mental fitness depends, in large part, on our capacity for controlling our own thought processes, and for encouraging and understanding the feedback we receive from our environment. Mental fitness is based on our life's purpose and the pursuit of our life-long learning processes, and those elements in life that interest, challenge, and nourish us. Mental fitness is especially important because it affects whether we think in a healthy way that produces the results we want. As this graph illustrates, *the way in which we think directly impacts the quality of our life and its results*:

How you think
is how you plan...
is how you act...
is how you are!

If you think you can't do something, you can't. Conversely, if you think you *can* do something, you usually can. As my superintendent at the U.S. Naval Academy, Admiral Minter, told us plebes (freshmen) in 1964:

*"Remember...you can do anything you put your mind to...**and don't you forget it!"***

(3) *Spiritual needs:*

There's no question that the consequences of good mental fitness extend to every part of your life. There's also no question that simply being mentally fit or physically fit isn't sufficient for a fully-integrated, highly functioning self. We are also *spiritual* beings—with a need for a sense of connectedness to something higher than ourselves.

In order to achieve this, we must feed our inner spirit, the core that is uniquely us. Whether that means a formal religion, a "New Age" spiritual process, a personal life philosophy and core values, or simply the concepts around which you base your life actions, it doesn't matter—what matters is that we continually work at creating in ourselves a character that we can respect and admire, with the right values and attitudes toward others. The focus on self-esteem, the "common good," and our interconnectedness to life all around us is crucial. Again, it's not just about self-aggrandizement or hedonism.

Growing and balancing each of our three distinctly human qualities requires, throughout our life span, continually increasing our knowledge, skills and abilities in each. Again, we must strive to take care of our physical *body*, exercising sufficiently, eating nutritionally, and building our skills. Working to maintain our *minds* and mental fitness is critical for directing and controlling our continuous involvement in the work, play, loving, and living that we need. We must also strive to maintain our "joy of living" and high self-esteem through maintaining fitness of *spirit.*

Having looked at each of these elements individually, however, we must not fail to incorporate another crucial principle of Systems Thinking...*all parts, in any system, can only perform in light of the purpose for which the whole exists.* Always, always remember that balance and fit with our vision and purpose in life is the key.

Integrating each of these elements of your being into your life can bring you a life of fulfillment, excitement, contentment—neglecting any of the three elements creates gaps and a sense of loss, which becomes an anchor tied to your ankle that slows you down. For each of us, the body—mind—spirit balance is, and should be, a uniquely personal decision and plan. Our body—mind—spirit balance can be achieved in many different ways, with many different results. In the final analysis, it doesn't really matter what methods we each adopt to achieve and maintain our balance, it only matters that we do. It is *the key* to becoming a personally effective leader and follower, envisioning the future, inspiring people, clarifying direction for others and taking part in positive actions to make a difference.

Skill #3 Controlling my own behavior

> *"Let him who would move the world first move himself."*
> —*Socrates*

Even an exquisite balance of body—mind—spirit means nothing, though, without control over our own behaviors on a conscious, intentional level. All of the external trappings with which we present ourselves to our world at large—keen intelligence, sharp wit, advanced degrees, spirited drive, etc.—are certainly ingredients that accommodate the accomplishments we may desire. However, without personal accountability, persistent self-discipline, and conscious action, we fall short every time.

"If I could only change one person to make the world better...it should be myself."

To borrow from Jacques Cousteau, *"No law, no regulation, can replace the kind of ethics [that] being a human being imposes on anyone."* Our current culture, with it emphasis on individual freedoms and rights to "life, liberty, and the pursuit of happiness," has left some of us with a lazy, self-indulgent mindset.

A personal observation is pertinent here. I spend most of my professional life facilitating strategic planning and strategic change processes and meetings. I work with CEO groups and senior managers of all types of organizations, public and private, across the U.S., Canada, and Internationally. I have averaged 100+ days (or 1,000 hours) of doing this each year since 1988. In 19 years, this is over 19,000 hours of personal observations of senior executives.

In my expert view, this lazy, self-indulgent mindset and lack of self-control and accountability is endemic in senior executives today. Somewhere around 50% of these executives I come into contact with today are on "autopilot," acting and reacting in the same ways over and over again. They are out of self-control and focus much too inwardly on "me, myself, and I"—their ego. In many ways, this book is for them, as the other 50% are an absolute joy to work with and assist in their journeys towards personal fulfillment through achieving some purpose outside themselves.

To summarize, in my view, we, as individuals and as a society have taken individual rights and self interest to a bloated extreme. Now, we need to step back and each of us re-think this from a societal and systems perspective.

When we re-examine it from the systems viewpoint that "the whole is greater than the sum of its parts," it is more crucial than ever for us individually to clearly delineate between rights and responsibilities. Though we need and want individual freedoms (reference today's most popular buzz word, "empowerment"), we must never forget that with such freedom comes great responsibility to serve others and make a positive difference in today's difficult world.

Those things that can take our focus outside ourselves and concentrate our lives on a higher purpose can be such simple but meaningful concepts as integrity, reliability, loyalty, honesty, or responsibility. We must also keep in mind that, as individuals, we are characterized by our relationships with the individuals that surround us—it is not possible for us to survive and thrive separate or apart from our environment. In pursuing self-mastery on an interdependent level, it is crucial to be honest with yourself about what you really want from life, and to bring a sense of integrity to the methods, ethics, and relationships in your life and career.

You must also make a conscious choice to act as if you are 100% responsible for creating the results and outcomes you desire in life...because, in fact, you are. A clear understanding that you are 100% committed to successfully achieving your desired goals is also necessary in gaining control over your behaviors.

When we are able to consistently hold ourselves accountable in our day-to-day life, it becomes a key ingredient to pursuing, reaching, and maintaining self-mastery. This level of commitment and accountability also directly impacts our life style, keeping us on track with our desired goals. In the U.S. Center for Disease Control, a survey was taken to evaluate sources of risk to physical health. The survey found that, among such sources as biological, environmental, and medical care risks, the major source of health risk is our lifestyle, at over 50%.

A final but important self-mastery ingredient is maintaining an awareness of our emotions, rather than letting emotions control our actions willy-nilly. Feelings and emotion are areas that we, particularly in our working lives, tend to overlook or even ignore—yet, left unacknowledged, they can play havoc. Emotional self-awareness can often make the difference in our gaining control over stressful life situations. When we are in touch with our emotions, we are better able to adjust our behaviors as needed to reach the optimal level of clarity for peak performance. Being aware of and acknowledging your feelings and emotions is Step #1—controlling them is Step #2 (a step which the 50% of executives I mentioned earlier do *not* do).

Emotional balance (Emotional IQ in the jargon of the day), accepting accountability, and responsibility for ourselves and our actions is key. So is acting with integrity, recognizing our interdependence, and controlling ourselves and our behaviors in interpersonal relationships—each of these are needed to gain control over our behavior on a conscious, intentional level.

WHAT?	1) *What happened?*
SO WHAT?	2) *So what did I learn?*
NOW WHAT?	3) *Now what am I going to do differently?*

Skill #4 Life-long learning

Achieving self-mastery, then, requires of us: 1) a vision, 2) body—mind—spirit balance, and 3) gaining control over our own behaviors. The fourth and final, yet equally essential ingredient we need for self-mastery is life-long learning. Though we talked about learning as a part of our body—mind—spirit balance, life-long learning is more of an entire, conscious orientation to life, a continuous commitment to the pursuit of learning and the associated feedback that is so crucial. Here, once again, self-esteem is a critical factor; it is core to being able to be open to feedback—without which we cannot have life-long learning. In fact, we believe that "*feedback is the breakfast of champions,*" as you'll discover in the last chapter of this book

Life-long learning is not as much about a learning process as it is an attitude toward life itself. People who pursue interdependent self-mastery are willing to retain a sense of humility about what they've just learned, because they understand that—no matter how much they've learned in one area of life—there are and always will be more areas about which they are still ignorant or incompetent or still need to grow in.

Life-long learning is about instinctively knowing that, while *knowledge* is always essential, ever-improving *skills* and *attitudes* are just as important to personal success. Without all three, we don't apply the learnings as a competency. It is well-documented that "adults learn best by doing"—it's the difference between "talking," which imparts knowledge, and "discovery," which can only occur when we apply action to the "talking." This holistic approach to life-long learning should encompass three specific questions to learn from our experiences:

Throughout our life-long learning, as we learn, process, and apply our knowledge, these three questions can help us avoid this familiar question: *"Did I gain ten years' experience or did I simply repeat one year's experience ten times over?"*

"There are two types of people in the world...the 'learn-ed' and the 'learners.'
The 'learn-ed' are the people who interpret today's world based on what they
learned 40 years ago and have not changed or grown since.
'Learners' are constantly in a changing progression. Based on mistakes and
failures, they change and grow."
—Greg Riddoch, former Baseball Manager

In order to continuously progress through our dependent and independent life stages to the reality of life as interdependent adults, we need life-long learning about ourselves. Throughout the course of our lives, we need to develop and acquire different skills for different purposes, and we can't do this without being committed to learning throughout life. The day of the forty year job or career with one company, with the pension and company watch at retirement is gone forever. Most experts believe we will have three to four careers in our lives—in my instance, writing is my fourth career...the Navy was my first.

Education, learning, and continuously gaining new skills and attitudes are also crucial throughout our life span because our environment is dramatically changing, as well. If we are not continually sensing our environment, gaining feedback from it, and learning, we are falling behind, running down, and, in general, becoming irrelevant (remember entropy, Characteristic #10 of Living Systems?).

Our individual career paths, for instance, take many different shapes throughout our life span. We continue to learn new functions; we move vertically up or horizontally across the hierarchy of different organizations. We serve at several levels simultaneously, too, from apprentice to colleague, to mentor or sponsor—and with each stage and transition, we learn about a brand-new array of issues and emotions—resulting in anxiety, excitement, challenge, reassessment, and change, to name but a few.

Today's global marketplace is forcing most of us to repeatedly reconsider our career choices and paths. As I've said, the day of retiring with a gold watch after 40 years service to one organization is long past, and it is changing too fast and in too many ways for us to anticipate what lies ahead. Those of us who stubbornly remain 'learn-ed' by shaping our choices around the reality we know today will soon be left in the dust by 'learners' who recognize change for what it is, embrace it, and continually update, train, and develop themselves to be ready for tomorrow's job market. We all need to embrace and master the value of life-long learning; it's a fact of life today that we must wake up to—even (or maybe especially) the increasing population of surreptitiously-laid-off 40-50 year-old, one-career employees who must continue to learn and grow in order to thrive. *If you know one of these people, give them a copy of this book and note this page!*

As we mentioned earlier in "Visioning," we also change roles in our personal lives. We go from being someone's son or daughter, to an increasingly independent adolescence, to husband, wife, mother, father, and so on. Throughout each of these roles and transitions, be they in our professional or personal lives, we must continually be open to new learning, obtaining new knowledge and attitudes, and developing new skills.

To achieve life-long learning, it is necessary to understand what we at the Haines Centre for Strategic Management call the Stairway of Learning (developed by my partner, Jim McKinlay), illustrated graphically here.

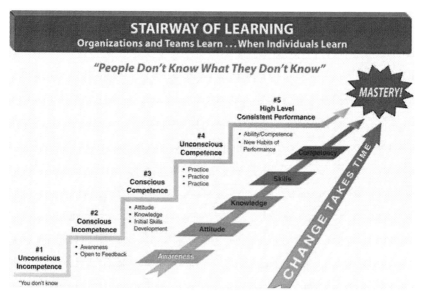

Figure: 6.2 Stairway of Learning

The Stairway of Learning issue is about going from *unconscious incompetence*—you don't even know what you don't know yet—to *conscious incompetence*—becoming aware that there are many things you don't yet know—to *conscious competence*—developing and practicing new attitudes, knowledge, and skills—and, finally, honing those skills to a level of *unconscious competence*. In fact, at the highest levels of mastery our consciousness competence becomes so ingrained in us that we *un*consciously select the appropriate behaviors in a given situation. Just be careful that this doesn't spill over to an auto-pilot mode, which is the reason we call this *life-long* learning.

Once we reach the level of unconscious competence, the learning cycle begins all over again, only this time we find ourselves at a different or higher plane of development. This is why a continuing commitment to life-long learning is so important—we truly only move forward when we're open to learning. We do not learn or advance to any higher planes when we remain fixed in a self-centered or defensive stance. When we approach life from a holistic view in which learning is necessary and wonderful, it enables us to humbly acknowledge and accept that naiveté, feedback, and learning is an ongoing part of a healthy, balanced life.

In order to change and grow, life-long learning is fundamental to self-mastery. Indeed, in the 21st Century, we each face more change of a far different kind than anything we could have imagined 15 years ago. If we want to succeed in today and tomorrow's world, we will need more than ever the kind of self-mastery that enables us to create, rather than simply react.

"The people who get on in this world are the people who get up and look for the circumstances they want, and, if they can't find them, make them."
—George Bernard Shaw

Of course, it's much easier said than done; it takes very hard work, persistence, and ingenuity to accomplish this. By continually concentrating, persisting, and persevering on all these necessary ingredients to self-mastery, and following through in setting (and *re*-setting) priorities and goals for unmet needs year to year, you can accomplish it. Focusing on one area or role in your life, for instance, may take you a little way down your path, but, ultimately, it won't get you where you truly want to go.

Where individual self-mastery is happening today...and where it needs to happen:
In the military:

Though individual self-mastery in a holistic way is not yet among the broad-stroke change concepts, there *are* places where it is beginning to take hold. The U.S. Naval Academy in Annapolis, for instance, believes that self-mastery is so important for character-building that they have a four-year course of study called Integrity Development Training. It is an unusual program, which breaks from the more typical training by lecture, into more contemporary training by discussion. The U.S. Naval Academy even goes so far as to state the underlying self-mastery concepts right in their mission statement:

The Mission of the Naval Academy:
To develop midshipmen morally, mentally, and physically and to imbue them with the highest ideals of duty, honor, and loyalty in order to provide graduates who are dedicated to a career of naval service and have potential for future development in mind and character to assume the highest responsibilities of command, citizenship, and government.

In education:

Self-Mastery as a part of Systems Thinking is also creeping into our community and educational systems. The U.S. Department of Labor, through its Secretary's Commission on Achieving Necessary Skills (SCANS), asked business and industry what capabilities were most desirable from students entering the job market, the response included most aspects of our individual self-mastery, based on Systems Thinking:

The Three SCANS foundation skills

1. **Basic skill development:** Reading, writing, mathematics, speaking, listening
2. **Thinking skills:** Thinking creatively, decision-making, problem-solving, visualizing, learning how to learn and to reason
3. **Personal qualities:** Individual responsibility, self-esteem, sociability, self-management, integrity

The Five SCANS competencies

1. **Resources:** Allocating time, money, materials, space, and staff
2. **Interpersonal skills:** Working in teams, teaching others, serving customers, leading, negotiating, and working well with people from culturally diverse backgrounds
3. **Information handling skills:** Acquiring and evaluating data, organizing and maintaining files, interpreting and communicating, and computer processing of information
4. **Systems:** Understanding social, organizational and technological systems, monitoring performance, and designing and improving systems
5. **Technology:** Selecting appropriate technology, applying the most effective tools for the task, and using good troubleshooting skills

Source: T.I.E. News, volume 5, no. 1

This indicates that the U.S. school system is beginning to understand and appreciate that self-mastery goes far beyond simple knowledge, however, it still has a long way to go. They are, at least initially, recognizing at the federal level the concept that knowledge must be taught *in conjunction with* the skills and attitudes needed to make real use of knowledge.

It is the skills and attitudes that make a difference in our lives and careers, not just knowledge alone. Schools today still persist, however, in placing 70-80% of their teaching emphasis on knowledge alone. This 70-80% emphasis is based on surveys I've conducted in numerous schools systems with which we have done strategic planning, plus numerous observations of others. Further, a key to life for all of us is our attitude of positive self-esteem. This is much more important to be conveyed and reinforced in schools than, again, knowledge alone.

Questions to Ponder...

- What are your own strengths and weaknesses in Self-Mastery?
- Do you have a strategic life plan? If not, when will you start to build one?
- Which of the SCANS competencies and foundation skills do you possess?

In families & community groups:

The same holds true for parents and adults in dealing with kids, whether within families, Girls or Boy Scouts, Big Brothers and Sisters, and all other children's groups and clubs. There remains an inherent need to focus on skills and attitudes, and especially, self-esteem. Further, it is crucial for schools, families, and clubs to help children vision and image their own positive Ideal Futures, and do their own mini-version of our strategic life planning (especially the visioning portion).

In corporations:

Today, organizations have seen the value to their success by "linking benefits and employee satisfaction to their Business Plan." These benefits are much more holistic in nature, taking into account all the individual employee and family needs.

Today's corporations are well aware that personal, family, and home concerns have a direct and potent impact on its employees' workplace performance. According to the March, 1995, issue of *HR* magazine, a mere decade ago, the number of work-life programs in U.S. corporations numbered 600; today, it exceeds 10,000 and continues to grow today over 90% offer some form of work-life support.

In the training & development industry:

Individual change expert Charles Garfield's "Peak Performance" seminars teach the integration of such self-mastering techniques as motivating yourself by having a mission, welcoming change and innovation, becoming results-oriented, developing teamwork capabilities, and, most importantly, viewing and developing yourself as your own best resource.

An organizational pioneer in this is author Stephen Covey, whose book and course on *"Seven Habits of Highly Effective People"*, is helping many people in organizations. Covey's Seven Habits consistently follow Systems Thinking, even though he himself seems to be unaware of the link—he is simply following the natural order and principles of life, which, of course, *is* Systems Thinking.

In the Human Potential Movement:

While this field has been around for many years now, it still plays a vital role in individual self-mastery. In fact, many of the more "touchy-feely" concepts and processes within the Human Potential Movement are becoming more and more mainstream all the time. Places like NTL (National Training Labs), of Arlington, VA, Gestalt Institute of Cleveland, and Esalen Institute on the Big Sur in California are some of the originators and are more useful today than ever.

In my mind, their main limitations are that their feelings styles are not for everyone and that they focus mainly on body/emotions. While they focus on the mind as important and "centered," it appears to be a more limited focus of the three.

In downsizing, outplacement, and retraining:

As our society continues to restructure itself in the Information Age and into the coming Systems Age, people are having two, three, even four careers. Thus, there are many firms assisting organizations with outplacement and downsizing. There are also many organizations focused on helping people with retraining for their next career or job. This last category includes not only private sector firms, but government-funded ones, schools, extension studies departments in colleges, Regional Occupational Programs (ROP), tied to the county school system in many North American states.

All of these organizations can assist tremendously with people in these critical "career transition" periods. The systems principles and ideas on self-mastery that are absolutely essential to people at this point in particular include: 1) strategic life planning (not just job training), 2) balance of body/mind/spirit, 3) life-long learning (versus forced obsolescence), and 4) control over self (with enhanced self-esteem being the key).

In all areas (holistic):

As we survive the changing ages and all that they imply, we will need more than ever the holistic approach that life-long learning and Systems Thinking bring to all areas of our lives. Noted author and Futurist, Ken Dychtwald calls this phenomenon an "Age Wave," and cited three primary training areas in which life-long learning will be crucial:

Three Primary Training Areas:

1. Job re-training

2. Cyclic strategic life planning

3. Inter-generational/community relationship skills

It is only through such a holistic approach to how we change and adapt in each area of life, making sure to give equal importance to all that we can hope to attain real self-mastery.

In general:

It's clear that the underlying concepts of self-mastery—developing a clear vision, balancing body, mind, and spirit, gaining control over our behaviors, and life-long learning—are gaining recognition and acceptance in many areas today. What we're still seeing, however, is that while one, two, or even three of these concepts are applied, it continues to be within a piecemeal, almost hit-or-miss framework—there has been no holistic approach to self-mastery prior to this book. To fully achieve our individual sense of a higher purpose, we must first consistently apply this fully integrated, Systems Thinking approach to self-mastery everywhere in our society.

Summary

"He who knows others is learned. He who knows self is wise."
—*Lao-Tsu, TaoTeh King*

As we examine the Systems Thinking concept of the Seven Levels of Living Systems and at the individual level, it becomes clear that self-mastery is the key to leadership and making a difference in the lives of others. Though self-mastery by its very definition is far from easy, it is clearly possible to progress quite far in this direction. Self-Mastery isn't easy to achieve; there will be many times when difficulties will arise and challenges will seem too steep. It is the persistence, and in the striving toward mastery that is important. Self-Mastery is never really "achieved;" it is a process and pursuit of a state of being and living in today's complex society. However, by:

1. *Keeping a strong sense of ourselves through self-esteem and integrity,*
2. *Setting aside our ego and becoming a 'sponge' to the world around us,*
3. *Incorporating strong, valid feedback mechanisms so that we know when we're doing something right or wrong...*

...we will experience the vigor, intensity, and satisfaction that come from being a part of shaping our own destiny.

> *"Nothing in the world can take the place of persistence.*
> *Talent will not...nothing is more common than unsuccessful men with talent.*
> *Genius will not...unrewarded genius is almost a proverb.*
> *Education will not...the world is full of educated derelicts.*
> *Persistence and determination alone are omnipotent."*

When we move higher and higher still toward this kind of mastery, we can begin to make a profound difference in the lives of others. Through developing strategies and working to become consciously competent at:

1. Shaping them into our own individual "game plan" through Strategic Life Planning

2. Controlling our actions and holding ourselves accountable for our commitments

3. Maintaining a balanced and healthy body, mind, spirit, and self-esteem

4. Continuing our life-long, knowledge-skills-attitudes learning process ...we can achieve mastery over ourselves and our lives. These four strategies—together with Systems Thinking for the approaching Systems Age—are needed in every aspect of our society—families, schools, clubs, organizations, churches, not-for-profit organizations, neighborhoods, and communities. What is particularly needed is for some leaders in all of these organizations to step forward.

In this chapter, we have explored how self-mastery affects life all around us at Systems Level #3, the individual as a system. We have examined how mastery over ourselves will be crucial to finding systems solutions in the Systems Age.

All Seven Levels of Living Systems are important to us. We need to function effectively at most, if not all, of theses **Six Rings of Reality**. Hence, the Centre's important research in developing our **Centering Your Leadership** model with its Six Natural Leadership Competencies and 30 Skills that correspond to each of the Seven Levels of Living Systems (and their relationships/collision of systems).

However, no matter which of these six rings you are focusing one in your life at work, at home, or in your community, Self-Mastery is the first and foremost life-long issue to pursue.

"If I can't change myself, what hope do I have of helping to change others?"

Learners in Times of Drastic Change

"In times of drastic change it is the learners who inherit the future."

Source: The Economist, March 25, 2006

In the next three chapters, we will look at how other Systems Thinking Concepts can be applied separately and also integrated with each of these Six Rings of Reality from the Seven Levels of Living Systems to make a difference in our organizations and world.

Chapter 6

The Seven Levels of Living Systems
Summary of Key Concepts

1. In this chapter we tried to look at these Seven Levels of Living Systems (Concept #1) in application; especially as it relates to Leadership Competencies at all key levels.

2. These are six natural Leadership Levels—one for each level of Living Systems and their **collision of these same systems**:

	Energy Source ⟼	Leadership Competencies ⟼	Some Outcomes
Level #1	Awareness	Enhancing Self-Mastery	Balanced Life
Level #2	Integrity	Build Interpersonal Relationships	Trust
Level #3	Interdependence	Facilitating Empowered Teams	Goal Attainment
Level #4	Valuing Service	Collaborating Across Functions	Customer-Focused
Level #5	Shared Vision/Values	Integrating Organizational Outcomes	Add Customer Value
Level #6	Synergy	Creating Strategic Positioning	Globally Competitive

3. Within each core competency there are five or more skills to learn. Since **Enhancing Self-Mastery** is the first competency and foundation for all others, going through (1) visioning and life planning, (2) building a balance in body—mind—spirit, (3) learning to control my own behaviors, and (4) pursuing life-long learning are crucial to fulfilling your potential as a person and as a leader.

4. Why does "thinking" matter? Remember, "how you think…is how you act…is how you are." Think holistically about all Seven Levels of Living Systems and which one(s) you are working or trying to change.

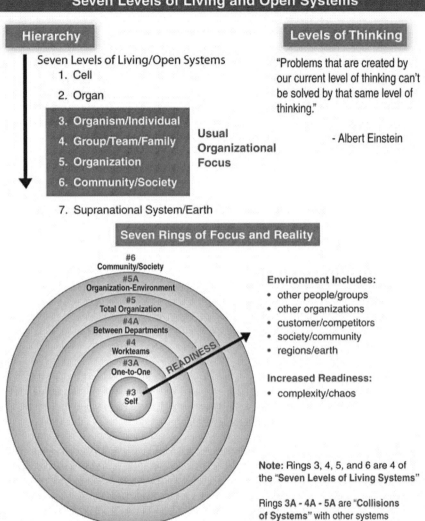

Figure 6:3 Concept #1 Seven Levels of Living and Open Systems

CHAPTER 7

Concept #2: Standard Systems Dynamics

"The Laws of Natural (Living) Systems…
systems and strategic consistency yet operational flexibility"

OVERVIEW

"Systems Thinking is a discipline for seeing wholes, a framework for seeing patterns and interrelationships. It's especially important to see the world as a whole as it grows more and more complex.

Complexity can overwhelm and undermine: 'It's the system. I have no control.' Systems Thinking makes these realities more manageable; it's the antidote for feelings of helplessness.

By seeing the patterns that lie behind events and details, we can actually simplify life."

—Peter M. Senge, The Fifth Discipline

Simplifying how we view life is what 12 Characteristics, or Laws of Natural Living Systems that were defined by the General Systems Theorists are all about. They have incredible and far reaching implications. After all, they are the predictable characteristics of how living systems at all Seven Levels of Living Systems act on our earth.

They lead to a set of "Standard Systems Dynamics" that allow us to discuss these living systems in similar ways throughout our personal and professional lives. It also allows authors such as us to write books such as these.

Think about it...without a set of standard and predictable dynamics of how individuals, teams, and organizations function, the scientific field of management and leadership would not exist!

In trying to understand the implications of these 12 characteristics as they interact with each other, we have only begun to "scratch the surface". Unfortunately for the "profession of management" these characteristics may be the natural way systems can operate, but most organizations experience a different set of dynamics.

For example, open and living systems have feedback on their effectiveness as a normal part of their functioning. However, in most organizations and in most teams and in most performance management systems, individuals receive little or no useful feedback. For this reason we have devoted an entire chapter later in this book to the problems with this dynamic.

In fact, in almost every one of these standard system characteristics and dynamics, the opposite seems to occur in many organizations as we mismanage them, violate them, and ignore these characteristics. Look at the full list of these natural laws and characteristics vs. the experienced dynamics.

CONCEPT #2: Laws of Natural Systems (Standard Systems Dynamics)

Natural Laws/Desired State	vs.	Experienced Dynamics
1. **Holism**-Overall Purpose-Focused Synergy/Transformational		1. Parts/Activity Focused/ Suboptimal Results
2. **Open Systems**-Open to Environment		2. Closed Systems/Low Environmental Scan
3. **Boundaries**- Integrated/ Collaborative		3. Fragmented/Turf Battles/ Separate/Parochial
4. **Input/Output**-How natural systems operate		4. Piecemeal/Analytic/ Sequential and Narrow View
5. **Feedback**-on Effectiveness/ Root Causes		5. Low Feedback/Financial Only
6. **Multiple Outcomes**- Goals		6. Artificial Either/or Thinking
7. **Equifinality**-Flexibility and Agility		7. Direct Cause—Effect/One Best Way
8. **Entropy**-Follow-up/Inputs of Energy/Renewal		8. Decline/Rigidity/Obsolete and Death
9. **Hierarchy**-Flatter Organization/Self-Organizing		9. Hierarchy/Bureaucracy/ Command and Control
10. **Inter-related Parts**- Relationships/ Involvement and Participation		10. Separate Parts/Components/ Entities/Silos
11. **Dynamic Equilibrium**- Stability and Balance/Culture		11. Short-term Myopic View/ Ruts/Resistance to Change
12. **Internal Elaboration**-Details and Sophistication		12. Complexity and Confusion

QUESTIONS TO PONDER...

As a result of these 12 Natural Laws of Characteristics of Living Systems:

- Why do you think we often don't follow them in organizations?
- Which two-three characteristics/laws are most violated in your organization?
- Which two-three do you pay the most attention to in a positive way?

As a result of this state of affairs, we have tried to identify some "Guiding Principles" for these natural laws to guide us in our organizations today. Along with them we have identified a *"systems question"* to go with each of them in order to assist you in using these principles in your organizations.

Some Guiding Principles of the Systems Age

To truly become the creators of our own future in the 21st Century, it will be imperative for us to resist applying *Systems Thinking* merely as a generic buzzword, and, instead, develop this new way of thinking to the point where it is the continuing, **unconscious** discipline of our daily lives.

As you begin to assimilate and master Systems Thinking, use the guiding principles, outlined here, as a map to keep you on track. As I said, these principles are underscored by key *systems questions* that can continually help you determine whether you're on track with Systems Thinking, versus partial Systems Thinking or analytic, reductionist thinking.

From these principles, the Centre has devised these Systems Thinking Questions to apply the principles in your daily work and life. These systems questions underscore why knowing and understanding the systems in and around us has been so difficult...*the tools and key questions to make it a useful discipline have been lacking*.

If you want a "show stopper" in a meeting, just use these questions—and refocus the meeting on a more productive one. These principles and associated systems questions need to become an inherent part of any leader's day-to-day Systems Thinking. They need to become as much a part of your daily tools as your computer, your car, paper, and pen. In time, as you become more and more adept with your Systems Thinking 'tools,' you will also find yourself refining and honing them for all of your needs and applications—thus, using Systems Thinking as the foundation upon which you base all your choices and decisions as a leader.

For all ten Key Systems Questions, Preconditions, and Tools in one place, please see the end of this chapter.

Principle #1 Look for the common superordinate goal whenever possible.

Too often in situations of conflict and disagreements, it is because we each focus on our own goals. In each case, if you will raise your sights higher to the level of a Living System that encompasses both of you; you will find a goal that is a common one. We call these a "superordinate" goal as it is at a super or higher level of systems thinking. It is here where you can find the 3rd alternative (as Steven Covey says) to create a win-win solution. This gives rise to the **Ultimate Systems Tool and Question:** "What is our common superordinate goal here?"

*This gives rise to the **Ultimate Systems Tool and Question:** "What is our common Superordinate goal here?" (This is the Helicopter View of Life)*

Principle #2 The entity to be changed must be clear. (Remember.... 'holism')

Challenge the obvious–always look for and define the presence of which of the Seven Levels of Living Systems you're dealing with. Be clear on the entity you are working to change–is it an individual, team, family, business unit, community, company, state, nation, or international country? What are its boundaries? Is it relatively open or closed in its environmental interactions?
This gives rise to the first Systems Precondition Question:
***Precondition #1** "What entity, system, or 'collision of systems' are we dealing with?"*
This must be clear and agreed upon by everyone before taking action.

Principle #3 Always begin any dialogue with a crystal-clear understanding of the desired outcomes. (Remember...multiple goal seeking).

Develop clarity/agreement to this before beginning any actions. Keep in mind there are usually multiple outcomes; not either/or questions from reductionistic thinking. Other words for outcomes include: vision, ends, goals, objectives, mission, purpose, (the "what"), etc.

*This principle gives rise to **Systems Question #1:** "What are the desired outcomes?"*

Without agreement on ends, our actions will never have a chance of succeeding. Once the "what" is clear, there are many ways to achieve the same end (the "how") through empowerment, etc.

Principle #4 There are many different ways to achieve the same desired outcomes, thus, involvement of the right people involved in planning and implementing the solutions/actions is key. (Remember... equifinality).

"People support what they help create." It follows that decision making should be as close to the actions and the entity we desire to change in #1 as possible. People have a natural desire to be involved and provide input into decisions that affect them *before* the decision is made. For leaders, this is called participatory management skills, which results in empowerment.

*This principle gives rise to **Systems Question #6:***
"What do we need to do to ensure buy-in/stay-in and perseverance over time (toreverse the entropy)?"

Principle #5 Feedback is the breakfast of champions—be flexible and adaptive. (Remember the feedback loop).

In today's complex and continually changing world, initial solutions are not even as important as the ability to gain constant feedback vis-à-vis our outcome measures of success. Then, we can continually adapt in order to better achieve our desired outcomes. The ability to be flexible and adaptive (i.e., to learn, grow, change and adapt to changes in the environment) are crucial. Economies of speed are replacing economies of scale as a key competitive edge.

Feedback relating to our outcomes is the key input into today's need for learning organizations that can learn, grow, and adapt at all levels of the organizational system (individuals, teams, and the organization as a whole). Leaders also need constant feedback on their own desired outcomes in order to continue to learn and grow.

*This principle relates directly to **Systems Question #2:***
"How will we know we've achieved our goals?"

Principle #6 The whole is more important than the parts—and the relationships and processes are key. (Remember holism and subsystems).

Synthesis of how the parts fit/link together in an integrated process in support of the whole outcome is the most important assessment to be continually made by any system.

Analysis of each part's effectiveness cannot be analyzed in a vacuum, but only in relationship to the other parts and the processes that lead to the whole. *Always remember, a system cannot be subdivided into independent parts.* Change in one part effects the whole and the other interdependent parts or processes. This is true whether talking about families, teams, departments, neighborhoods, organizations, or society as a whole; something we all still need to learn and understand.

This gives rise to **Systems Question #4:**
"What is the relationship of X to Y?"
(And, how do they contribute to the overall objective of the whole system and its desired outcomes?)

Remember to employ 'backwards thinking,' start with what is changing in

Principle #7 Work and align the entity to be changed from the outside-in–not inside-out. (Remember...open systems view).

the environment, and the wants and needs of the customer and desired outcomes to gain clarity. Then work backwards in the organization to determine how to meet those current and future needs while still meeting the multiple outcomes of other key environmental stakeholders.

Align all employees, suppliers, the entire organization, and business processes across departments to meet these outcomes. This is the conceptual basis for business process re-engineering in today's organizations. However, it is often fragmented into departmental elements or internal cost-cutting activities only without regard to customer impact.

This principle most directly aligns with **Systems Question #3:**
"What will be changing in the environment in the future that will impact us?"

Principle #8 All systems are linked to other systems—some larger; some smaller–in a hierarchy. (See hierarchy characteristic).

No system is independent of any other. We are all, as human beings, linked in a hierarchy of systems to all others on this planet, to a greater or lesser extent, *whether we like it or not.* Pay close attention to both the system and system-system linkages as well. Supplier—organization—customer is one set of linkages; individual—family—community would be another example of system-system linkages. It is crucial to make this hierarchy work together for you in a synergistic fashion.

This gives rise to the second Systems Precondition Question: **Precondition #2**
"Within our identified system, what level(s) of the system are we trying to change?

Principle #9 Root causes and effects are usually not linked closely in time and space. (See open systems and systems boundaries).

Our simplistic, knee-jerk, cause-effect analyses and desire for quick fixes often *cause* more problems than we solve. Our world/earth is composed of seven levels of complex and interdependent systems, multiple causes with multiple effects are the true reality, as are circles of causality-effects. See, for example, how our local weather and crops are effected by the ocean/clouds/rain/wind/plants/food, etc.

Delayed time—the time between causes and their impacts—can have enormous influences on a system. The concept of 'delayed effect' is often missed in our impatient society and it is often too subtle, ignored, and almost always under-estimated. When we feel that results aren't happening quickly enough, it shakes our confidence—causing unnecessary violent 'knee-jerk' reactions.

Decisions often have long term consequences years later. Mind mapping, fishbone diagrams, and all sorts of creativity/brainstorming tools are quite useful here. However, *keep in mind that the complexity encountered is often far beyond our human ability to fully assess and comprehend intuitively.* For this reason, it is crucial to flag or anticipate delays; understand and appreciate them–and learn to work *with* them–rather than against them.

*This principle aligns with **Systems Question #9:***
"What are the root causes?"

Caution: Dig deep, and dig again, for the root causes; they are rarely obvious—just like there are six sides to a Rubiks Cube that interact with each other

Figure 7-1: Rubik's Cube

Principle #10 The KISS method really is best—reverse the entropy! (See entropy and neg-entropy characteristic).

Systems can continuously increase in complexity until they become very bureaucratic and ossified, ultimately resulting in the death of the system. All living systems require constant energy and inputs (i.e., feedback) into them if they are to reverse this entropy. Otherwise, all living systems eventually run down and die.

For example, while human beings and families obviously have a finite life cycle, it doesn't have to be this way for neighborhoods, communities, and organizations. For them, the renewal process that reverses the entropy is key to long-term success. Fortunately, chaos and disorder are a precursor to renewal and growth at a higher level. Don't let this short-term disorientation prevent long-term success.

In addition—and this is the good news in our worldwide instantaneous information transmissions—we now have a virtually limitless supply of constant feedback which provides us with new input toward change. On the reverse side, however, we often have the problem of information overload, leading to more and more complexity in our lives. We need to eliminate the waste that complexity brings. Remember, the KISS method is more powerful than many economies of scale. Focus on the fundamentals, *not* the fads. In the future, the virtual corporation may very well be more effective than the more traditional, vertically integrated complex organizations.

This principle gives rise to **Systems Question #10:**
"How can we go from complexity to simplicity and from consistency to flexibility,
in the solutions we devise?"

Reverse the Rubik's Cube Effect and our *unintended consequences.* Instead *understand the consequences* and keep it simple.

> **Principle #11 The steady state equilibrium we all want can kill us. In a rapidly changing society, the biggest risk is to stay the same. (See steady state, entropy characteristic).**

However, our normal and natural inclination is to maintain the status quo and its comfortableness vs. the pain, awkwardness, uncertainty, and ambiguity of change. Change requires the difficult issues of (1) admitting and becoming willing to change, along with (2) acquiring the new skills and abilities to function more effectively.

Knowledge and information is just an input, and not enough of an input to be effective by itself. Further skills in working with systems need to be developed if we want to learn, grow, and change. Short-term creative destruction can sometimes be key to long term advances; today's 'steady state' is one of constant change.

This gives rise to **Systems Question #7:**
"What are the new structures and processes we are using to ensure successful changes?"

> ## Principle #12 Focus and strengthen the basic units/systems of organizations and society. (See holism characteristic).

In our view, the basic unit of organizations and society is not the individual alone. It is also the relationships of individuals to one another. Thus, we believe the basic units to be: (1) the diverse family, home or department team, and then (2) the community or organization.

We need to balance our strong North American natural tendency to glorify the individual at the expense of community and society (see Eastern Oriental society for the reverse). The old nuclear family or functional department team in organizations is often not the unit either; it is both 1) today's differently defined and diverse family, and 2) the cross-functional teams in organizations, as well. We need to strengthen all these units!

> ## Principle #13 Change is an individual act. (See the Seven Levels of Living Systems...the individual is the smallest conscious system).

Organizational change is a myth. Organizations and institutions change only when people change. Processes and procedures change when people change their behaviors. Accepting responsibility for yourself and your actions and being accountable for them is key. Each of us needs to understand how we link to and fit in with the rest of society.

Unfortunately, in terms of wisdom and maturity, *interdependence* is the third or highest order, coming after the 1) dependent and 2) *in*dependent stages. Truth is, independence is really a myth! Thus, focusing on assisting individual change within the interdependent family/team/unit-as-a-system and context is the only way to assist real individual change.

This principle directly relates to the Foundation Tool of the Systems Questions: "What is it that I can contribute to the problem and can change to be a positive and proactive leader on this?"

> ## Principle #14 Systems upon systems upon systems are too complex to fully understand and manage centrally. (See internal elaboration, complexity).

Thus, liberation from regulation, shaping corporate bureaucracies into smaller units, privatization, and free market economies are generally more efficient and effective than government or big business can ever be in understanding the complexities of systems. It is the thousands and thousands of little decisions we all make daily in our businesses that shape and meet these market needs; not central government regulations. Clearly, government has a role to play in today's society, just not an all-encompassing one! The same is true for big corporations.

This principle most closely aligns with **Systems Question #8:**
"What do we centralize (mostly 'what's') and what (mostly 'how's') should we decentralize?"

Principle #15 We are holistic human beings—in search of meaning. (See multiple goal seeking).

Our search for meaning in our lives is crucial to our own success and failure. This meaning only comes from the "ends" and "whats" of serving others outside of ourselves, as opposed to the many more self-serving activities we undertake in our lives. Rather, we need to align our activities–or 'means' or 'how-to's'—to our 'ends' or what we are doing to serve others. Again, this requires understanding of our own interdependence with others in our world.

And, the more we can be a balanced, holistic human being in body, mind, and spirit, the better we can serve others. Starve any of these three essential elements and we starve as human beings. Dehumanize us in our work settings and we don't perform anywhere near to our true potential.

This principle gives rise to **Systems Question #5:**
"Are we dealing with means or ends?"
Only "ends thinking" or" destination thinking" or "backwards thinking" is true Strategic and Systems Thinking

Principles #16-17-18 "You tell me..."

Above all in Systems Thinking is the understanding that we learn about our systems and ourselves as we evolve, grow and change. The learning never stops, nor should it; so you tell me, what other General Systems principles there are in *your* field of vision. Call us (619-275-6528)...we'd like to know, too.

QUESTIONS TO PONDER...

- Which three or four of these principles are most useful to you? Why?
- Which three or four of these key system questions make the most sense to you? Why?
- Which of these principles and/or questions are not clear or useful to you? Go back and read over the information on it presented here again.

MULTIPLE OUTCOMES—CUSTOMER FOCUSED
(Standard Systems Dynamic #6)

Systems Question #1: "What are the desired outcomes"?

This is often a highly enlightened and thought provoking question when asked in organizations. Of course, the only real answer to this for organizations of all types is "customer satisfaction". Customer satisfaction takes many forms with today's demanding consumers—speed, responsiveness, quality, service, **and** low cost, to name a few. This is what gives rise to the positioning of many organizations in the marketplace as providing "customer-value" through being "market-driven", "customer-focused/centered", "customer-oriented" and other like sounding phrases.

Some of the more highly publicized management change concepts have been "Six Sigma", "Business Process Reengineering", and "Total Quality Management"; all of which purport to being ways to improve customer satisfaction and value. Without trying to argue the merits of one vs. the other management concepts, it is clear that they have failed, in many cases, to delivery these *multiple outcomes* desired by customers (Standard Systems Dynamic #6).

Our research of current business trends and our client assessments show, however, that—despite their positive aspects—these Six Sigma, Reengineering, and Quality efforts are still separate and fragmented solutions to customer needs. Though it seems hard to believe, ***most organizations today still do not have regular and systemic customer feedback mechanisms, so they still don't know what their customers really value.*** I have observed this first-hand in my CEO talks through TEC (The Executive Committee, now Vistage International), where, in the 14 CEO's of each TEC group, it is rare to find more than one or two CEOs with systemic customer feedback. (Standard Systems Dynamic #5)

The truth is, there is still a significant gap between words and attitudes, best practices, and actions. Though many organizations give lip service to the old adage, "the customer is king", and to being customer-focused/centered the figuratively-bestowed crown does not often elicit the deference and regal service the phrase implies.

According to an extensive survey conducted by Rath & Strong, a management-consulting firm based in Lexington, MA, most companies do not live by their "customer is king" credo. Their survey asked more than 1,000 managers from Fortune 500 companies how customer-centered their organizations are. While 87% of the respondents said that delivering value to customers is critical to success, 70% also admitted that their performance was driven more by internal operating measures than by external (outcome) ones. In addition, 80% said that compensation for all employees is not tied to a defined measure of customer satisfaction.

Another personal, first-hand experience came out of field research for my doctoral degree at Temple University. My initial hypothesis was that the more customer-focused organizations would also be more profitable. However, the reports that I got back indicated that almost *all* of the organizations surveyed were, indeed, customer-focused. What I found was that, while everyone said they were customer-focused, few of them, in reality, were. What actually turned out to make the most positive difference in profitability was in those organizations that had **fewer**, and thus more focused, core strategies—in these "focused" organizations, profitability was significantly higher.

Today, especially, organizations must keep pace with changes in their environment and often must reduce current overhead, waste and operations to be globally competitive. As well, they often must completely reinvent their future vision and outcomes to create customer value. Then, they must ***begin thinking backwards to this future*** with the strategies needed to remain successful in serving their customers. Lastly, they must commit passionately to the disciplined management of the changes that occur along the way towards creating this customer-focused, high performance organization.

What, specifically, does *"creating customer value"* mean—is it Six Sigma, TQM, business re-engineering, or customer service? It is these and many other elements. Creating customer value is about focusing in a holistic, intensive manner on your customer's wants and needs for receiving value from you. It must be your entire organization's vision and driving force—both now and in the future. Creating customer value potentially means radically redesigning the entire spectrum of your business processes and competencies that create this value. It also means redesigning the fundamental support and capacity-building components of your organization to better fit, integrate, and align towards this ideal vision.

There's no question that, at the bottom of it all, being 100% customer-focused is the key to creating a successful, high-performance organization. Without true customer focus and satisfaction, no organization will be able to maintain such an environment over the long-term. Of course, the customer-friendly approach, like everything else, has evolved over the years.

In fact, it would be a gross understatement to merely say the history of providing customer value has changed over the past twenty years. From order taking, to zero defects, to Deming, to business re-engineering, to Six Sigma creating customer value to achieve a business advantage has come of age and is now essential for every organization in today's global economy. Focusing on outcomes and serving the customer is the key Systems Thinking approach and outcome for today's successful organization.

The mass production and mass marketing of the Machine Age manufactured products for the "average" customer, thus creating "order-taking" behaviors. Customers were given the choice of selecting products only from what was available through mass production. Later, in the 1970's, quality control and "zero defects" attempted to refine this internally oriented process even more. In the 1980's many of the quality methods made popular by the Japanese came to the US—Deming, Juran, PDCA, JIT, Kaizen, Service, etc. In the 1990's, cut-throat global competition began and has intensified today. Cost-cutting, waste elimination and outsourcing now dominate.

Today's would-be high-performance, customer-focused organization understands clearly that it must focus *all* of its ongoing efforts on their customers, using research-based best practices, such as our Centre's researched and synthesized list of the "Ten Commandments of a Customer-Focused Organization":

10 COMMANDMENTS OF CUSTOMER-FOCUSED ORGANIZATIONS

1) **Stay close to your customer**—This is especially important for senior executives (i.e., see, touch, feel, meet, and dialogue with them face-to-face, out of your office, on a regular basis).

2) **Know your customers' needs, wants, and desires**—The driving force of your entire organization should be not only to meet, but to surpass these customer needs.

3) **Survey your customers' satisfaction**—Know what value your customers place on your products and services on a regular basis. A constant flow of customer information is essential, whether it is positive, neutral, or negative. Don't resist it, welcome it!

4) **Focus on all your value-added benefits to the customer**—Pay attention to such elements as quality and service, environmentally improved, cost effectiveness, responsiveness, and delivery speed. Service, versus the total cost of doing business with you.

5) **Include your customer in your decisions**—Don't freeze them out; ask them to participate in focus groups, meetings, planning, and even internal deliberations.

6) **Require everyone in the organization to know your customer**—Every member of the organization should meet and even serve your customer directly at least one day or more each year. There is no substitute for everyone feeling the pulse of your business and its customers.

7) **Re-engineer your business processes based on customer needs and perceptions**—Do this horizontally across all functions within the organization.

8) **Structure your organization to the marketplace**—Align the organization to fit your markets (i.e., 1 customer = 1 representative).

9) **Have a Customer Recovery Strategy (CRS)**—Reward CRS behaviors, especially in cross-functional teams that work together to serve the customer.

10) **Hire and promote only "customer friendly" people**—Though this may seem an obvious, common-sense notion, the fact is that most organizations (and this is particularly true in the public sector) have gotten so buried under their own paperwork, activities, bureaucracies, and hierarchies that they have lost sight of their raison d'être...the customer.

Use these Ten Commandments in questionnaire/survey format to determine if your organization is indeed geared toward both customer focus and even, when necessary, *Customer Recovery* (#9 above).

MARKETPLACE POSITIONING AND VALUE
"Value" is in the eyes of the beholder.

When exploring customer-focused activities, organizations are wise to remember that value, per se, is not an objective term; it is subjective. It is defined as what the customer perceives they receive from choosing and using your products and services—in relationship to their total cost (financial, psychological, environmental, and otherwise) of doing business with you. In systems terms, it is the "output" they receive from their "inputs"(Standard Systems Dynamic #4).

It is the *multiple outcomes* customers desire from the range of five possible world-class "Star" results positioning, shown here:

Figure 7-2: Value-Added Star Positioning

While Six Sigma, customer service, and the like are certainly crucial customer-focused change strategies, the only way to know whether these are appropriate for your particular organization is to, again, collect real data and work/feed it backwards from the range of possible "Star Results Positioning" the customer may desire. Otherwise, these strategies are each a fragmented "solution in search of a problem". Unfortunately, even today, it is the rare organization which has a strong market research arm for collecting this real customer data on a regular basis.

In reality, the key to any organization's competitive edge or positioning is to make one (and only one) of these Star points their edge, while ensuring they

are "ballpark" competitive in all the others in their marketplace.

Call this whatever you want—your competitive edge, your positioning, reputation, image, driving force, strategic intent or grand strategy—it's all the same thing. *It is your one uniqueness that is different and better in the eyes of the customers versus your competitors that makes them prefer to do business with you.*

In addition, today's customers often seek individual relationships with their providers—they most definitely do *not* want to be treated as just another sale. The intelligent, Systems Thinking organization understands that it is not market share alone, but individual customer loyalty that matters, as well—both immediately and down the road. In this perspective, economy of scope and organizing for the customer become important, not simply economy of scale and organizing for efficiency. Collaboration and intimacy with your customers from "cradle to grave" has become key, as opposed to superficial, occasional contact only when you have something to sell. This means long-term responsiveness by you to your customer's desire for choice, thus cementing a longer-term loyalty (and repeat business).

In the 21st Century, there's no question that an organization's competitive advantage depends on creating customer value that is customized for each market segment and niche, and ultimately each individual customer's choices. It is Systems Thinking that can give organizations clear, holistic strategic decisions and integration—within our simple and consistent A,B,C, systems framework and Systems Concept #3 in the next chapter—that will help them maintain and grow their successes over the long-term.

Note: For a more detailed view of Positioning see our free article on *Marketplace Positioning* on our website www.hainescentre.com.

QUESTIONS TO PONDER...

- Does your organization say it is "customer-focused" or some such phrase?
- How does it rate on the 10 Commandments of a customer-focused organization?
- Specifically, does your organization have a clear "customer recovery strategy" and does it have regular ongoing feedback on customer satisfaction?

OTHER STANDARD SYSTEMS DYNAMICS

Every one of these 12 Standard Systems Dynamics could have a whole section or chapters written about its application (or lack thereof) in teams and organizations; thus creating an entire book. The applications are endless. Thus, the author of this book has also written a companion book to this one entitled, *The Complete Guide to Systems Thinking and Learning* (HRD Press). It has 64 practical tools that apply these Standard Systems Dynamics in great detail.

For Example:
Some of the ways to utilize these Standard Systems Dynamics might include the following:

- **Predicting Outcomes:** Since multiple outcomes occur on almost everything you do, can you predict not only your desired outcomes, but also the negative or by-products as well? What are they? (The helicopter view).

- **Run Down Entropic Effect:** Since everything runs down and dies over time, left to their own devices, how do we continually add power, energy and follow-up into any system, project or change process?

- **Elaboration and Rigidity:** Since most systems acquire more complexity, elaboration and bureaucracy/rigidity over time, how do we keep things useful, simple with the KISS method (Keep It Simple Sweetheart/Sam)?

- **Dynamic Resistance:** Since most organizations (and especially organizational structures) exist in a steady state, dynamic equilibrium, how do you use it positively to effect change? The answer is it is very difficult because the steady state structure naturally resists change as it is often not in their own best interests. Who is resisting? Why?

- **The Gift of Feedback:** "Feedback is the breakfast of Champions" is so true—so the organizations with the most open boundaries that seek feedback from their environments and see feedback as not good or bad, but just feedback, make their needed corrections and adapt better to their dynamic changing environment. What feedback do you get? (See full chapter later in this book)

- **Equifinality, Empowerment and the Hierarchy:** Since there are many ways to achieve a desired future vision (the "what"), that is why empowerment (the "how") is so important. The person closest to the issue usually has the best view and is the most committed to solving the issue (not higher up in the hierarchy). Who is closest to the issue?

- **Boundaries-Integrated/Collaborative:** Most systems require cooperation within the system and have competition with other systems (at times). Do you know which is appropriate and when? Be conscious of this.
  For Example: The "turf battles" and politics between departments/individuals in an organization reflect this lack off "broader corporate and holistic view". If your organization has this and I compete with you, I am very happy to see these four struggles. While I am competing with you, you have taken your "eye off the ball" and marketplace.
  These adversarial cultures and turf battles often include: Managers versus those being managed, line departments versus staff departments, manufacturing versus marketing, headquarters versus field, division versus division. Where are the turf battles in your organization?

- **Inter-Related Parts:** Becoming the whole system is primary and the parts are secondary; trying to maximize the elements (i.e., departments) actually suboptimizes the whole system. Too much of a good thing is the operable situation here. Instead it requires the cooperation of the elements (i.e., departments) to only optimize each part so as to maximize the outcomes of the whole system (i.e., organization). How does your organization function? (The Rubik's Cube Effect).

SUMMARY

The 12 Standard Systems Dynamics presented in this chapter are what to watch for and make work naturally in your favor. In particular these are: four standard systems dynamics that really differentiate Strategic and Systems Thinking vs. mechanistic thinking in our five phase A-B-C-D-E Model. They are:

- **#2 Dynamic open systems**—open to environment (**Phase E**);

- **#6 Dynamic multiple outcomes**—the focus on goals, results and ends (**Phase A**) vs. the internal, means, or relatively closed system;

- **#5 Dynamic feedback**—on effectiveness (**Phase B**);

- **#10 Dynamic inter-related parts**—all parts/elements of any system are embedded in a web of relationships; not separate components (**Phase D**—The Rubik's Cube Effect).

When all is said and done, we will only successfully integrate systems solutions to our systems problems when we make the transition from unconscious to conscious systems applications of these 12 Standard Systems Dynamics.

When we look at resolving today's problems in order to grow and thrive in the 21st Century, we must always remind ourselves that: 1) *how* we approach it and 2) how we think about it are just as crucial as *what* actions we take. One thing is certain—if we continue to engage in an analytic, reductionistic approach—the resulting entropy will, guaranteed, grind our systems to a halt.

There are many systems aids in this chapter as translated to the Guiding Principles and Key Questions of the Systems Age—that we can use to make certain we're staying on a Systems Thinking track.

If we remember to consistently pose these questions first–and if we always remember that every system is an indivisible whole–we will be well on our way to **no longer applying analytic approaches to systems problems.** The next chapter will take some of these Standard System Dynamics and formulate them into our practical A-B-C Systems Model and its many applications as well.

In one way or another, we are forced to deal with complexities, with "wholes" or "systems" in all fields of knowledge.

This implies a basic reorientation in "Scientific Thinking"!
—*Ludwig van Bertalanffy*

Chapter 7
Concept #2: Standard System Dynamics
Summary of Key Systems Questions:

Precondition #1
What entity/system or 'collision of systems' are we dealing with?

Precondition #2
Within our identified system, what level(s) of the system are we trying to change?

Systems Question #1—Phase A
What are the desired outcomes?

Systems Question #2—Phase B
How will we know we've achieved our goals (i.e., feedback loop of outcome measures)?

Systems Question #—Phase E
What will be changing in the environment in the future that will impact us?

Systems Question #—Phase D
What is the relationship of X to Y?

Systems Question #5—Phase D or Phase A
Are we dealing with means or ends?

Systems Question #6—Phase D
What do we need to do to ensure buy-in/stay-in and perseverance over time (to reverse the entropy)?

Systems Question #7—Phase D
What are the new structures and processes we are using to ensure successful change?

Systems Question #8—Phase D
What do we centralize (mostly 'whats') and what should we decentralize (how)?

Systems Question #9—Phase C
What are the root causes?

Systems Question #10—Phase D
How can we go from complexity to simplicity and from consistency to flexibility in the solutions we devise?

The Foundation Tool and Question—Phase C
What is it that I contribute to the problem and can change to be a positive and proactive leader on this?

The Ultimate Tool and Question—Phase A
What is our common superordinate goal here?

CONCEPT #2: Laws of Natural Systems
(Standard Systems Dynamics)

Natural Laws/Desired State	vs. Experienced Dynamics
1. **Holism**-Overall Purpose-Focused Synergy/Transformational	1. Parts/Activity Focused/ Suboptimal Results
2. **Open Systems**-Open to Environment	2. Closed Systems/Low Environmental Scan
3. **Boundaries**- Integrated/ Collaborative	3. Fragmented/Turf Battles/ Separate/Parochial
4. **Input/Output**-How natural systems operate	4. Piecemeal/Analytic/Sequential and Narrow View
5. **Feedback**-on Effectiveness/Root Causes	5. Low Feedback/Financial Only
6. **Multiple Outcomes**- Goals	6. Artificial Either/or Thinking
7. **Equifinality**-Flexibility and Agility	7. Direct Cause—Effect/One Best Way
8. **Entropy**-Follow-up/Inputs of Energy/Renewal	8. Decline/Rigidity/Obsolete and Death
9. **Hierarchy**-Flatter Organization/Self-Organizing	9. Hierarchy/Bureaucracy/ Command and Control
10. **Inter-related Parts**- Relationships/ Involvement and Participation	10. Separate Parts/Components/ Entities/Silos
11. **Dynamic Equilibrium**-Stability and Balance/Culture	11. Short-term Myopic View/Ruts/ Resistance to Change
12. **Internal Elaboration**-Details and Sophistication	12. Complexity and Confusion
12A. **Cycles of Changes**- Chaos and then Elegant Simplicity	12A. Individual/Sequential Change/ New Problems Created

15 Key Principles of Systems Thinking

1. Look for the common superordinate goal whenever possible.

2. The entity to be changed must be clear.

3. Always begin any dialogue with a crystal-clear understanding of the desired outcomes.

4. There are many different ways to achieve the same desired outcomes, thus, involvement of the right people involved in planning and implementing the solutions/actions is key.

5. Feedback is the breakfast of champions—be flexible and adaptive.

6. The whole is more important than the parts—and the relationships and processes are key.

7. Work and align the entity to be changed from the outside-in—not inside-out.

8. All systems are linked to other systems—some larger; some smaller -in a hierarchy.

9. Root causes and effects are usually not linked closely in time and space.

10. The KISS method really is best—reverse the entrophy!

11. The steady state equilibrium we all want can kill us. In a rapidly changing society, the biggest risk is to stay the same.

12. Focus and strengthen the basic units/systems of organizations and society.

13. Change is an individual act.

14. Systems upon systems upon systems are too complex to fully understand and manage centrally.

15. We are holistic human beings—in search of meaning.

CHAPTER 8

Concept #3: The A-B-C Systems Model
The Whole Before the Parts...Backwards Thinking

Generally speaking, there has been considerably more movement towards Systems Thinking in today's world. In this chapter, we'll explore the ways in which the A-B-C Systems Thinking Concept applies to individuals, teams, and to senior executive leadership of organizations.

Application #1: Strategic Thinking on a Daily Basis

These five Systems Thinking Phases interrelate for the most powerful results. For review sake, look at the A-B-C Template that follows. Its use is universal as Systems Thinking is the "natural way the world works". Use it in every daily situation you find yourself—focus on your desired outcomes first.

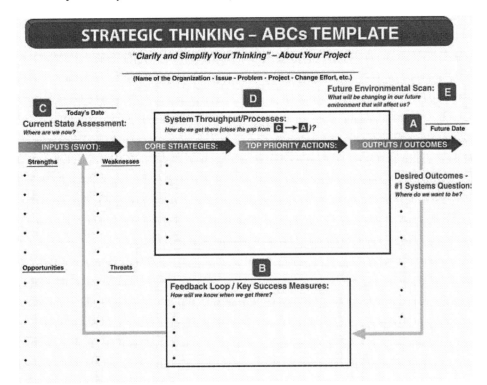

Figure 8-1: Strategic Thinking Template

In addition, there are many, many integrated organizational applications which make full, holistic use of this A-B-C Template. Here are some of these organizational applications:

Application #2: Reinventing Strategic Planning

As is the case with our individual self-mastery (Chapter 6), so, too, must organizations reassess how they achieve their desired outcomes and interact with their environment? Our Reinventing Strategic Management Model (planning, people, leadership, and change), shown here, provides organizations with this clear, five-phase A-B-C systems framework that works within the ongoing reality of changing times. With its systems focus, it is the only planning and change model that "begins with the end in mind" and views the customer as the primary purpose of all organizational enterprises. (See my book, *The Systems Thinking Approach to Strategic Planning and Management*, available from SystemsThinkingPress.com for thorough and complete details on its applications.) Our Reinventing Strategic Management Model comprises ten Systems Thinking steps in our five distinct, A-B-C phases:

Figure 8-2: Reinventing Strategic Planning into Strategic Management

Phase E: Future Environmental Scanning

Environmental scanning is the foundation for strategic thinking and planning. True scanning breaks out of the internal focus and limiting paradigms that keep us from seeing and understanding the driving forces in the environment. Environmental scanning is not fortune telling. You can't predict the future, but you can prepare. Even a modest head start can assure you of a marketplace advantage.

The environment to be scanned is not that of the present, but of the future. It scans out to the end of the planning horizon time frame. The idea is to try to understand, as much as possible, what the future holds in store that could affect your organization.

The results of a future environmental scan will show up as implications for the SWOT analysis: the **O**pportunities and **T**hreats of today.

We have identified eight broad and general "baskets of categories" for environmental scanning. These form the acronym SKEPTIC:

- **S**ocial
- **K** Competition/Substitutes
- **E**conomic and **E**nvironmental/Ecological
- **P**olitical
- **T**echnological
- **I**ndustry/Suppliers
- **C**ustomers

In fact this analysis can be one of the most insightful and rewarding parts of the scan. Having done their respective research, your various team members come together to run through dozens of "what if" scenarios, playing this social factor with technological or Legal factors. Don't short change yourself, your organization, or your team by severely limiting the time for this exercise.

Tip: It is best to have each scanning team assigned one letter based on the SKEPTIC framework.. It also helps if you get a senior management sponsor for each team, using the natural roles that the different functional executives play, i.e., S (socio demographics) to the VP of HR, E (economics) to Finance, etc. In addition, ask volunteers to assist them.

An environmental scanning should no longer be conducted once a year as part of the planning process. We recommend it be performed quarterly as part of the Change Leadership Team, guiding the implementation of the plan. As a minimum, conduct the scans no longer than six months apart. The world is changing too fast now, don't get left behind.

Step #1: *The Plan-to-Plan Step.*

This is a critical step in focusing organizational strategic planning; one in which visions are established and a commitment to leadership is made. The Plan-to-Plan step is valuable in its own right as a unique diagnostic and learning event, and is composed of four elements:

(1) Conducting an Executive Briefing including Educating, Assessing, Organizing, and Tailoring in a day long session for senior management.

(2) Begin developing the six natural leadership development competencies and their associated knowledge, practices, and skills, for the CEO and top executives

(3) Establishing and training an Internal Support Cadre.

(4) Fine tuning the organizing and tailoring of the process to achieve the desired results

Once the Plan-to-Plan step is completed, then the A-B-C's of strategic planning and change begin in earnest.

Phase A: Creating Your Ideal Future
(Outputs of any Organization as a System)

Step #2: *The Ideal Future Vision Step*

This second step has its primary purpose as formulating organizational dreams that are worth believing in and fighting for. At this stage in beginning the actual strategic planning process, the cry of "It can't be done!" is irrelevant; how to turn it into reality is pursued after the vision is created. Five important challenges are met during this step:

Challenge #1) *To conduct a visioning process and develop a shared **vision statement** organization-wide of your dreams, hopes, and desired future.*

Challenge #2) *To develop a **mission statement** describing why your organization exists, what business it is in, who it serves, and your competitive positioning in the marketplace.*

Challenge #3) *To clarify your desired **positioning** in the marketplace.*

Challenge #4) *To articulate **core values** that guide day-to-day behavior, and collectively create your desired culture.*

Challenge #5) *To develop a **rallying cry**— a crisp and concise statement (eight words or less) of the entire strategic plan and the essence of your positioning.*

Note: Be clear here, especially on defining who your primary customers should be, and anticipate what their wants and needs will be, and contrasting it with our five-point World Class Star Results Model in Chapter 7.

Phase B: Quantifiable Outcomes
(Measurements of Success)

Step #3: *The Key Success Measures (KSM)/Goals Step*

This is a critical step, in that it requires organizations to develop those quantifiable outcome measurements of success that demonstrate the achievement of the organization's vision, mission, and core values on a year-by-year basis. The maximum preferred number of KSM's is ten, because this forces the organization to focus on what's really "key" to success. KSM's should always measure what's really important—not just what's easy to measure—including, as a minimum:

1. Customer satisfaction,
2. Employee satisfaction,
3. Financial viability, and
4. Community/Society contribution.

Phase C: Converting Strategy to Operations
(The Input to Act)

Step #4: *The Current State Assessment Step (Gap Analysis)*

This is the step in which internal and external analyses, sometimes called SWOTs—Strengths, Weaknesses, Opportunities, and Threats—are conducted. In traditional forms of strategic planning, this step is the first and main step, leading only to long-range planning that merely projects the current state incrementally into the future. In our framework, it highlights the gap between Phase A and Phase C (Ideal vs. Actual)

Step #5: *The Strategy Development Step (Gap Closure)*

Step Five, the strategy development step, creates the Core Strategies that will enable organizations to bridge the gaps between the Ideal Future Vision and the Current State Assessment; resulting in *three to seven focused Core Strategies* to be implemented organization-wide.

Note: The 21ˢᵗ Century has seen a proliferation of new strategies as businesses try to cope with these revolutionary times. In looking at these strategies, beware of those that are usually of the *cost-cutting* variety only. These might include reorganizations, layoffs, business re-engineering, outsourcing budget cutbacks, etc.

Cutting is definitely necessary, yet not sufficient for success. Building for the future type strategies, focused on quality products and services that satisfy the customer, is where the strategic answers are found. *Thus, both cutting and building strategies are needed.*

Note: It is also key to deal with two other kinds of strategies. **The first is the economic and efficient alignment of the delivery system. The second is the attunement with the hearts and minds of your employees to create your culture** in support of the customer (more on this later in this chapter).

Each Core Strategy also needs to be supported by a set of Strategic Action Items/Priorities to achieve that strategy over the three to five-year planning horizon. These become the major activities and changes required over time. Further, organizations need to identify the top three to five annual Action Priorities for each Core Strategy over the next 12 months. *These Core Strategies and their Action Priorities become the organizing framework and priorities used by everyone* to set annual department work plans, strategic budgets, and individual goals for performance appraisals.

Get rid of the concepts of "Department Goals" and individual "Key Results Areas". Use the Core Strategies as your business glue at every level of the organization—for every department as their department goals for every individual as his/her individual goals. The synergy you will get when doing this is just amazing—much greater cross-functional teamwork/collaboration and much less conflict as everyone and every department has **the same superordinate goals** (Core Strategies).

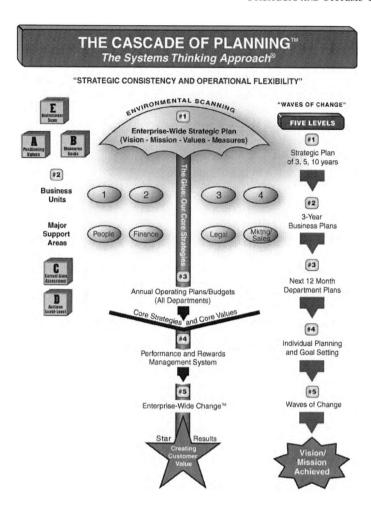

Figure 8-3: The Cascade of Planning - The Systems Thinking Approach

Step #6: *The Three-Year Business Planning Step*

This step is actually the replication of the A-B-C Systems Phases here again at a lower level Strategic Business Unit (SBUs) level and Major Functional Area (MFAs) of the Seven Levels of Living Systems. However, when working a three-year Business Plan within the context of the organization-wide strategic plan; remember the whole is primary and the parts are secondary. Thus **business plans should link to the strategic plan,** *not the other way around,* as is frequently done.

Note: In most of the strategic planning literature, scant attention is paid to three-year business plans for Major Functional Areas (departments). This is a big mistake and a serious strategic omission. **Why should they be exempt from strategic thinking, strategic planning, and strategic change?**

Step #7: *The Annual Plans/Strategic Budgeting Step*

This is where "the rubber meets the road". It is where you develop department and unit plans based on your overall prioritized tasks, and then provide the resources to actually achieve your Core Strategies. It is not enough to have each unit develop their own isolated annual plans. What is needed is a large group meeting of the full collective leadership (i.e. top 30-50 people—sometimes called a "search conference") where all draft plans are critiqued and refined based on their fit with the strategies and top priorities above.

Once this is accomplished, it is time to change the way budgeting is traditionally done. It needs to be more strategic, use the top priorities as a guide, and *follow*, not lead, annual planning. Such strategic budgeting will enable organizations to achieve a focused allocation of resources based on the strategic plan and the action priorities it set for the next fiscal year under each Core Strategy (Step #5) above. **Remember, organizations are a web of interdependent relationships. Thus, the strategic plan drives the business plans, then the annual plans, and then the budget.**

Step #8: *The Plan-to-Implement Step (A "Smart Start" for success in making desired changes)*

The Plan-to-Implement Step is designed to bridge the gap between strategic planning and the difficult implementation process. The key to this step's success is installing the following nine crucial concepts:

1. A Strategic Change Leadership Team led from the top

2. A yearly Comprehensive Map of the implementation process

3. The use of cross-functional Project Teams to begin to create a critical mass for change

4. Selecting an internal change management support cadre (or even a Program Management Office) to coordinate the day-to-day implementation process

5. Clear communications and roll out of the final approved document

6. Assigning a Key Success Measure Tracking Coordinator (to actually track success)

7. Allocating resources to support the change process/priorities

8. Personal Leadership Plans for each senior executive as to how they are going to personally lead implementation

9. Modifying performance appraisal and rewards processes to support the strategic plan.

Phase D: Implementation
(The Processes or Throughput: Real Actions)

Step #9: *The Strategy Implementation & Change Step*

This is the step that ensures successful implementation of the organization's strategic plan. It results in transforming the strategic plan into thousands of individual plans, and tying a rewards system to it.

Throughout implementation, organizations need to focus on the following Vital Few Leverage Points for Strategic Change, which were developed from our research and that of others regarding best practices of successful organizations. These leverage points are:

Vital Few Leverage Points for Change

(1) *Increasing the range and depth of your collective **leadership and management practices**, including all your human resource management practices*

(2) ***Customer-focused, business process reengineering** to eliminate waste throughout the firm*

(3) ***Organization redesign and restructuring** to support the vision, values, & strategies*

(4) ***Becoming more customer-focused through high quality products and service**, vis-à-vis the five-point World Class Star Results Model & best practices Ten Commandments*

In addition, monthly meetings of a Strategic Change Leadership Team are absolutely essential. *Of all the organizations we at the Centre for Strategic Management have worked with, none have successfully implemented their strategic plan without this Change Leadership Team.*

In addition, the CEO needs to conduct weekly or bi-weekly meetings with his or her staff with the first part of the agenda, which is focused on reviewing the status of the top annual priorities previously agreed to under each Core Strategy (with internal support cadre help). *Then*, cover day-to-day issues—not the other way around.

Step #10: The *Annual Strategic Review and Update Step (including a Strategic IQ™ Audit)*

Similar to a yearly independent financial audit, this critical step is needed to keep pace with and be flexible to changing environments. This is the key to sustaining high performance over the long term, and includes:

(1) *Formally auditing and reviewing the strategic plan's status (especially Key Success Measures and Core Strategies/ priorities). i.e. determining your organization's Strategic I.Q.™*

(2) *Reacting to changes in the environment/updating annual action priorities for the next 12 months*

These, then, are the ten Systems Thinking steps of Reinventing Strategic Planning into a yearly Strategic Management System designed to enhance the organization's ability to reach its desired outcomes while dealing successfully with change, to create customer value. Perhaps the greatest value to this model lies in its flexibility. Like people, no two organizations are the same—or are even at the same stage at the same time—this Systems Thinking model allows organizations to enter into strategic planning and change management according to their own unique requirements. Actually—*as a system is circular (as opposed to linear)—organizations may enter this model at any starting point, and go from there.*

The key is to pick the most logical point and just get started!

Figure 8-4: Yearly Strategic Management Cycle using the Systems Thinking Approach

Questions to Ponder

- Does your organization have a strategic plan? A Strategic Management System?
- If so, how does it compare to the first seven steps listed here?
- Do you have a good Strategic Change Management game plan (Step #8)?

Application #3: Changing to a high-performance organization through the "Organization as a System" model—the Business Excellence Architecture.

Using the Strategic Management System to create and implement a strategic plan will set an organization well on the path toward becoming high-performance and customer-focused. At the same time, however, an organization must employ the Systems Thinking Approach™ throughout implementation. Only in this way can the organization deal consistently and successfully with ongoing change and change management.

Just as with individuals and groups, the real beauty of a systems approach within organizations is in how it allows and plans for change—as a natural, expected characteristic of every system and its environment. By applying the same A-B-C phases used in the Reinventing Strategic Planning Model, our copyrighted Organization as a Systems Model—the Business Excellence Architecture Model, shown here, enables organizations to analyze and assess the status of all components of the organization—versus: 1) our best practices/benchmark research, 2) the Malcolm Baldrige Quality Award Criteria, 3) the fit of each component with other components, and 4) in support of the overall desired outcomes or vision, and values.

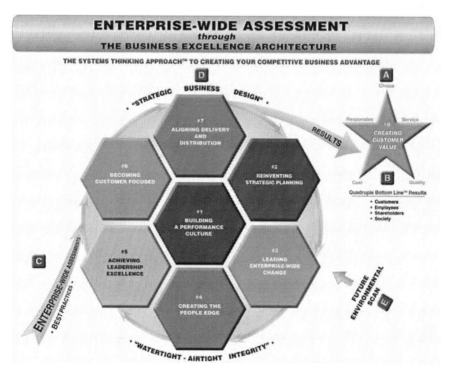

Figure 8-5: Enterprise-Wide Assessment through the Business Excellence Architecture

There are a number of very practical uses for this model, including the following assessment tool/survey. Our clients prefer this to the "SW" of the SWOT assessment as it gives *seven times* the depth of analysis—seven elements instead of one generic SW(OT).

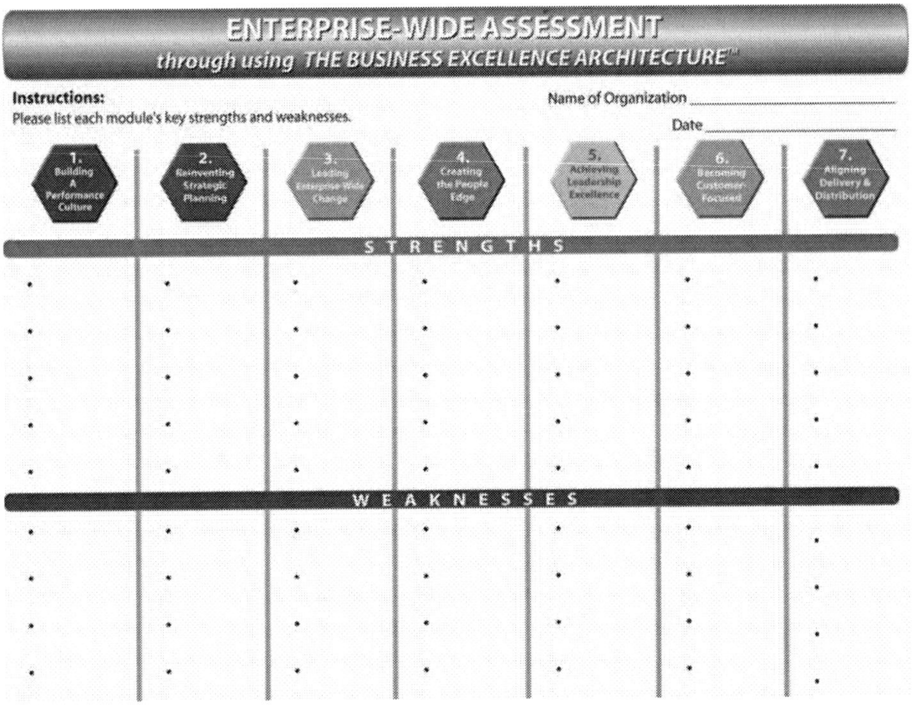

Figure 8-6: Enterprise-Wide Assessment

Keep in mind two points: 1) that the relative numbers of the survey will tell you, realistically, where each component ranks within your organization, and 2) they will show you the fit of each component with all other components. If, at the end of the survey, for instance, you find that one component is a "2", and another shows up as a "4", this is an indication of non-alignment or integration within your organizational components. In some respects, it is more desirable to have mainly "3's", because this shows that most of your components, though imperfect, have alignment and fit with one another.

Questions to Ponder

- Does the "Organization as a System" model—Business Excellence Architecture—make sense? Review it again.
- How does your organization rank in the survey? Why?

Using the A-B-C framework in planning allows you to 1) accelerate and advance the changes you want and need to make, and 2) tie in and increase the importance of these major changes that should be correlated with corporate strategies (but most often aren't) to gain total buy-in and ownership.

Finally, remember that *Systems Thinking is really the art of trade-offs; for every problem solved, another is created.* Systems Thinking is science and the art of deciding which problems we want to live and cope with in this imperfect, interrelated world of ours.

Application #4: Strategic Human Resource Management System— "The People Edge"

Another major A-B-C Systems Thinking Approach application for becoming high-performance and customer-focused deals with an organization's people. Without the passionate commitment of your people being strategically "in tune" (i.e., on the same sheet of music), you cannot hope to achieve ongoing Star Results Positioning as discussed earlier. Thus, the *cultural attunement* with people's hearts and minds in support of creating customer value is crucial to success as well as the "*economic alignment* of the delivery system".

As in the other applications we've looked at, changing to a high-performance organization requires viewing human resource management in its own A-B-C systems model and flow of people over time, such as the one shown here:

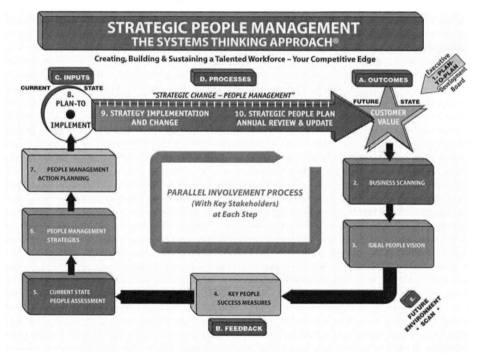

Figure 8-7: Strategic People Management

The creation of people management practices of any organization should be viewed as a strategic plan also using this A-B-C system. A healthy and aggressive human resource management approach, based on a systems model such as this, should be one whose programs and processes are linked directly to your organization's strategic plan, particularly your vision, values, and strategies.

Organizational leadership should place equal emphasis and attention on each step of the HRM model, building your "people edge" through the nine systems steps and utilizing our Best HR Practices research, as described here:

10 Best Human Resource Practices
(to create the "People Edge")

1. Create a common HR systems framework and terminology on strategic human resource management.

2. Create a successful executive/employee development board and process.

3. Develop and implement an HR department strategic plan. Using our A-B-C Systems Model.

4. Win the game on hiring and selection, versus just development alone.

5. With limited development funds, the key to organizational success is a leadership development system. Focus first on trainer skills—coach, facilitator, influencer—and self-mastery, as well.

6. Match up individual needs (Systems Level #3) and organizational needs (Systems Level #5) through tying succession planning and development to career and strategic life planning.

7. Tap the discretionary effort of all employees. Use their hearts and minds in support of your business, not just their hands. Work toward empowering each of them as they are ready, willing, and able.

8. Use your organization's core goals, strategies, and core values as the organizing framework for your performance management system—including all job descriptions—to coach and sustain high performance.

9. Tie your total rewards system; both pay and non-pay, to your organization's strategic plan (remember the importance of connecting our web of relationships). Create a "manager of rewards" position, rather than the old, tired "manager of compensation".

10. *People support what they help create.* Remember, people want involvement in all decisions that effect them prior to the decisions being made.

...and the five absolutes

11. Treat all people with dignity and respect, regardless of their roles relative to your role.

12. *Feedback is the breakfast of champions.* Create HR measurements and learn to "speak finance", not just English.

13. Make sure the KISS principle is applied to all these practices and policies (simplicity again).

14. Develop a clear and specific reward system for teamwork, both functional and cross-functional (Systems Levels #4 and #5).

15. Develop programs for rewarding actual results and outcomes (Phase A) *not* the usual suggestion programs (ideas only rewarded).

Application #5: A Strategic Leadership Development System (an organization's only true competitiveness over the long-term)

Senior management leadership, skills, and competencies are crucial for your organization to ensure Star Results. The skills of trainer, coach and facilitator are key—as are the abilities to become passionate customer advocates and develop close relationships with your customers. Leadership is the foundation for everything else, and leadership development must be a primary and ongoing organizational priority.

Senior management leadership in the organization is so critical that each and every organization should have a Strategic Leadership Development System. Making all this happen falls within the responsibility of the organization's senior management, with HR support. Typically, it is best if done through an Executive/Employee Development Board—made up of senior management—whose sole task is to focus on this development system and framework to create management as a competitive business edge (the most important subset of the "people edge", Application #3).

Like all else, successfully integrating a strategic leadership development program in your organization depends upon incorporating the following five phases of the Systems Model, like the one shown below.

Phase E: *Scan the future environment for the number and kind of future leaders you need from your strategic direction.*

Phase A: *Creating your vision and philosophy of leadership, principles, and practices*

Phase B: *Developing measures for tracking your success in developing leaders*

Phase C: *Developing an overall, collective leadership current state assessment (as well as the individual executive's "leadership gap", with plans for closing it through a Personal Development Plan (PDP))*

Phase D: *Actual implementation of the leadership development process*

Within this A-B-C framework for this leadership development system, the goal is for senior management to develop the skills and competencies to effectively function at all the key levels of the Seven Levels of Living Systems (and the collisions of each of the systems levels, as well).

See Chapter 6 for our **Centering Your Leadership** model that covers these Seven Levels. It calls for fast developing self-mastery skills at the individual level, also interpersonal, team level, cross-functional, and organizational levels. It even requires skills at the community and public level (see Chapter 10). Again, we need to tie the A-B-C Systems Approach to all of these Levels of Living Systems

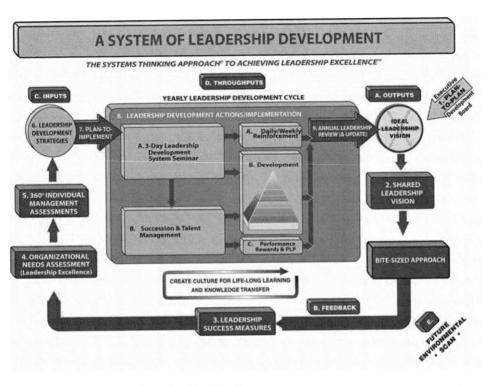

Figure 8-8: A System of Leadership Development

Application #6: *The Learning Organization*

The desire for a true learning organization creates an ideal environment for strategically applying our Systems Thinking, A-B-C framework to achieve the very best results.

There is much research on learning today that is making us more aware overall of what makes us learn—one such learning theory, adapted from the Kolb, Rubin, & McIntyre learning model, shows us that our learning is comprised of: 1) awareness and knowledge, 2) skills, and 3) attitudes and motivations. The application of this learning is our *ability* (or lack thereof) to actually put the learning into practice in a more and more competent way over time. Ultimately our ability to effectively apply this learning becomes our learning *competencies**

* Adapted from D. Kolb, "On Management & the Learning Process"

The truth is, most of our modern learning research—from Montessori on up to today—has direct impact for management applications in creating an organizational learning environment, as well. At the Haines Centre, partner Jim McKinlay's research produced this Stairway of Learning, showing how we progress, in five distinct steps, from unconscious *in*competence to the ultimate goal of a high level of consistent performance (see earlier Chapter for the visual model)

What, defines a true learning organization?

*"A learning organization is an organization skilled at creating, acquiring, and transferring knowledge, **and** at modifying its behavior to reflect new knowledge and insights."*
—*Harvard Business Review*

How can a systems approach be applied to create a learning organization? To build a learning organization—as in all else in Systems Thinking—it is critical to apply learning strategies at all seven levels, as shown here:

How to Develop a Human Organization Systematically?

Level of Living Systems	Examples	
#3 Individual	• technical training	• personal growth
	• managerial training	• individual career development
	• new hire orientation/assimilation	• continuing education
	• job design	• time management
	• OJT/cross training	• management development
#3a One-to-one relationships	• process skills	• coaching/counseling
	• goal setting performance appraisal	• communication skills
	• boss-subordinate relations	• influence, power skills
#4 Teams	• staff meetings	• department systems and processes
	• team building	• meetings skills
#4a Inter-department	• design review teams	• integrity mechanisms/task forces
	• interdepartmental meetings	• conflict resolution
	• liaisons	• interdepartmental team building

#5	Organization-Wide	• communication systems • HR Management system • committees • large systems change	• management conferences • cross-sectional task forces • strategic planning
#6	Organization-Environment Interfaces	• briefings • outside seminars • trade/professional associations	• customer contacts • customer service training • industry conferences/publications

The learning organization is characterized by many things. Though subject experts Pedler, Burgoyne, and Boydell, along with us at the Centre, remain convinced that no full-fledged learning organization exists, they suggest the following characteristics would support a learning environment:

• An organization which considers strategic planning and policy-making a learning process, viewing management decisions as experiments, rather than edicts.

• Encouraging all organizational members—employees, customers, suppliers, owners, and neighbors—to participate in major policy decisions.

• Applying information technology to inform and empower its workforce.

• Structuring all accounting and control systems to assist learning.

• Working to please internal customers through constant interdepartmental communication and awareness of overall company needs.

• Employing new and meaningful ways to reward people for ideas and actions contributing to innovation and growth.

• Creating organizational structures that invent opportunities for individual and business development.

• Relying on all organizational workers who contact external customers, suppliers, and neighbors for market information.

• Learning from other companies through joint training, investments, research and development, job exchanges, or benchmarking.

• Providing opportunity and encouragement to all workers for taking responsibility for their own personal growth and learning.

To engender a true learning environment, organizations must be certain to religiously contrast what they're learning against: 1) what's happening in their environment on an ongoing basis (environmental scanning—Phase E), 2) how the learning affects expected organizational outcomes (Phase A), and 3) a continual feedback loop (Phase B), to tie the learning in with ongoing results.

As you see here, building these phases provides the opportunity for successful learning throughout the organization:

Phases: Learning Everywhere		
A	Outcomes	**Developing Common Anchoring Points**—in which all change pivots around (i.e., desired common core values and culture, vision, and mission).
B	Feedback Loop	**Having all Executives with a Continuously Naïve Learning and Problem Identification Orientation**—to keep growing and changing with the environment; to keep valid organization information flowing to you with a minimum of filtering
C	Strategies	**Developing Short Term Clear Strategies**—and Annual Priorities as the glue and organizing framework to drive day-to-day decision making.
D1	Attunement with Peoples Hearts and Minds:	1) **How to Promote/Manage Innovation Empowerment and Continuous Improvements**—to ensure operational tasks to lead to high quality products and quality service by everyone. 2) **Developing and Maintaining a High Quality Executive Cadre/Succession with the following characteristics:** • teamwork/collaboration • strategic conceptual thinking • intelligence • high energy • leadership skills (trainer/coach/facilitator) • common interpersonal and management skills and practices 3) **Promoting and Rewarding Cross-Functional Teamwork and Collaboration**—as a hallmark of the organization, along with self-initiative and cooperation towards the common vision

D2	Alignment Delivery Process	1) **Having a Clear Understanding of the Organization Design**—a philosophy and criteria to preserve as the organization grows and changes 2) **Simple**—efficient, few, and nonbureaucratic policies, practices, workflow, and approvals. 3) **Managing Complex Information**—quickly and accurately for the right people and the right time
D3	Mega Track	1) **Having a Systems Thinking Orientation**—to understand how complex parts/issues in an organization impact each other, with a specific emphasis on human behavior impacts. 2) **How to Manage Strategic Change**—constantly shifting resources and focus on new strategies over time. Implications of the human behaviors on the "rollercoaster of change" are paramount.

Also, a key point to remember here is that—like the three *content—process— structure* elements mentioned earlier, that must all be present in any group or team interaction—in a true learning environment there must also exist the same three specific elements, only in different form: *skills (structure), knowledge (content), and attitudes (feelings and process)*.

More often than not, most organizations give lip service to all three of these necessary learning environment attributes, but in reality, target only one—knowledge. This is a mistake, for without the right skills and attitudes, you'll basically just end up with a bunch of knowledge in search of its intended application. Besides in today's internet world, knowledge is the easiest to acquire.

Senior organizational management needs to establish the mindset that real learning in an organization requires knowledge, skills, and the right attitude. Also—while strong leadership is crucial—senior management should act as guide and rudder, not as dictator or know-it-all. *Always remember, it's much more effective in the long run to act as the "guide on the side" posing questions, rather than the "sage on the stage" with all the answers.*

From this same mindset should come the realization that a well-thought out rewards and recognition system can go a long way toward cementing employee motivation and ongoing commitment to learning. Rewards—both financial and non-financial—for individuals and teams that are timely, meaningful, and personally significant are key for successfully creating a true learning organization.

In the end, strong leadership is what gives organizations the vision to create an ongoing learning environment—a necessity, we believe, for organizations to thrive in the coming 21st Century and Systems Age. Only with such senior management leadership can organizations withstand the buffeting of today's changing marketplace.

As we've said earlier, *knowledge isn't enough; it's putting that knowledge to productive use through our leadership skills that will be key to success.*

Application #7: Teams and Effective Teamwork

To become something more than an assorted group of people passing through each others' professional lives, teams need to understand and develop their interdependent effectiveness. Developing effective teams on a conscious, intentional level requires: 1) a balance of content/process/structure, 2) strong interdependent goals— roles and relationships, and 3) ongoing best practices throughout each of the A-B-C Phases.

Phase E

In teamwork, most of us look inside the team for its effectiveness. However, outside the team is the environment and all its key stakeholders to the team's success. Therefore it is crucial to know who these key outside impactors are and what demands they make on the team—and—what the team's responses are to these demands.

In addition, it should be obvious that the culture of the organization or unit **around** the team is a huge environmental impactor of team behavior and success. Understanding the culture's strengths and weaknesses as they have implications for the team is also key.

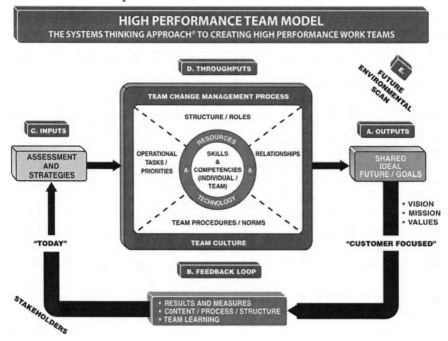

Figure 8-9: High Performance Team Model

Phase A
Where the team wants to be in terms of vision and values (desired future outcomes)
Vision

Within Phase A of the team systems model, teams need clear, agreed-upon, established visions—i.e., what the team's members, both individually and collectively, expect to accomplish. For instance, is there a shared understanding and ongoing clarity as to desired outcomes? Nothing can damage effectiveness more quickly than when there are conflicts between team members regarding undefined individual and overall visions. Also, does each member have a sense of ownership and agreement, or buy-in, with all these visions?

Values

In addition to establishing the team's vision, team members also need to agree and model the values they will live by in their pursuit of the vision. Setting such standards as team expectations and values up front can save enormous amounts of confusion and time lost in the team's effort to achieve its vision. It is equally crucial to clarify and follow clear consequences of any violations.

For example:

Determining the values under which it will proceed is crucial for teams, because it establishes an overriding spirit of individual cooperation for the common good. No matter what personal agendas a team leader may have, for instance, they must be subverted to the team's ongoing direction—otherwise, *no one's agenda is met.*

Phase B
How will the team know when they've successfully achieved their goals?
Feedback

Though we have devoted Chapter 11 of this book to discussing the concept of feedback in detail, it needs mentioning here. As in all Systems Thinking, the idea that change is a norm should be accepted by teams, and planned for, rather than avoided. This is the primary reason that, in Systems Thinking, environmental scanning and a feedback loop are so very vital. Whether it's about building in clear success measures or milestones, establishing regular, ongoing status check meetings, creating a formal method for reporting achievement, or all of the above, a feedback loop gives both the team and individual members a standard against which they continually check and recheck ongoing progress—making corrections where necessary.

A feedback loop can also make the difference between "buy-in" and "stay-in" for team members. "Buy-in", which encourages forward motion, is created in the initial phases of developing clear visions. "Stay-in"—which motivates team members to persevere and "stick with the program" and carry on to the finish line even when the going gets tough—can only be accomplished through continual spot checks and an effective feedback loop.

Phase C
Current state of the team.
Current State Assessment

In order to achieve their visions, teams need to create a base by focusing clearly and honestly on where they stand today. A current state assessment is not about future hopes and desires or playing the "what if" game—it is a precise analysis of the current realities, warts and all. It is only through this kind of real-time honest assessment that teams will prepare themselves for developing the necessary, most effective processes and strategies they'll need to move ahead.

Phase D
What actions (and behaviors) will be needed to close the gap between the present and the future desired state?
Roles (i.e., structures)

Clarity of roles plays an equally important part in Phase A for teams. Any team, be it departmental or other, cannot be effective where there is a lack of clarity as to who does what and when. In addition to buy-in to vision and values, each member must similarly be in agreement and feel a sense of ownership about what role they (and others) are expected to play.

For example:

This can be found in sports teams. Teams found in the winners' circle are invariably those without an abundance of superstars, but ones in which all team members are clear on and committed to their given roles and interdependence for the overall good of the team. There are obviously at least a few superstars on winners' circle teams—just not an entire team of them.

Processes

Another team effectiveness factor lies in the way in which members work together to accomplish team goals. In organizations, for instance, all processes—including decision-making, communications, meetings, conflict management, leadership style, and rewards—must be sharply defined and understood before beginning. *Otherwise, it's a given that the team will lose its way or even disintegrate.* This is such an important criteria that an actual checklist for clearly detailing and delineating various processes, such as the one shown here, is strongly advisable:

Some Team Processes and Procedures

1. Decision-making
2. Communications methods & styles
3. Meetings management
4. Leadership styles
5. Conflict management
6. Performance & results management
7. Rewards management
8. Relationship maintenance
9. Diagnosing team effectiveness & norms

10. Giving & receiving feedback
11. Self-disclosure & openness
12. Encouraging & supporting each others' task

Actions—Implementation

For teams—as in any other application of the systems model—Phase D is where the rubber meets the road. This is when team members determine the series of actions and behaviors necessary to achieve their desired future goals—and then they "just do it." In order for teams to carry out these actions over the long-term, they will also need to understand how change affects individual behavior, as well as the interaction of the team dynamics overall.

The rest of Phase D Throughput on this High Performance Team Model needs attention to fit, alignment, and attunement to the desired outcomes as well. An entire book could be written about this alone—but we will leave that to others who have written extensively on team development...albeit without the systems framework for teams.

Application #8: Creating Customer Value

"Value results from a total effort rather than from one isolated step in the process"
—Alvin Tofler, *Creating a New Civilization*

This last A-B-C organizational systems application is actually a **summary** of the combined first earlier applications, as you will see. When all is said and done, there is a problem with focusing exclusively on the bottom line of applying this to the alignment of delivery processes above. Re-engineering and organizational design should not be viewed as separate strategies, but as complimentary strategies to other, more customer and product-related strategies. They are often primarily the first steps toward organizational survival. Senior management must continually be aware that lowering costs alone improves the bottom line only in the short run.

At the Centre, we consider this application as a synergistic and more holistic variation that combines both the alignment and attunement applications. Well-thought-out, consistently adhered-to customer and product strategies and people innovations are the only true strategies for building long-term customer value—and it is only in the hands of truly differentiating leadership, combined with a clear competitive edge, that these new strategies become effective. The ultimate goal of any organization's leadership is to create the level of customer value that translates into long-term customer loyalty.

Key steps in differentiating your product or service to achieve this competitive business edge include:

Key Steps to Creating Customer Value

1. Determine the real customer—the user is not necessarily the actual customer—*market research is key.*

2. Analyze what your customer values and your ability to deliver it vs. the World Class Star Results criteria—then rank order it.

3. Assess how your organization's value chain differs from its competitors—*can you improve quality, service, reliability, maintainability, etc.?*

4. Estimate the cost of each of these differences. Adding features usually increases your cost/complexity. *Improving quality almost always simplifies and reduces cost over the long term.*

5. Test each source for sustainability by you vs. the competition.

6. Reduce activities and/or waste that do not affect your organization's chosen forms of differentiation—*don't waste resources on bells and whistles that do not contribute to the customer's value chain.*

7. Implement, protect, and continuously improve your customer value and competitive edge.

When organizations focus on all the components of the organization as a System Model—the Business Excellence Architecture, they accomplish both:

(1) A strategic *economic alignment* of their delivery system and

(2) A strategic *cultural attunement* of their people as a competitive edge.

Alignment of the Delivery System: "The Process Edge"

1. Organizations must strategically realign their entire set of operational tasks in the delivery system to ensure they provide value to the customer each and every time. Star Results are delivered through the operational, value added process chain (supplier—employee—customer) which might include:

   • *Choices and customization controlled by the customer.*

   • *Quality products and services delivered through Quality and Six Sigma concepts (Deming, Juran, Crosby, etc.) This includes the "continuous improvement" (or Kaizen) concept as well as the relatively unknown QIDW (quality improvement in daily work).*

   • *High-quality customer service (Legendary, Raving Fans, etc.).*

   • *On-time delivery, speed and customer responsiveness vs. the total cost of doing business with your organization*

2. Alignment of Delivery also includes the need for strategic budgeting and resources of all types to support the selected strategies—this is crucial for achieving customer value and Star Results. Indeed, it takes resources of all types to make this level of customer value a basic instinct through the organization, including people, money, facilities, space, technology, information, etc.

3. In addition the overall organizational design and structuring management include making sure all of the following support the creation of customer

value:

- *Formal and informal work flow and job design*
- *Organization design around the customer*
- *Horizontal and cross-functional teams*

4. Business process improvement—is almost always required to make the organization more effective. Some key points organizations should continually reassess include:

- *Being as simple, fast, and efficient as possible*
- *Eliminating all waste (non-value added activities) and "Blowing out Bureaucracy"*
- *Combining related sub-processes from diverse disciplines such as customer service, manufacturing, marketing, in bound and out bound logistics, distribution, sales, R & D, product development, etc.*
- *Utilizing the appropriate technologies, including automation and telecommunications, in an integrated system throughout the organization*

5. Obviously, effective horizontal and cross-functional teams must be built to conduct this successfully. Thus team development is the final key to alignment and attunement as we saw in Application #6.

Cultural Attunement of "The People Edge"

Attuning with peoples (1) hearts and minds to create the "people edge" as a competitive advantage, has much to do with organizational leadership, (2) human resource management, and (3) strategically communicating your direction to create a shared vision/values/culture. From the organization's macro systems viewpoint, the people edge is developed within (4) the organization's values and desired culture changes with (5) employee involvement crucial in this regard. While we've covered all these people attunement strategies earlier in the chapter, a short recap is warranted here.

"Centering Your Leadership" with consistent, committed, and skilled management most directly impacts this attunement. The other organizational components that relate in detail to the development of the people edge are best practices in your HR programs and practices—and teamwork at all levels and across all functions of the organization.

Application 9: Project Management and Problem Solving

Project Managers are always having to deal with problems and conduct problem-solving meetings. However, most of these meetings start with the problem or symptom (Phase C) and go right to brainstorming solutions (Phase D).

This is simplistic problem-solving at its worst—definitely not focusing on enhancing daily problem-solving into a more "solutions-seeking" focus.

Our Seven Step sequence below rectifies this and is recommended as the better approach to finding longer-lasting systems solutions.

Enhanced Daily Problem Solving

Solution-Seeking Sequence: Seven Steps

[C]   Identify problem, issue, or pain

Now Use Systems (and Backwards) Thinking:

[A]   1. Set ideal desired objectives or goals that also solve the root
        causes. It usually is a weakness in analytic thinking.

[E]   • Within your scanning of the relevant future environment.

[B]   2. With quantifiable outcome measures of success.

[C]   3. Identify Current State Strengths/Weaknesses and root causes,
        not simple cause and effect symptoms.

        • Be sure to collect data and facts about the issues.

[D]   4. Brainstorm alternative strategies and actions to achieve these
        ideal outcomes or desired solutions. Do not just lock on quick
        answers.

        • There's always a third alternative. Find it.

[B]   **Double back—*gain more feedback***

        • Troubleshoot the action plans. This is usually a weakness in
          analytic thinking.

        • Examine your biases and assumptions.

        • Include a "Parallel Involvement Process" with key stake-
          holders (both internal and external) to increase buy-in and
          ownership, and generate more ideas for correct systems
          solutions.

        • Remember to focus on the "relationships" of all the parts to
          each other, the potential Rubik's Cube Effect of unintended
          consequences, and the overall desired outcomes

☐D 5. Develop first draft of strategies and integrated action plans.

☐D 6. Implement action plans with speed and flexibility.

- Include rollout and communications as part of a "Smart Start".

- Predict and prepare for the Rollercoaster of Change™, the natural way the world works—that is natural, normal, and highly predictable.

☐B 7. Continually provide feedback about how close you are to meeting your goals. Give frequent status updates. Timing and goals may change, given the complex and changing environments that you are dealing with.

In sum:

Most problem-solving approaches are, again, an analytic approach (left to right sequence) to a systems problem. All problems are embedded within a system (such as a team) or multiple systems (such as cross functional teams), so considerations of the environment (Phase E) around the system and clarity of the project's objectives or goals (Phase A) are a must before brainstorming alternatives. Solve the System's issues to achieve the desired future outcome, not just to resolve the problem and the past. This requires that every organizational element be efficiently aligned (i.e., "the process edge") and effectively attuned (i.e., "the people edge") into one system delivering customer value. This includes strategic plans, operations, policies, measures, structures, resources, technology, competencies, business and human resources processes, as well as leadership...i.e., all organizational elements of the Business Excellence Architecture.

Application 10: Top 10 Everyday Tools for Strategic Thinking

- **Tool #1: Desired Outcomes**—Always ask the #1 Systems Question First: *"What are the desired Outcomes?"*

- **Tool #2: Environmental Impact**—Keep asking the Systems Question: *"What will be changing in the environment that will impact us?"*

- **Tool #3: Backwards Thinking**—The Ideal Vision Question: *"What is impossible to do today, but if it could be achieved, would fundamentally change what we are?"*

- **Tool #4: Feedback is a gift**—The Systems Question: *"How will I know I've achieved my desired outcomes?"*

- **Tool #5: Helicopter View**—The Ultimate Systems Question: *"What is our common higher level (superordinate) goal?"*

- **Tool #6: Booster Shots**—Systems Question: *"What do we need to do to ensure buy-in and stay-in over time?"*
- **Tool #7: Operational Flexibility**—Key Systems Question: *"What doe we centralize (outcomes) and what should we decentralize (means)?"*
- **Tool #8: A Web of Relationships**—Systems Question: *"What is the relationship of X to Y in all aspects of our lives?"*
- **Tool #9: Root Causes**—Systems Question: *"What are the root causes?"*
- **Tool #10: Simplicity**—Systems Question: *"How can we go from complexity to simplicity and from consistency to flexibility in the solutions we devise?"*

Questions to Ponder...

- Is the focus of your organization on outcomes such as creating customer value? Or is it internally focused?
- How well does your organization align your economic delivery system in support of the customer?
- How well does your organization gain the cultural attunement with peoples' hearts and minds?
- How clear are you on the Systems Model as a problem-solving Template? How does it differ from other problem-solving models?

Systems Thinking applied to an organization... Where it's happening today and where it needs to happen

In terms of Systems Thinking being actively applied to organizations today, it's clear that the private sector is picking up on it and incorporating it in a much more aggressive fashion than in the public sector. Currently, many public and private sector organizations have been caught up in throes of mass outsourcing, cost-cutting, and performance measurements—only the first part of a total systems application. Customer-related strategies and service need to be there as well. The not-for-profit sector is even further behind in any kind of Systems Thinking applications, in our view.

So, where is this happening?

1. Having said this, I must apologize to those in the public sector who are using the A-B-C Systems Thinking Template in their organizations— people such as Don Fast in British Columbia, Bob Reeves, former Superintendent at California's Poway Unified School District, and the City of Henderson, Nevada, to name a few.

2. Where, specifically, are our A-B-C Systems Models being followed in the private sector? Our Centre's 38 partners in 20 countries are one such group applying it to organizations of all types.

3. The call for a Systems Thinking Approach® to improve organizations

has become a loud clarion call. Deming taught that we must reject the one-best-way and widen the scope of our lens to look instead at the whole system in which individuals operate. To improve the quality of an organization's products and services he believes you need to fix the system; where over 95% of all problems lie. The problem is not with people; it is with the system.

4. Peter Drucker, the 20th Century's leading management guru, also believed that the entire organization as a system must be looked at in order to achieve the kind of results organizations need. Review any of his extensive bodies of writings and you will see it more clearly.

5. No less than Stephen Covey, the author of *The Seven Habits of Highly Effective People*, and *The Eighth Habit* also articulates a systems view of human effectiveness. He sees the building of relationships and having a set of principles based on the natural laws that govern human and organizational effectiveness as the keys to change. The natural laws he articulates such as "begin with the end in mind" are the embodiment of Systems Thinking.

6. John Kotter, professor of leadership at Harvard Business School, chimes in with similar perspectives. He sees far too many change efforts failing as management often has a culture of complacency rather than creativity, risk taking, and achieving impressive gains in culture and performance. In order to make these successful transformations he sees committed teams of leaders and managers guiding the effort, but somehow involving the entire organization and all of the people in the system with change. Based on the shared vision and values, this holistic view is crucial to successful change in organizations.

7. Russ Ackoff, Professor Emeritus at the University of Pennsylvania's Wharton School of Business has been a General Systems Theorist throughout his life, with his many books and other works. He continues to write and teach this today more than ever and is a key intellectual mentor of mine.

8. Jay Forrester, professor at MIT in Cambridge, MA also is a systems thinker and father of Systems Dynamics. He sees systems as pervasive throughout society. Yet he wonders why the concepts and principles of systems are not clearly articulated and utilized in today's organizations. He sees it as three-fold; there has been no need to understand the basic nature of systems; systems seem to possess no general theory and meaning; and the principles of systems are so obscure that they have evaded protection. While all of these are true, he acknowledges that systems dominate life as we know it. A systems structure, he believes, is essential to providing knowledge and learning for human beings in order to improve the effectiveness of themselves and of their teams and of the organizations within which they operate.

9. Peter Senge, MIT Professor is a direct descendant of Jay Forrester's teachings. He says that the most important issue facing domestic and

international business today is the **whole system of management**. We still operate our businesses like 17th Century Newtonian mechanists while the world operates in natural systems perspective. Thus, the whole set of processes, practices, assumptions, norms, and highly developed habits in the ways we operate organizations are now obsolete. We need a different language and set of core competencies in order to be effective as leaders and managers in the future. Systems Thinking is this language, its just obscure in his book, *The Fifth Discipline*.

10. Margaret Wheatley, in her books also knows it is time to change the way we think about organizations. They are living systems and must be reviewed and understood as living self-ordinate systems that can be much more effective if we just follow the systems perspective.

11. As the American Quality Foundation and Ernst & Young's study mentioned previously has found, there are better ways that organizations can function. And there are organizations that are effectively achieving their shared vision and operating in highly effective best practices ways.

12. It can be done and it is being done. The Baldrige Quality Award also has seen world class quality status emerging in a cross-section of American industry. Now that the Baldrige Award has re-created their criteria and model into more of a **systems view**, their decisions also identify those companies operating more from a systems perspective in the future.

13. Jim Collins' best seller, *Good to Great,* really focuses on the proven Best Practices of excellent organizations—ones that are not flashy, but do the basics well—over and over again—until they "take off" in terms of dynamic and positive results. This is perfecting your system—your organization as a system.

This systems approach to customer satisfaction and organizational excellence is popping up in more and more different places. In the past we have been fads, formulas, and one-best-way driven whereas the Japanese, the Germans, and many other countries are relationship driven. We are now changing this as the US is part of a global business economy.

Top managers are becoming systems thinkers who see their businesses as a complex system (Rubik's Cube Effect) whose subsystems such as ; people, technology, money management, processes, etc. have to mesh together if performance and quality are to be expected. These leaders are also leading their companies from one view and paradigm of the mechanistic world to the other one of the systems and organic world view of the future. In fact, some business leaders such as Jack Welch, former CEO, of General Electric, actually anticipated these shifts and understood how to move organizations across these paradigms.

The really good news is that as more and more women move beyond the glass ceiling as executives, they bring with them some different ways of functioning and managing. Study after study has shown women outscoring men. This correlation between improved management and leadership practices and women moving more and more to top management is a positive trend. It is helping to transform our information age concept of knowledge management into systems solutions that allow us to plan, lead, and manage our business in a more holistic and effective manner.

In summation, the research shows that global organizations can become complex and still function effectively if they look for simplicity on the far side of complexity. Looking holistically from the helicopter, rather than finding the one knee-jerk best way, builds a climate of high probabilities for success. This kind of view has been substantiated by research again and again, ever since the mid 1980's when I conducted my initial masters and doctoral research on Systems Thinking.

The data has been consistent for the past 20 years that organizations can create their competitive advantage only through a more holistic view of their organization and the changes that it requires. Having a systems view and a systems model creates the potential for clarifying and simplifying the complexities of organizational life. Systems Thinking is not a fad, but a fundamental and natural way organizations should think and operate in today's global environment.

These and other examples are a healthy indicator that Systems Thinking is alive and growing rapidly. See our extensive bibliography for many more sources. These represent a positive new beginning. However, Systems Thinking needs to be a significant part of society and our organizations at all levels—individual, interpersonal teams, and cross functionally; both in the private and public sectors, and society at large.

Whether your organization has any of the "desired outcomes" listed below—applying this A-B-C Systems Thinking Approach® will virtually ensure that every selection or decision is successfully geared toward meeting your overall goals, creating customer value, and achieving world-class Star Results.

Which Desired Outcomes Do You Want?

1. Higher Profits?
2. Greater Revenue?
3. Lower Costs?
4. Enhanced Market Share?
5. Drive Competitive Advantage?
6. Increase Customer Service & Satisfaction?
7. Deliver Better Customer Value?
8. Implement New Product/Service Offerings?
9. Growing Community/Society Reputation?
10. Change the Employee Culture?
11. Execute a Merger or Acquisition?
12. Enhancing our Commitment to the Community?
13. Develop Strategic Alliances or Partnerships?
14. Turn Around an Underperforming Business?
15. Enhance Safety?

16. Protect and Enhance the Environment?

17. Decrease Waste/Simplify your Bureaucracy?

Now it is time to look at the fourth Systems Concept, the Rollercoaster of Change and how systems naturally change. While the A-B-C framework can work at every level of the Six Rings of Focus, actually changing these systems effectively requires an in-depth understanding of the nature and natural cycles of change.

Success

The great successful men (women) of the world have used their imagination...

They think ahead and create their mental picture, and then go to work materializing that picture in all it's details, filling in here, adding a little there, altering this a bit and that a bit, but steadily building—steadily building.

—*Robert Collier*

Chapter 8
The A-B-C Systems Model
Summary of Key Concepts

In the final analysis, the true beauty of the A-B-C Systems Model and the Seven Levels of Living Systems is that they can be applied to virtually any organizational change strategy, at any level, and to whatever degree is required. Here are just some of the ways in which the Systems Thinking applications we've shared with you can be utilized by your organization:

1. *Comprehensive Strategic Plan*—Apply the five-phase systems model comprehensive strategic planning process to the entire organization.

2. *Strategic Planning Quick*—Develop a shortened, less comprehensive version of strategic planning for the entire organization.

3. *Business/Functional Strategic Planning*—Create a three-year business planning process for a line of business unit or major support function or single organizational element.

4. *Micro Strategic Planning*—Use the five-phase systems model to plan strategy for a small organization or business.

5. *Strategic Life Planning*—Create your own personal life plan and strategies, viewing your family unit as its own organizational system.

6. *Strategic Change*—Plan for a major project or task force, such as Six Sigma, TQM, service, business process re-engineering, empowerment, partnerships, teamwork, technology, etc.

7. *Strategic Human Resource Management*—Use a five-phase systems model on which to develop the people edge in your organization.

8. *Talent Management and Leadership Development System*—Apply Systems Thinking to enhance organizational leadership roles and competencies along with succession and talent management as a competitive business edge, at all six levels of leadership skills.

9. *The Organization as a Systems Model, (our Business Excellence Architecture)*—Employ this Systems Model to systematically implement any change effort and dramatically increase your probability of success.

10. *Teamwork*—The A-B-C systems model can be applied to dramatically improve team development, as well.

11. *The Learning Organization*—Use a five-phase systems approach to develop a true, self-generating learning environment organization-wide.

12. *Creating Customer Value*—Create improved value and delivery to customers by utilizing many of these applications together.

13. *Conducting any Project Management Process or Problem-Solving Issue*—this ABC Template has virtually a universal application.

Reinventing Strategic Planning
(Application #2)

Phase E: **Future Environmental Scanning**
Step #1: Plan-to-Plan

Phase A: **Creating Your Future Ideal Vision**
Step #2: Ideal Future Vision

Phase B: **Quantifiable Outcomes**
Step #3: Key Success Measure/Goals

Phase C: **Converting Strategy to Action**
Step #4: Current State Assessment (Gap Analysis)
Step #5: Strategy Development (Gap Closure)
Step #6: Three-Year Business Planning
Step #7: Annual Plans/Strategic Budgeting
Step #8: Plan-to-Implement

Phase D: **Implementation**
Step #9: Strategy and Implementation
Step #10: Annual Strategic Review and Update (including a Strategic IQ ™ Audit)

CHAPTER 9

Concept #4: The Rollercoaster of Change®
"Changing Systems...The Natural Cycles of Change and Life"

Concept in Detail:

T he Rollercoaster of Change® is the key natural and normal way a system changes. It doesn't matter whether the "system" is the individual, interpersonal relationships, a team issue, cross-functional project team work, or a total organization change. This Rollercoaster is the only concept that you need to know, because it is a summary of over 20 change process concepts that are all the same, just different words and visuals. The Roller Coaster of Change® applications are many, nearly universal.

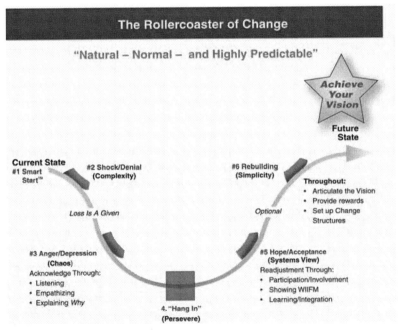

Figure 9-1 The Rollercoaster of Change

Once you kick off a change project, it is a given that Stages II and III will occur. As you can see, shock and denial is Stage II of the Rollercoaster. Stage III is the depression, anger, and emotional Stage. It is a given that both of these will happen.

However, to make change your ally, you need to prepare for changes **before** Stages II and III. Since the Rollercoaster is "natural, normal, and highly predictable", we always have a pre-meeting before beginning any change. We call it the "**Smart Start**" of Stage I and in it we ensure we "educate—assess—organize and tailor" the change process **before** kicking it off. Stages II and III will occur. However the real issue is what happens after that—do you control the change or does it control you?

The only real question is whether you help yourself or others through Stages III and IV through acknowledging them, by listening actively, by empathizing with them and yet still explaining the importance of why the change is necessary (in this order). As people go through these Stages they bottom out at what we call the "hang-in point". At the hang-in point people need to persevere and persist in the change process rather than giving up or trying to reverse or undo the change. This is part of how you move through to Stage V which is the hope, acceptance, and readjustment Stage. It is where you begin climbing the right hand (positive) side of the Rollercoaster.

It is not a given that any Rollercoaster achieves full completion by climbing up the right hand side. While the loss and the depression left side (Stages II and III) is *a given*, the right hand side is *optional* (see chart below)—with five options. It requires some level of self-management plus the leadership of others to help people through the change. This readjustment Stage is best assisted through the involvement and participation of people in building towards the new vision; both for themselves and as a team. It is also helped by showing people "what's in it for me" (or WIIFM). Any kind of new learning that helps people feel they are growing is also very helpful at this Stage.

THE FIVE CHOICES OF CHANGE AND LEVELS OF EXCELLENCE

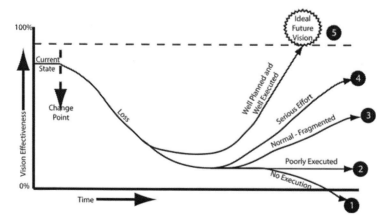

Figure 9-2: The Five Choices of Change and Levels of Excellence

Only at Stage VI: Rebuilding; can you really allow people to be empowered effectively on their own, or for teams to be able to proceed effectively as high performance units as well. This is because Stage VI is the **only stage of high**

performance.

Throughout the complexities and the chaos of this entire Rollercoaster, people, teams, and organizations also need to continually:

- reinforce and articulate the vision of why this is important,
- continue to provide rewards, reinforcement and recognition to others in a positive way as they proceed towards this vision, as well as
- set up mechanisms and structures to assist with the change process.

We will cover this last one, the change mechanisms and structures, later on in this chapter.

While any model is a simplistic representation of a complex reality, the full complex Rollercoaster **is** the reality of change. I coined this term "Rollercoaster of Change" in the 1980's because, when viewed from afar, it does not look like this simple cycle here, but rather like a rollercoaster. It has so many curves and cycles that it looks almost like a maze.

Rollercoaster Questions:

The following kinds of questions and issues regarding the Rollercoaster show its true simplicity...on the far side of complexity:

- Question #1: It is not **if** you go through shock and depression but **when** will it occur

- Question #2: How **deep** will the trough be? This depth is the depth of psychological change that takes away from the energy for performance in a person or a team's life.

- Question #3: Deals with how long it will take to get over to the right hand side and Stage VI's rebuilding. It is not a given that the Rollercoaster has to have a major dip during a change process. The depth and the length of the change is frequently dependent on your ability to manage yourself and others through this change curve so that the curve itself is a "mini-curve".

- Question #4: Is whether we will get up to the right hand side of the curve and rebuild at all. The left hand side is a given. The right hand side is optional and requires proactive responses to the change.

- Question #5: Deals with whether or not we will rebuild to the highest level of new achievement that makes the entire change process and pain worthwhile. When viewed from the current state over to the rebuilding stage the question is whether you rebuild at a higher level, the same level, or some lower level than where you were before. The only reason to undergo change is to end up with an improvement that is worth tolerating the pain and the dysfunctional behavior through the chaos, complexity, and emotions of the Rollercoaster's dip.

- Question #6: Deals with how many different Rollercoasters we experience at any one time? This was particularly true in the 90's when we were living with a global, economic environment and constant dynamic change. While you may look at changes as if they occur one at a time, the truth is we usually undergo many different Rollercoasters at the same time. Our personal and professional lives are intertwined. We experience a confluence of many different changes at the same time. Thus, the conflicting emotions that we have about change are often because of these multiple changes.

- Question #7: Deals with whether we will hang in and persevere through the change? The hang-in point is where many change processes fail. The key is to recognize this Rollercoaster, understand when the hang-in point feels like it is occurring, and persisting forward despite your depression and/or anger.

Regardless of what anyone might feel or say about former U.S.A. President Bill Clinton, everyone would agree that he had the ability to persevere and persevere in very difficult situations.

The Only Alternative to Persistence is Failure!
"Nothing in the world can take the place of persistence. Talent will not; nothing is more common than unsuccessful men with talent. Genius will not; unrewarded genius is almost a proverb. Education will not; the world is full of educated derelicts. **Persistence and determination alone are omnipotent.**"
—Calvin Coolidge

This is what we mean. No matter how difficult the situation, you must continue on. To not do so is what leads to failure.

- Question #8: Deals with how to deal with normal resistance? The reality is that Stage III's depression, anger, emotions and the accompanying resistance is normal. So, we can either assist it by the methods described earlier, or we can make it far worse by saying things like "you shouldn't be upset" or "if you don't change, I'm going to fire you". Dealing with resistance is better done through the kinds of "martial arts flexibility" rather than the massive pushing of people often done by inexperienced and incompetent managers.

- Question #9: (and the last question) Is how to create a critical mass in support of the change? There are always some early adopters, but the large groups of the silent majority take a "wait and see" attitude. A few people are often strong resisters. We usually fail in change when we focus on the small group of resisters, rather than trying to work with the early adapters and some of the silent majority to create a critical mass in positive support of the change. It has a lot to do with how we involve people and show them what is in it for me (WIIFM). They can then become informal leaders of our critical mass to eventually assist the resisters in adapting to the change. Then the change becomes a steamroller that cannot be stopped.

Example: To illustrate this Rollercoaster, look at the example of the Stages of change an organization goes through in just a reorganization. Unfortunately, Stages I, IV, and V are often overlooked, prolonging or even stopping the Rollercoaster at the bottom hang-in point.

Figure 9-3: Six Stages of Enterprise-Wide Change

Questions to Ponder...

- Are you clear on the details of how the Rollercoaster operates?
- Can you apply it to a change you have recently undergone in your personal life (or one you are currently undergoing)?

The importance of this Rollercoaster cannot be overestimated. In fact, when people are going through change, just the acknowledgment of its existence is extremely helpful to people. This means that it is natural and normal to be depressed during change: just don't live there on a permanent basis. It's extremely important to realize that the loss experienced during the Rollercoaster creates a feeling of depression for most people. It is a difficult experience to handle, and the loss must be mourned if you are going to let go and continue forward through this process, therefore, Stage III is the most critical. This is where you must acknowledge the loss and create a psychological wake or funeral to help people let go so they can move forward. Most organizational change flounders here because this experience of loss is not taken into account.

To undertake successful organizational change, every executive and manager must anticipate in Stage I (Smart Start) and provide the means of working through the losses of Stage III (not to mention helping with all six Stages).

> The "Basic truth of management—if not of life - is that nearly **everything looks like a failure in the middle**...persistent, consistent execution is unglamorous, time consuming and sometimes boring."
> —*Rosabeth Moss-Kanter*

Finally, realize that chaos and complexity are a normal and natural part of the process of change. They are important to experience in order to discover new ways of acting and being. They are a necessary part of achieving one's vision. While we don't like to believe things get worse before they get better, in fact, that is the reality.

Now let's look at the different ways we can utilize this one Rollercoaster concept in changing systems in their many forms — and at all of the Key Levels of Living Systems (i.e., by tying the Systems Concepts together).

Major Use #1: Self Change

The first issue with change is making sure that each of us work our way through this Rollercoaster of Change personally. The key for each of us as individuals and employees is not to overreact to the shock. Then, as we go through depression and anger, to ask questions, express our feelings, and realize it is O.K. to be depressed and skeptical. However, we must not give up on the change, but hang-in personally despite our emotions. Again, persistence and resilience are keys.

Then, in order to move up to Stage IV we must answer the question of WIIFM or what's in it for me? Focusing on answering this question is key to feeling some sense of hope. It allows ourselves to participate and be involved in actions and activities that will help us build the new vision. At this stage, focusing on the future is crucial. Let go of the past and move forward.

And finally, once we understand the vision, it is important to be committed to it and to take independent and proactive initiatives within the overall system we are trying to re-build. Being a team player at this point is very crucial.

Thus, as an individual, it is important that we know this curve well. Recognize it as normal and natural in today's world of constant change. We have to be somewhere on this curve at all times, since change is a constant in today's world. Don't deny your feelings and emotions when you are in Stage III. Acknowledge and honor them, just don't stay there forever. It's also important in Stage III to take care of yourself and adopt coping mechanisms and behaviors such as taking time off if necessary, eating healthy, getting enough sleep and exercising. The important thing to remember in personal change is to keep in mind the big perspective. All things too shall pass over time. The key is not to overreact.

Major Use #2: Interpersonal Changes

In dealing with change we often close ourselves off from others. It is important at this level of change in dealing with others to realize that all of us have these same issues during change. We need the support of others, even though we often close ourselves off to others during Stages II and III of change. It is important during this shock Stage that managers provide a directive response to employees and tell them directly and honestly about the change, recognizing that many of them will not remember or understand fully what you have told them. You'll have to explain it to them two, three and even four times. As a manager, it is important that you go through the change process first yourself so that you understand and appreciate how others feel during it. Remembering that everyone changes at different rates and depths, it is important to be ready to deal with all six Stages of change at the same time.

If you are in a coaching situation, it is important to establish a purpose and contract to help the person you are coaching all the way through the Rollercoaster. As people begin to go through Stage III's depression, realize that there are issues of control at this juncture. This is why it is important to be highly supportive by listening and asking questions and being empathetic. However it is also why it is important to be directive in explaining why the process is so important and the vision is worth the pain. At this point you have to be an effective coach. Ask, listen, and only then sell people on the change ideas in an effective way. Many managers and supervisors alienate employees rather than being supportive at this Stage. Realize that "skeptics are my best friends" and that it is O.K. to be skeptical. Don't try to convince them that they are wrong at this Stage or the depression will last far longer. Again, listen, emphasize, and only then explain why the change is necessary.

It is also key at this Stage for supervisors to be in face-to-face conversations, rather than avoiding employees at this point. If you are willing to induce shock and depression by telling people about a change, you must also be strong enough to go out and deal with them and their emotions on a face-to-face basis. Again, rather than trying to convince them, what you want to do is listen and empathize first; then explain why. This skill and approach, if understood by managers, makes dealing with the depression and anger far easier. Develop your coaching skills!

As a supervisor it is important to realize that people generally want to learn and grow. Therefore, you need to model and to learn and grow yourself. Don't be defensive. Be consistent, persevere, and model the way during the hang-in point. Maintaining continuous relationships with people and don't allow them to be alone all of the time. Use group sessions to show people they are not alone, helping them to transition towards Stage V's hope.

The way to tell if someone else is moving in Stage V's direction is whether or not they can answer the WIIFM question for themselves. If they can answer it, they are moving towards a sense of hope, adjustments, and openness at Stage V. Now it becomes easier as you can become more supportive and a little less directive with them. Create involvement and participation opportunities to assist them along the change process. While they will still challenge the process in this Stage it is usually done in a more positive way. They can still be skeptical, but positive movement (and the celebration of it by you) is crucial. Don't celebrate perfection, celebrate progress.

The fifth Stage of hope is where you really want to make sure you have a solid agreement regarding the kinds of expectations you both have of each other. That will allow you to move toward more and more collaboration and empowered work on Stage VI's rebuilding and restructuring.

At Stage VI people are working toward high performance. This is where you are able to empower people within the overall system and direction that the vision and values of the organization provide. At this Stage being low in supportiveness and directiveness is fine as the motivation and control come from the vision, values and the understanding of their role in achieving it.

However it is still important to articulate through stump speeches and other mechanisms the shared vision and values. It will continue to enable more and more people to join the critical mass and assist with the overall alignment, attunement, and integrity of what you are attempting to do.

Overall, at the Interpersonal Level of Living Systems it is important for you to study these situations. Decide for yourself in very practical terms how you can be flexible in your own style to deal effectively with others. Be clear on how you want to interact with others. Deal with your own needs as well as theirs for inclusion and control; the two big issues. Realize that your own and others need to control often stifles growth. Also examine your own level of openness. Do you self disclose first to others, or do you hold your cards close to your vest? Whichever way you model will come back to you.

It also means you must be willing to be open to feedback from skeptics even if it hurts. Only this way can you continue to learn, grow and be more effective in interpersonal situations. As a supervisor and/or a parent, realize that you need active listening and questioning skills as well. Most of us tend to be good at only one or the other (asking or telling) in our interpersonal relationships.

In addition, learn to be flexible to match up your own management, parental and/or peer style to the needs of the other person in the situation. This flexibility is the key to the long term popularity of the famous Situational Leadership Model of Hersey and Blanchard. Will Shutz, of FIRO-B Fame, is another consultant who has dealt with control and inclusion as very important issues when helping people through interpersonal change. Both of these models are their own applications of this same Rollercoaster.

Finally, the Rollercoaster is the only concept you need to know; use it to perfect your application of it in coaching and working with others.
- learn effective listening and questioning skills
- have a goal to maintain the relationship even when strong corrections and sanctions are necessary
- build healthy norms between yourself and the other person including a clear sense of purpose
- and outcomes, the #1 Systems Question.

Major Use #3: Team Change
(including both Department and Cross-Functional Project Teams)

The Rollercoaster of Change also applies to teams. Teams are where most productive work gets done in today's organizations. Therefore forming groups of people into effective teams doesn't just happen automatically. Whenever you get together a new group, it is natural and normal for all of you to go through the Rollercoaster; both as a team and as individuals.

Most people assume wrongly that by putting groups of people together into a meeting they have formed an effective team that can immediately do productive work. Nothing could be further from the truth.

Thus, it becomes very important for us to recognize that teams go through this Rollercoaster of Change as well. The Stages of group dynamics that teams go through is very well researched and known. It is just another application of the Rollercoaster:

- Stage V induces shock by **forming** the team. Then the group goes immediately into depression and anger (or the **storming** Stage III for the group) as people try to make sense out of the people, the roles, the group processes, and the group goals.

- If the group does hang in, then setting up **norms** of behavior for Stage V is crucial to moving up the right side of the Rollercoaster—key is to answer all the questions listed above in Stage III. Only then can the group form a true effective team for high level performance.

Questions to Ponder...

- How effective are the key teams (department or otherwise) that you are on?
- What Stage are you in on these teams? and
- What questions above in Stage III have you, unfortunately, not answered clearly?

In other words - the Rollercoaster can be described as forming, storming, norming, performing. These are also the Stages of group dynamics; turning groups into effective teams .

Learning this set of four words above can help you tremendously as teams go through change. Most of us usually are on a number of teams in organizations today. So this set of group dynamics is one of the absolute keys to successful organizational change.

This whole process of a group becoming an effective team is part of what we also talk about as dialogue and discovery in today's world. This occurs when we go past the forming and storming Stages that deal with denial and defending our own territory. The problem with dialogue and discovery is that we can either defend our own territory and our own opinions in Stage III or we can begin moving with others through the hang-in point that will lead to the two-way dialogue and learning of Stage V. We can defend our territory and ideas, or we can be open to dialogue and new learnings .

This is what occurs in Stage IV-V among team members. It leads to the rebuilding of the team towards the vision and the discovery of lots of new learnings and applications. Only by two-way intellectual honesty and openness can we go through Stage IV's dialogue to the discovery of new applications and ideas in Stage VI. This is crucial in today's world as teams often are groups of cross-functional people going through change at different rates and different speeds. It all depends on their different personalities, backgrounds, professions, experiences and functional expertise.

Change equals learning! Whenever we go through learning we are also going through change. The Adult Learning Cycle is a change and rollercoaster cycle as well. The four Stages of the adult learning cycle include first the shock of the activity and experience which is why we say "adults learn best by doing". However, we only learn if we and the others around us in the group or team process the activity and the feelings and trends of the depression stage of change. Answering the question "What occurred" is crucial here.

Transitioning from there, through the hang-in point of Stage IV to Stage V allows teams to look at the learnings and the actions and applications needed for effective change. The question we ask in Stage V is the openness question of "So What have we learned as a result of these activities and the processing?"

The third key question is "Now What do we do to apply the learnings in our real life experiences and situation?" Thus, learning is something that can occur readily as long as trainers, facilitators and leaders understand to ask the "what", "so what", and "now what" questions in that sequence.

If people resist the "so what" question it is because they are still in Stage III or the hang-in point Stage IV. Therefore, by definition, they are not ready to learn. They may need to process the "what happened" question for a longer period of time until you can transition them to the "so what" and eventually to the "now what" questions. Without answering this last question, it is not always clear to people what the experience was all about and now what they can do different the next time.

What - So What - Now What? Remember these questions.

Finally, in dealing with teams and groups of people, conflict is the norm. Very often the activity and experience of Stage II creates some form of disagreement and/or potential conflict. At this point we often go into the depression Stage and move in one or two dysfunctional directions.

Option #1. We may continue to talk politely to people even though underneath the surface, our stomach is churning. We liken this to how a duck swims in the water where they appear to be nice and calm as they move along on the surface, but underneath, their feet are paddling like crazy.

Option #2. The other way that people handle depression poorly is through raw and emotional debate, with yelling and abusive kinds of behaviors common place. Unfortunately, the hang-in point is one where people must have a desire for resolution and letting go of their anger and frustration in Stage III. Since it is not the point of this book to cover conflict resolution in all its detailed skills, we want to point out to the reader a book entitled *"Ethical Persuasion"* by Dr. Tom Rusk. It is the best book we have seen on resolving conflict. The skills of *"ethical persuasion"* go through three stages on how to deal with conflict and they are Stages III, IV, and V of the Rollercoaster.

Tom Rusk's Stage III is where he explains that you must be the "learner" and deal with conflict effectively just like you do in any interpersonal situation; by asking questions and listening actively to the other person. He wants you to make sure you allow the other person to explain "why" to you first before you can ethically ask them to listen to why you feel differently. Being the Learner and learning the other person's point of view is crucial in conflict resolution. Contrast this with the traditional reaction—as soon as you are in a defending mode you cut off all possibilities of resolution.

Once you move on to Stages IV and V (hope and adjustment) Rusk's book has you becoming the Explainer. Here you use a more disciplined dialogue and a set of skills on how to involve the other person in the solution. The basic problem with conflict is that we try to influence without first being willing to be influenced by other people. Unless you first allow the person to influence you, you will never really influence them in most situations. Only after involving them in hearing your explanation can you move to the last Stage of dialogue in Rusk's book. There, he has you both seeking a third alternative and discovering the answers for resolving the conflict (i.e., rebuilding the relationships - the last Stage in the Rollercoaster). This issue of conflict is particularly true in cross-functional teams where people have different backgrounds, experiences, and perspectives.

Both personally and professionally, you need to understand the group dynamic stage sof forming, storming, norming, and performing. Since most productive work today requires groups of people to function effectively in teams, the Rollercoaster is the framework for these dynamics. You must learn the techniques for speeding up and shortening the depth and breadth of this Rollercoaster to really build effective teams more quickly. Some of the ways to do this include the following:

- Spend time at the beginning of your group formation to define your purposes and goals;
- Also spend time up front developing your norms of what are excepted behaviors and ground rules. Especially build clear norms of decision making and dealing with conflict;
- Not only set up the goals and purposes, but also the timeframes and timetables upon which you are functioning;
- Also acknowledge the different and interdependent roles and accountability as teams must function together;
- And finally, set up how to continually gain feedback, so that the team can undergo continuous improvement and learning

In addition, work with each of the teams you are a part of to learn how to be intellectually honest with each other. Learn how to utilize the **dialogue and**

discovery that creates better solutions. Learn to *"leave your shield at the door"*, stop defending all your ideas and taking issues personally. You can either defend your position and ideas or expand the range of information for better decision making.

Consensus decisions mean that I can **"actively support"** the decision that is made, even if it is not the one I would have personally made. Work towards making this consensus tool an effective part of your teamwork. However, realize that not all decisions require or can achieve consensus. This is due to the fact that the issue of decision making always deals with two issues they are: (1) ownership or "buy-in and (2) quality of decisions. Don't let the desire for buy-in be so politically correct that you begin to make poor quality decisions.

As state earlier, effective conflict resolution always goes through these Rollercoaster Stages. Stifling anger and emotions in the name of politeness (which occurs in most teams) is only to suppress conflict and its potential benefits. What are its benefits? There are many. In order to become more effective in dealing with conflict utilizing the Rollercoaster I again direct you to *Ethical Persuasion* by Dr. Tom Rusk.

"Adults learn best by doing" is also a basic truism. Therefore, to learn from anything that you are doing, whether it is a formal training program, a meeting on whatever, learn to gain feedback and insights for improvement at the end of each activity. Do this by asking three simple questions that only take two-three minutes of debriefing. These questions are the **What—So What—Now What Questions:**
- **What** just happened?
- **So What** can we learn or generalize from all this experience?
- **Now What** can we do differently to improve ourselves by applying these learnings?

Major Use # 4: Organizational Change

"Organizations change when people change" is a basic truism. However, there still is a collective set of behavioral changes that organizations need to undergo organization-wide to deal with constant and dynamic changes. This is the ultimate Level of Living Systems; dealing with improved organizational effectiveness. Just as within the hierarchy of the 7 Levels of Living Systems, organizational change also includes **all** of the Rollercoaster dynamics of the previous three uses, as well as this one. The Rollercoaster of Change operates at the individual, interpersonal, team and cross-functional levels as part of collective organization-wide change. **Therefore, you can now see how difficult cultural change really is.** **Effective** organization-wide change requires everyone, and every team, in every relationship, to undergo some kind of behavioral change.

Most organizations attempt organizational-wide change in a piecemeal haphazard fashion. This is why up to 70-80% of all major and complex change fail. As this book on simplicity shows, major change requires close attention and fit among all aspects of the web of relationships in support of the overall objectives of the organization.

There are some clear techniques on how to help an organization through the six Stages of the Rollercoaster. They include:

Ways to unfreeze an organization: (Rollercoaster Stage II: Shock and Denial)

1. Share what competitors are doing.
2. Explain your organization's finances and P/L statement.
3. Share your organization's vision and future ideal.
4. Clarify the impact on the organization and employees of a particular situation or issue.
5. Conduct an organizational survey. Feed it back to Senior Management then staff.
6. Collect interview data and feed it back to Senior Management then staff.
7. Re-explain job expectations and standards of performance.
8. Expand the reward system (individual – team—organization-wide).
9. Discuss changes in the environment that impact the organization.
10. Discuss why there is a need to change.
11. Explain the organization's strategic plans and direction and their logic.
12. Set goals with employees for each of their jobs.
13. Examine employee data, such as turnover, etc.
14. Conduct an unfiltered upward feedback meeting.
15. Change the roles of key informal leaders.
16. Feedback on customer perceptions and data.
17. Conduct focus groups of employees and customers.
18. Change the location of management offices to be closer to the employees.
19. Set up task forces to analyze issues and recommend solutions.
20. Explicitly evaluate employee performance (including senior management) against your desired values.

Factors needed to go through the Stages of Change successfully:
(Rollercoaster Stages III, IV, and V: Depression/Anger, Hang-In, and Hope/Adjustment)

1. This is a time of high uncertainty and anxiety:
   a. Communicate frequently about the change and change process.
   b. Develop feedback mechanisms to hear the employees' questions and concerns and then a way to conduct two-way dialogues.
2. Don't react emotionally to employee concerns and resistance. Empathize and understand them. Let people talk it out. Then try to deal with the underlying issues (i.e., read between the lines).
3. Let people have a clear understanding of why the change is necessary.
4. Let people have an opportunity to critically cross-examine the leader(s)

and verify for themselves the necessity for change.

5. Give people occasions to talk through their feelings of loss and detachment from the old ways.

6. Have methods by which people affected by the change can participate in some aspect of change to control their destiny.

7. Have management develop and organize new support systems to establish the new state.

8. Develop a positive climate about the change by evoking a clear and positive "common vision" of what the end state of the change will look like.

9. Show people how the change can personally help them and their needs (WIIFM).

10. Relate the change to employee values.

11. Develop teams—not just groups or departments—and implement values and rewards for teamwork.

12. Work closely with the informal leaders of the organization.

13. Provide employees with an opportunity to increase their learning and competence about their jobs and about the change.

14. Develop and communicate about your well-planned "change management process" to give employees a sense of security and knowledge that you are in control and in charge of the changes.

Ways to institutionalize changes in an organization: (Rollercoaster Stage VI: Rebuilding)

Note: While it may be good to think of institutionalizing change in an organization, the practical reality is that once you institutionalize this new changed state, you will immediately begin to make other changes in response to changing conditions. This continues indefinitely (i.e., continual improvement/ renewal)!

There are ways to insure changes are successfully completed and maintained. They include:

1. Conduct an organizational assessment to see the status of the change and problems that need improvement in order for the change to reach its full effectiveness.

2. Conduct refresher training courses on the change topic.

3. Hold yearly conferences on the subject (renewal).

4. Have the basic change and also the improvements listed in #1 above as part of senior line management's goals and performance appraisal.

5. Conduct a reward system's diagnosis and make appropriate changes so that the rewards (both financial and non-financial) are congruent and consistent with the changes.

6. Set up an ongoing audit system such as the yearly Strategic IQ Audit. Also find ways to statistically measure the change effectiveness. Line

managers are used to statistics and generally like them.

7. Have ways to discuss and reinforce the change at periodic staff meetings of top management and department heads.

8. Place the desired changes into policies and procedures of the ongoing organization; then have someone accountable for them. Staff up permanent jobs to maintain the changes or put the accountability into existing job descriptions.

9. Use a variety of communications avenues and processes for both one way and two way feedback on the change.

10. Hold periodic team meetings on the subject across the organization.

11. Have top line managers conduct "deep sensing" meetings on the subject down into the organization on a regular basis.

12. Have periodic inter-group or inter-department meetings on the subject and its status.

13. Set up a process of yearly renewing and re-examining the change in order to continually improve it.

14. Have outside consultants conduct periodic visits on the subject and assess the status of the change.

15. Be doubly sure that the top team continues to model the changes.

16. Set priorities and deadlines for short-term improvements to the change.

17. Look closely at the key environmental sectors to be sure they are reinforcing the changes.

18. Create physical indications of the permanency of the change (offices, jobs, brochures, etc.)

19. Develop "stay agents" or multiple persons who have a strong interest in maintaining the change (particularly among line managers and the informal leaders).

20. Refine change procedures to make them routine and normal.

21. Link other organizational systems to the change. Encourage specific and formal communications, coordination, and processes between them.

22. Keep the goals and benefits of the change clear and well known.

23. Assess the potential dangers and pitfalls of the change and develop specific approaches and plans to minimize these dangers.

24. Be alert to other changes that can negatively affect this change. (Unintended negative side effects and consequences.)

25. Have a different person manage the stability than the one who managed the change. They are different tasks involving people with different personalities. **Change agents** are poor **stay agents**.

Questions to Ponder...

Go back over these last few pages and these checklists:

- Which of these actions do you use in helping yourself and others through change (circle them)?

  ...*And*...

- Which of these actions should you be doing

Three Major Change Issues Always Present

Now, let's get even more specific about the process of change at the organizational level.

When dealing with organizational change there are almost always three major kinds of change issues to pay attention to as the graph shows.

Change Issue #1:

We must deal with the economic alignment of the delivery processes of your organization. Economic alignment is based on the strategies you have chosen and need to implement to achieve your world class customer value outcomes. This often requires strategies for the organization about the shock/denial and depression/anger around "cutting"; such as staff cuts, reorganizations, and low cost focus. It also requires a focus on the right hand side of the Rollercoaster and how to "build" your organization towards the future and the vision of serving the customer. This is where quality, service and customer orientation are crucial (see cycles of change below).

In order to help an entire organization through the Rollercoaster of Change you must not only deal with the *cutting* and left side of the Rollercoaster but the positive right hand *building* side. The hang-in point is where you need to continue to focus on both sets of strategies, but, especially on the *building* side. You will need to build the fit and alignment of the entire system of delivery together after the change. This is why, at the hang-in point, it is important to persevere, be resilient, and not back off.

Change Issue #2:

It is also crucial to deal with the **cultural attunement of people's hearts and** minds in support of the new values and desired culture, as well as customer satisfaction. This requires people at all Systems Levels; individual, teams, and cross-functionally to go through the change.

The shock, the unfreezing of the status quo, is the second Stage. However, in the third Stage of cultural change, you have to control the same three things that the revolutionaries have know for ages to overthrow a government. Those include:

(1) Education,

(2) Communications, and

(3) Rewards and sanctions.

So you as the leader of cultural change need to control these same three areas. While rebuilding the morale and the motivation of people through these changes, create a critical mass for change. Eventually you will need to move that critical mass up the rebuilding side of the Rollercoaster. Key is empowering and rewarding them for supporting the new culture.

Change Issue #3:

The third major need in organizational change is to build a Strategic Management System to control, adjust, correct, and keep the fit and relationships of all the changes going in the same direction. This overwhelming task includes almost everything that we discussed in this book and the four concepts of Systems Thinking applied to organizations. It really requires the overall assessing of where you are as an organization, holding on when necessary, but eventually letting go to build the economic alignment and the fit of the delivery parts and the cultural attunement of the hearts and minds of people in support of rebuilding towards the overall future vision, values, and measurements of success.

In other words, you must design and build a system of coordinating, managing, and leading in a strategic and *integrated* way. Rather than just singular, tactical, or operational excellence.which people confuse frequently.

Operational or tactical excellence is not the same as building a system of defining, leading, and managing *strategically* towards a clear and shared vision and values of customer satisfaction. The web of relationships in an integrated organization as a system requires this kind of approach. It is what Jim Collins discussed in how to go from **Good to Great** in his book.

This requires the creation of a *"strategic change management system"* that includes the overall organization-wide processes and structures necessary to help people at all levels go through change effectively. In other words, achieving major, large scale or transformational change of any magnitude is very, very difficult with a low probability of success. Your choices of success or failure include the five Rollercoaster potential results shown earlier in the Chapter. Which do you want?

What price are you willing to pay to achieve it?

In other words, do you want your change to be:
- Unplanned or poorly executed,
- To have a normal fragmented analytic approach,
- To make a serious effort but not do all the many things that are needed or
- Awell planned and well executed change process that leads you to actually creating your ideal future vision?

The choice is yours!

Cultural and organizational-wide change can be overwhelming unless you pull back and look at Systems Thinking Concept #4, the Rollercoaster of Change™, and how to help change occur successfully at all Levels of Living Systems simultaneously. Thus, it is crucial in all these major levels of systems changes for you to internalize the Rollercoaster and its predictable consequences. Be sure to remember that any model is only a simplistic representation of a complex reality. It is much more complex than anyone can put down in a book as we all know. However with this model change is *"highly, highly predictable"*.

Teach and share this model with people whenever you are involved in any type of change. Ensure that people know it is *natural, normal* and highly predictable—i.e. expect in every change for things to get worse and for a loss of energy to occur before things get better. Persevere and hang-in throughout this Rollercoaster.

Summary of Concept #4: The Rollercoaster of Change

This Rollercoaster is the major way to learn to assist in changing systems at all of the different levels within an organization. The Rollercoaster is the natural and normal cycle of change and of life. It should be recognized, shared, and appreciated as such. Utilizing the major questions identified at the beginning of this Chapter for each of the different levels of application is crucial. Exactly how change occurs at the self-level, the interpersonal-level, the department-level, the cross-functional team, and the organizational-level is operationally unique. Yet strategically, and systems-wise, all levels still follow the Rollercoaster in concept. While organizational change when viewed in all its details is quite complex, **it is the simplicity of knowing the Rollercoaster that is key**.

Then apply it to all the Levels of Living Systems within an organization. This is a framework of simplicity, yet it helps to ensure the comprehensiveness of effective transformational changes.

Major Questions	Major Uses
1. How deep is the trough? How long?	1. Personal transitions/Learning
2. Will we get up the right side and rebuild?	2. Interpersonal relationships
3. Are there other changes occurring?	3. Coaching
4. Will we hang-in and persevere?	4. Conflict management
5. How to deal with normal resistance?	5. Team effectiveness
6. How to create a critical mass for change?	6. Overall change management

Figure 9-4: Concept #4 - The Rollercoaster of Change

Chapter #9
Concept #4: The Rollercoaster of Change®
Summary of Key Concepts

1. The Rollercoaster of Change® is natural and normal - and is the only concept you need to know about changing systems.
2. It's applications to all Levels of Living Systems are numerous and crucial. Relate all other learning and change applications such as coaching, group dynamics, situational leadership, FIRO-B (Will Schulz) to it.
3. Forming, storming, norming, performing is the Rollercoaster in group dynamics terms.
4. What? So What? Now What? are the three key questions of the Rollercoaster in The Adult Learning Cycle. "Adults Learn Best By Doing."
5. Anger and depression is natural and normal in change. Don't deny it; listen, empathize and explain "why" the change is necessary.
6. The only alternative to persistence is failure. Hang-in.
7. WIIFM is key in change (What's in it for me?).
8. Learn to use dialogue and discovery techniques in conflict resolution. You either defend your position or expand your range of information for better decision-making.
9. Consensus Decisions means I can actively support the decision that is made, even if it isn't the exact one I would make myself.
10. Teamwork is key to implementing change. The "Plan-Do-Control" cycle for teams to learn is key to their success.
11. Strategic Implementation and Change requires a focus on the issues at all Levels of Living Systems in an organization simultaneously. They include: self, 1:1, department, cross-functional teams, and the integration of organization-wide change.

Some Principles of Change: (Based on Systems Thinking)

These principles of change are research-based; they are not matters of personal opinion.

1. Any change in any one part of the organization affects other parts of the organization—the "Rubik's Cube Effect" (The organization is a system.). Leaders need to pay constant attention to an integrated fit and corporate view; entropy will take over if not.
2. People are funny. Change they initiate is viewed as good, needed, and valuable. Change that is forced on them is met by some form of resistance, no matter what the nature of the change.
3. People need predictability—physical, psychological, and social. It's an

offshoot of the basic need for security.

4. People will feel awkward, ill-at-ease, and self-conscious; they need information over and over again.

5. People will think first about what they will have to give up; let people cry and mourn the loss.

6. People will feel alone even though others are going through the same change. Structure interactions and involvement for people.

7. People also need variety, new experiences, growth, breaks in routine, and creative outlets.

8. The communications power in explicit vision and values is enormous. People want to believe.

9. Only one to three themes (maximum) should be chosen in order to focus people.

10. People change at different rates and speeds; they have different levels of readiness for change.

11. Excellence is doing 10,000 little things right—that's strategic management and execution.

12. "Processes" exist—only issue is their focus and effectiveness.

13. The stress of change on people is enormous...but it can and must be led and managed for successful change to occur. People can only handle so much change; don't overload—it causes paralysis.

14. Being open to feedback doesn't have to be a sacred cow...but it is painful.

15. Employees can be a bottom line competitive business advantage—but only if management first becomes the advantage.

16. People will be concerned they don't have enough resources; help them get "Outside the Nine Dots".

17. If you take pressure for change off, people will revert back to old behaviors; relapses are natural and will occur.

18. We rarely use what works despite the fact that proven research is in on change management.

PART FOUR

IN CONCLUSION...

A Challenge
Be deadly serious over the long term...
or don't even attempt change...
You'll screw it up!
"In life, what you resist, persists!"
Constant reinforcement is needed.

SYSTEMS THINKING

The Science of Living Systems
The natural way the world works.

Backed by over 50 years of scientific Research—it is the most holistic, integrated, organizing framework available in the world today.

GENERAL SYSTEMS THEORY
The only science-based research in the management field!

General Systems Theory is not a theory but the natural laws of life on earth just like:
  • *mathematical laws*
  • *laws of physics*
  • *laws of thermodynamics*

THE SYSTEMS THINKING APPROACH
In summary:
  • We are governed by the natural laws of life and living as opn/living systems on earth
                                    —*so*—
  • a successful participant must learn the rules

Analytical thinking is old Industrial Revolution Thinking

CHAPTER 10

Feedback..."Breakfast of Champions"

Overview

*T*hroughout this book, we've referred to feedback in general, and its fundamental importance to true Systems Thinking. In Part IV of the book, we'll cap all our arguments for and explanations of Systems Thinking with what is truly the centrifugal force of every aspect of the systems approach: *feedback.* It is feedback; after all, that transforms linear, left/right analytic thinking into the circular mindset of Systems Thinking. In this chapter, we'll get down to the nitty-gritty of feedback, both its definition and the critical role it plays in each and every systems application.

The unfortunate fact of the matter is that—though many of the best futurists and strategic thinkers in our modern organizations suggest Systems Thinking as the right way to *go—none of them integrate feedback as the inherent, focal characteristic around which Systems Thinking revolves.* Without feedback at the center of Systems Thinking, all the best intentions in the world will ultimately falter and fail.

So what, exactly, is feedback? To clarify, let's go back to the 12 Characteristics of Living Systems. We defined two different types of systems— 1) open and 2) closed. Percentage-wise, few systems are categorized as true closed systems—totally self-contained mechanical systems would be an example of the closed systems category. On the other hand, almost any biological or social system is inherently more of an open system.

Open systems are those systems which exchange information, energy, or material with their environment. If this characteristic of open systems sounds familiar, it is because, by its very nature, it fundamentally defines feedback. *It shows us that, without feedback, information, and energy from the environment, an open system will run down and fail to survive. Its life force— feedback—is missing.*

Feedback, Characteristic #5 of Living Systems, is integral for systems to be able to maintain or improve their dynamic future state—this circular, input/throughput/output/feedback quality of systems, in which information concerning the outputs of the system are fed back as inputs to the system. Feedback leads to changing and correcting the transformation process, as well as improving future outputs.

It is important to understand that feedback can be both positive and negative in nature—and, as we have repeatedly inferred, both are necessary. Though it is human nature to gravitate toward the positive, we must incorporate positive *and* negative feedback in order to receive balanced and informative input—which then allows us to monitor and adjust our systems so that they may maintain or improve their desired future state.

Characteristic #8 of Living Systems, entropy, shows us more clearly *why* feedback is key. Entropy causes all living systems to run down and fall in upon themselves—entropy means that available energy diminishes, until all energy needed for progress is extinguished. In systems, the tendency toward maximum entropy is a movement to disorder, complete lack of resource transformation... and death.

In a more open system, however, the system imports resources from its environment. As a result of this, entropy can be arrested in open systems, and may even be transformed into negative entropy (or negentropy)—a process of more complete organization and the ability to transform resources into more positive results.

The final Living Systems Characteristic that makes the case for feedback is Characteristic #12, internal elaboration. From this characteristic—which states that all living systems move toward entropy and disorganization, while more open systems move in the direction of greater differentiation, elaboration, and a higher level of organization—comes the concept of incremental degradation— The Rubik's Cube Effect™.

In the absence of feedback, incremental degradation—the opposite of internal elaboration and growth—occurs. Probably the best illustration of this is that of our physical bodily systems. Though were superbly designed to remain healthy and resist the encroachment of illness and disease, we cannot maintain the necessary energy to do so without the proper feedback i.e., intake of nutrition, exercise, water, and rest, among others.

Regardless of what type of system we look at—be it our bodies, teams, organizations, or communities—resisting the feedback through which change and growth occurs creates a one-sided scenario of entropy and death, rather than building and growth for the future. When we insist on clinging to whatever's worked in the past, and avoid implementing any new directions that may be indicated by feedback from the environment, our systems will invariably experience entropy and begin to die, increment by increment.

Years ago at a NTL Institute session in Bethel, Maine, strategist Tony Petrella put it in practical terms:

"Suppose a new buyer comes in and says, 'You know our customers will never notice it if we substitute B for A and B costs a little less.' We do it, and we reward the buyer for the good idea.

*Then an engineer comes along and says, 'You know if we change the process here we can use less of this costly ingredient and the customer will never know it.' We do **it** and reward the engineer.*

Three years later, after 15 of these kinds of changes, our customer notices. There has been an incremental degradation to the point where we are not satisfying the customer with our quality. And now we wake up to discover that we no longer remember how to make the product the way we used to!"

This is an excellent example of incremental degradation and lack of feedback from the customer. It is certainly one most of us can relate to.

Another example would be Great Britain's changing political power, described here by Charles L. Schultze, a Senior Fellow at the Brookings Institute:

"The UK did not become a third-rate power by a series of crises. it became so gradually over 40 to 50 years. In no one year was it obvious that a continuation of current policies would do that. The test of the maturity of a democratic country (and organization) isn't whether is responds well to a crisis. Most countries (and organizations) do. The real test of maturity is, can you make the difficult decisions when they don't seem immediately necessary?"

Thus, feedback on outcomes enables us to measure the consequences of our actions. This is critical to virtually every systems application. Remember, "what we think, what we know, or what we believe doesn't matter—it is only through our actions and feedback that we create the results we want."

Another type of feedback in Systems Thinking comes from our processes or throughputs. Like outcome feedback, it is essential in all systems applications. In organizations especially, feedback on processes is integral to the success of the current popularity of business process re-engineering and total quality management applications.

The simple reason for its importance is obvious; if we fail to track, analyze, and continuously improve and adjust our processes, the outcomes we're attempting to measure will rapidly disintegrate. Thus, even in these internal applications we need customer feedback to be sure the quality and the efficient processes make sense in their perspective to customers...the ultimate perspective.

Lastly comes the feedback type that is most familiar to us—that of counting input activities. One example of this would occur when, say, we try to judge crime prevention success by the amount of funding or new police officers hired. Though this may seem a more superficial feedback type than outcome and process feedback, the truth of the matter is that it is also important.

Example:

A perfect example of how things can go awry where just limited input or process feedback is used is most government agencies. While today's politicos cry for instituting strong "performance measures", that's usually where it ends. The tendency is to focus on tracking input activities or processes versus outcomes. The real feedback is, therefore, missing. In order to become even moderately effective, such government agencies are among those who most need to develop a clear understanding and appreciation of the circular, systemic quality of *outcome feedback.*

Example:

Another example of this faulty, pick-and-choose approach to feedback is in the private sector. Though we've heard much of the lip service given to the concept of a "balanced scoreboard", the private sector in general fails to accurately and continuously measure the multiple outcomes of success.

In the end, feedback creates the glue that makes it possible for us to learn and to improve how we work well and cohesively within the complexity of our systems. Feedback is what makes it possible, as Meg Wheatley puts it, for "order [to] emerge out of chaos". It is being open to feedback and learning that will enable us to continue to grow and improve our open and permeable systems. Over time, it's a sure bet that those systems—be they organizations, teams or families—that encourage and develop the strongest, most flexible feedback structures are the ones that will be the most successful.

Example:

One of the best nationally recognized examples of using feedback to work cohesively within systems was that of General Electric, where CEO Jack Welch's concept of "boundary-less-ness" created an open and permeable system that incorporates 360° feedback from all areas. Another success story is Wal-Mart, whose state-of-the-art satellite system has integrated constant and simultaneous feedback from all store locations, creating enviably efficient logistics for just-in-time store management.

Another such story on a smaller scale was the medium-sized San Diego-based Maintenance Warehouse, who would virtually guarantee same-day delivery of maintenance repair and operations equipment and parts to 90% of U.S. apartment and condominium complexes, due to an extremely efficient delivery and feedback system they've created. Home Depot bought them to create a new division based on this concept—Home Depot Supply.

Giving and Receiving Feedback..
"Seek first to understand, and then be understood"

The Bible's timeless words—more recently borrowed and adapted by Stephen Covey—"Seek first to understand, then be understood", are critical to making feedback a two-way, giving, and taking event. In other words, we usually must earn the right to give someone feedback, and that can only happen when we first make ourselves open to receiving it from them. Think about it for a minute in terms of influence—if you want to influence someone else, you really need to first earn that right in your willingness to be influenced by them. You must demonstrate that, rather than only being interested in giving feedback, you are interested in receiving and respecting their feedback, as well.

Receiving feedback

To frame the receiving of feedback in a more tangible way, let's look at how it affects our day-today existence. Take driving your car, for instance—certainly of great importance to our daily life. We all look to the gas gauge to give us the feedback of how much farther it can take us before it will require more fuel. Our physical health is another example of our getting continual feedback in a tangible way. We are constantly receiving feedback from our bodies—when they need food, when they need rest, when they need exercise, water, and so on.

In organizations, we often receive feedback in the form of problems or crises.

When we receive any of this feedback, we may act on it in a variety of ways. We may choose to ignore it or we may decide to work harder at using this feedback for constructive change and growth. The point is, we are continually being given feedback; it is incumbent on us—especially those in leadership positions—to develop our individual feedback skills in order to: 1) encourage it, 2) receive it, 3) understand it, and then 4) act on it.

Feedback is clearly an area of paramount importance to our individual self-mastery. In fact, it would not be an understatement to say that the development of fundamental feedback skills on an individual leadership level is key to attaining self-mastery. In their books, both Stephen Covey *(Seven Habits of Highly Effective People)* and Dr. Tom Rusk *(Ethical Persuasion)* also speak to the importance of developing individual skills, not only in *giving,* but also in *receiving* feedback.

> *"To influence, we must be willing to be influenced"*
> *—Anonymous*

It's important to understand that feedback is important to our progress and growth, even when it's not exactly what we want to hear. Therefore, even when we feel overwhelmed by it, we still need to acknowledge it as a gift and try to reflect it in our actions. Be aware of the negative reactions you will experience—shock, surprise, frustration—and take care not to act on these feelings until you've sorted through them privately. In other words, "Skeptics are our best friends" is key.

Leaders
"Feedback as a gift"
"Feedback is a gift. Allow others to give it to you."

For leaders in particular, feedback truly is a gift—one that is both given to you and one that you give to others. Successful leaders are not only those who give feedback effectively—more importantly, they also welcome and receive feedback as it is given to them, using it to improve, expand, and strengthen their leadership styles.

The most successful leaders are invariably those that don't superimpose their egos over feedback; they understand that *all* feedback has value, and that without it, progress and growth aren't possible. With that end continually in mind, they create a "feedback friendly" environment, one that invites and encourages ongoing feedback.

For leaders in pursuit of the highest level of effectiveness, feedback is a leadership tool. It is the skill of being open and receptive to, and even encouraging feedback from all areas: 1) customers, 2) employees, 3) direct reports and peers, and 4) virtually anyone who can help you learn and grow as a human being and leader.

For many of us, the immediate reaction to feedback, particularly if it's negative, is to close ourselves off from the people around us and go into hiding. Giving into this feeling, however, is clearly not the stuff of which leadership is made. The fact is, all feedback, whether positive or negative in nature, gives us the ongoing opportunity to evolve, and to continually improve ourselves to our own advantage. In learning how to welcome and integrate feedback for growth, it's helpful to keep a few guidelines, such as these below, in mind:

- **Put yourself in the other person's shoes.** *If the situation were reversed, would you have experienced the same reaction?*

- **It's not a sign of weakness to say, "I'm sorry".** *Even if you're right 99 times out of 100, be willing to assess each situation individually, and, if warranted, apologize.*

- **Accept all feedback honorably.** *View feedback as constructive input that helps you improve upon your leadership style, and, even if it's meant that way, don't take it personally. Learn from it instead; turn it around and imagine how you might handle the same situation better the next time*

- **Put your ego on hold.** *"Leave your shield at the office door." Criticism is hard for all of us to take, but effective leaders accept that everyone has shortcomings, even them. Also, they keep their cool and take time to frame an appropriate response.*

- Adopt the *"Skeptics are my best friends"* mantra—and mean it!

- *In sum, the key question is:* "Do I want to learn and grow—or——defend where I am now?"

For leaders especially, understanding the various methods through which we communicate with one another is vital. The graphic of the "Ladder of Communication Effectiveness", shown in Chapter 2 illustrates the various *types* of communication which take place between us. Note, for instance, that it is only at the handwritten letter to telephone conversation step on the communication ladder that communication changes from one-way to two-way. Two-way communication, of course, is the essence of all effective feedback.

An element that is critical to leaders in feedback is **active** listening. A while back, researchers at the University of Michigan observed the behaviors of several hundred organizational supervisors in an effort to determine the levels of their leadership and career achievement. *Of those supervisors that attained the most success in their careers, researchers found one primary common behavior—each one practiced attentive, respectful listening—to everyone.*

This is still true today. Warren Bennis, well-known professor and author of *On Becoming a Leader,* agrees that successful leaders "are superb listeners, particularly to those who advocate new or different images of emerging reality... that's how they stay on the leading edge of change."

His research also found that the most successful leaders were found to be askers of great questions; they continually want to know "what" and "why".

This was also the key to legendary consultant Peter Drucker—his well-known ability to ask questions…and listen to the answers!

Questions to Ponder...

- Do you believe "feedback is a gift"? Why? Why not?
- To effectively communicate with others, what are the key ways we remember things?
- How much repetition is needed for effectively communicating change?

Clearly, listening—essential to virtually all two-way communication—plays a key role in feedback. To reap the most benefits, leaders need to understand the set of behaviors that accompany fruitful listening. At all costs, avoid being defensive. Temporarily drop your own agenda and just listen—otherwise, you'll run the risk of driving away the person you're supposed to be listening to. Responsive expressions and maintaining eye contact with the other person, as well as attentive body postures, also project genuine interest in what that person is trying to communicate.

One of the reasons we stress feedback for leaders so strongly is due to the unfortunate fact that the more senior your position and the higher you travel—in organizations of all types—the more difficulty you will experience in getting candid, rather than superficial, feedback.

This is particularly true with organizational members. To get maximum feedback from members of your team, you'll need to be diligent in asking for it. Don't be shy about this. Be clear as to the specific areas in which you'd like feedback, and explain why it is important. Once you've listened to the feedback, engage team members in conversation and paraphrasing, making certain you've correctly understood what's been said. Don't leave it at that, however. Acknowledge their contribution and, where appropriate, let them know what you plan to do with it. It is this type of careful attention and follow-through that encourages future feedback.

Since feedback is so crucial to the shaping and growth of your path, not just as a leader but also as a human being, you should be prepared to seek it from many sources. Ultimately, you should seek feedback from anywhere within a complete, 360° circumference, including direct reports, superiors, team members, and any other source you can think of be inventive and don't stick with the known; look for it in places not normally associated with feedback. Look to your peers, suppliers, and customers for feedback—usually, they're more than willing to give candid input from a different point of view that can help you greatly.

Renewal

Another area that can produce extremely valuable feedback for leaders is what Robert H. Waterman, Jr., in his book of the same name, calls "The Renewal Factor". Organizational renewal—the process of initiating, creating, and confronting needed change in order for organizations to become or remain viable, adapt to new conditions, solve problems, learn from experience, and move toward greater organizational maturity—is what most organizations surviving in today's global change are experiencing.

Renewal: *the planned and purposeful abandonment of the old and unrewarding is the essential prerequisite to successful pursuit of the new and highly promising —Hal McAlindon*

This "renewal factor" comes from a different way of looking at and approaching the inevitable:

Change. It's about seeing the glass as half-full, rather than half-empty. It's about systems design and redesign, and understanding that, as soon as a design is implemented, its consequences indicate a need for redesign. Finally, it's about welcoming, rather than resisting, change, seeing it as opportunity for valuable feedback.

Ten clear indicators of the need for organizational renewal are:

- Are labor costs too high? Is the work force structured to create low productivity through restrictive work practices, "feather-bedding", and excessive job classifications?

- Are product quality and first-pass yields up to best practice standards on a worldwide basis?

- Are prior investments in automation resulting in escalating indirect-to-direct labor rations that were unanticipated at the time such investments were made?

- Are there persistent problems in inventory utilization and/or continuing scheduling snafus?

- Are new technologies emerging in the marketplace that the business did not foresee, and/or for which the internal view has been cautious or negative?

- Are new product development schedules slipping?

- Are the new products that have been introduced as successful in the eyes of the business' customers as anticipated?

- Is the business meeting its profit forecasts? Are product prices being raised to prohibitive levels to meet these forecasts, even at the risk of current and future share erosion?

- Is the marketplace creating new demands that the business cannot respond to because its products or services don't match customer needs, or because it cannot develop the distribution channels and sales needed to serve these demands?

- Is the balance or economic power between the business' suppliers and the enterprise itself shifting adversely?

The most successful leaders view self-renewal as the process an organization experiences as it continually revamps and adapts itself to constantly changing circumstances *before* a crisis occurs. While routine managers tend to accept things the way they are, leaders recognize the ongoing need to revise structures and processes so that they meet changing realities. *They do this by integrating a feedback system in a number of areas,* including:

Environment

Self-renewal means systematically monitoring your environment, including products, customers, markets, and competitors as a basis for changing decisions and direction. Always remember, information is a competitive weapon. Think down-board, continually analyzing your relationships to the larger realisms of the environment; set up an Environmental Scanning System (ESS).

Outputs

Here, renewal is about providing incremental, evolutionary, and/or revolutionary change in response to market changes. Make your vision, mission, and values crystal clear, reiterating their rationale frequently. Gain consistent feedback on how you are doing versus your vision.

Strategies

In renewal, goals and strategies are established, but with the expectation that there will be revisions needed. Stay away from self-limiting, cost-only mentalities, and promote mobility, flexibility, quickness, and smallness as a strategic weapon. Adjust as you go, based on data and valid feedback.

Feedback and curiosity

Perhaps the supreme need in a successful self-renewal system is the creation of an internally-propelled, deep-sensing, and uncensored feedback system that provides a continuous, unfiltered flow of data on the changing realities your organization faces. *Establish curiosity as an organizational norm and part of the desired culture.*

Learning from and rewarding honesty in reporting mistakes

Self-renewal systems constantly model change, continuous improvement, and a renewal mindset—in which uncertainty is confronted, not denied—as organizational priorities. *In organizational renewal processes, honesty in reporting failures, mistakes, and setbacks is rewarded.* As long as people learn from their mistakes, the messenger of bad news is not shot, but rewarded.

"Skeptics are my best friends"

In organizational renewal systems leaders view "skeptics as their best friends", treat facts or opinions as friendly, and honor disagreements or resistance prior to decision-making. In setting up a renewal system that gives more than lip service to feedback, leaders should see themselves as monomaniacs with a mission, allocating organization-wide attention to a vision. They do not let themselves be distracted by cries from habit-seekers nor by the status quo.

Strategic Change Leadership Team

To stay ahead by managing continuous change, organizational renewal systems should clearly delineate "an attitude of continuous renewal", with permanent issue-management teams serving as devil's advocate. There should always be a Strategic Change Leadership Team in place led by the CEO and meeting monthly, to ensure successful renewal and change management.

After all, change is now the third constant to life along with taxes and death.

Empowerment and accountability

Renewal systems that hope to succeed must empower employees to take self-initiative. This can be greatly enhanced when leaders push decision-making activities down the corporate ladder, and delayering management. Also, prevent departmental inbreeding by establishing a mix of internal promotions, external hires, and personnel rotation across departments. Don't forget, empowerment is *responsible* freedom.

Feedback on values

Feedback will be healthiest in renewal systems that value risk-taking and innovation. It is also important to reward and promote organizational members that are fully committed to renewal, teamwork, and trust, versus power or office politics. Actions that stray from organizational values must be discouraged, and every organizational decision should consistently be based upon those values.

Informal culture

As leaders, your best bet for steady, honest feedback will be to thoroughly educate the entire organization about the significance of your renewal efforts—while ensuring the fit of your strategic plan with all parts of the Business Excellence Architecture, i.e., the Organization as a Systems Model, first introduced in Chapter 3. This can be accomplished through heavy emphasis on your vision, values, and motivation, making them more real to all organizational members. Keep your Rallying Cry alive and ensure that your entire organization is involved, owns, fits with, and reinforces these intangibles in all details.

Other renewal mechanisms

Organization renewal affects the functioning of the system, confronts a real situation, and helps the organization mature while being responsive to the environment. The multiple programs of management and organization development may contribute to and be a crucial part of renewal, but successful renewal is a total response by the human resources of the organization.

Though renewal is an end in and of itself, leaders should also view it as the prime opportunity it is for establishing an ongoing, tangible organizational mindset around feedback. Specific feedback and renewal mechanisms for building organizational mindset and culture around feedback could include:

- *Issues management process (government, community, stockholder, and stake holders)*
- *Environmental Scanning System (ESS)*
- *Competitor analysis*
- *Financial reports (short-term/long-term)*
- *Industry financial comparisons*
- *Customer data, surveys, perceptions, feedback, focus groups*
- *Non-customer data, surveys, perceptions, focus groups*
- *Technology trends*
- *Socio-demo graphic trends*

- *Employee opinion surveys—yearly, by units (morale, motivation, and communications)*
- *Rewards—matching surveys, programs, diagnosis*
- *Culture surveys, focus groups*
- *Administrative MIS reports*
- *Deep-sensing employee perceptions*
- *Advertising, marketing ROI, and research*
- *Management data, opinions, meetings*
- *Task forces, think tanks, discussion groups*
- *Strategic planning process*
- *Unfiltered upward feedback meetings*
- *Team building, diagnosis, executive retreats, and check-ups*
- *Action research*
- *Structured experiences, feedback, and learning*
- *Job design, work simplifications*
- *Organization effectiveness suggestion programs (not just productivity)*
- *Employee involvement programs, meetings*
- *Peer evaluations*
- *Meeting evaluations—three summarizing questions*
- *Employee/management meetings*
- *Offsite meetings, overnights, Outward Bound team experience*
- *Performance evaluation, including company values*
- *MBWA*
- *Strategic Change Leadership Team*
- *Feedback, feedback, feedback*

Through continuous, viable feedback that is not only absorbed, but acted upon, leaders can build an organizational renewal system which enables its human resources to also become increasingly viable to cope with the future, and to contribute to it in a relevant manner. This is also the emphasis in TQM or continuous improvement.

Personal Leadership Plans

Successful leaders *are* successful because they see feedback for what it truly is: a gift. Though it can be difficult to face at times, the ones that push through it and persevere, using feedback as the best educational tool there is, will always be rewarded. Sometimes the results will vary greatly from what you imagined in the early stages, but the point is that there *are* results. Final postscripts to this are these great thoughts from *Keeping Current (May 8, 1995):*

It is not easy...
to apologize,
to start over,
to be unselfish,

to take advice,
to admit error,
to face a sneer,
to keep trying,
to be considerate,
to endure success,
to profit from mistakes,
to forgive and forget,
to think first, then act,
to get out of a rut,
to curb an unruly temper,
to shoulder deserved blame,
to recognize a silver lining,
...but it is always rewarding.

Feedback for teams and organization (Living Systems Levels 4 and 5) ...the key to the learning organization

Teamwork—including that of departmental, cross-functional, and self-directed teams—is an important working tool in today's learning organization. In a true learning organization, leaders must work with organizational teams, teaching them to take a high performance initiative that focuses on future-based objectives or outcomes, as opposed to just reactive problem-solving in crisis.

As we saw in previous Chapters, true team interaction occurs when—as is best evident in the volleyball team—team members act not just as a unit unto themselves, but as individual systems with clear roles coexisting within a larger, overall system. Truly effective teams are those in which *everyone* wins not just one member or another.

Obviously, feedback plays an enormous role in creating the scenario just described. Without an active, healthy feedback system, the learning that is so vital to teams and their organizations cannot take place. Since we know that adults learn best by doing, organizational leaders will need to guide and direct teams in processes that reinforce active feedback. They need to hear that the organization appreciates the fact that they are working together effectively as a team. In addition, check-up meetings are scheduled quarterly to ensure the reinforcement [feedback] and new team behaviors actually take in the day-to-day rush of business.

Think of these meetings as similar to the check-up tune-ups we have done on our cars, as well as our annual physical exams and dentist check-ups. Sports figures really understand the importance of feedback. In baseball, retired San Diego Padres' star Tony Gwynn always had his "at bats" videotaped. In this way, if he felt something didn't go quite the way he felt it should, he could go back into the clubhouse to immediately watch his mistakes, and then get a base hit the next time up at bat. It's no wonder he was acknowledged as *the* best hitter in baseball during his prime playing time.

Leaders must realize that, because teams are complex by nature, they will need to have multiple feedback mechanisms in place. Such team feedback measures—in the form of "meeting takeaways" I've developed over the years—that can greatly improve team effectiveness can include:

- An economic model (income statement/balance sheet) to gauge implications/ feedback on decisions made.
- One-on-one comments, in the nature of "friendly facts", given individually where issues exist
- Meeting effectiveness postmortems at end of meeting (ask what to: "continue", "do more of, "do less of", etc.).
- Meetings management norms, guidelines, and structured agendas should be checked for agreement.
- Clarity of our different communication styles, and language tools, and a willingness to flex styles.
- Superordinate goals, future visions, values, and strategic plans as a decision-making umbrella/criteria.
- Continual checking..."Are we on track?"
- Listen-think-act versus listen-react
- Clear decision-making agreement for each agenda item: 1) information only, 2) decision needed, 3) discussion/input only, 4) consensus.
- Underlying concept of a "to do" list to: 1) deflect off-track, yet important issues for later discussion, 2,) follow-up and feedback on agreed-upon actions.
- Incorporate rewards and recognition in meetings as reinforcement and feed-back for desired behaviors.
- Use the well-known Pinch Theory ("I have a pinch"—versus a crunch) as a way to begin conflict resolution in a rational, less defensive way.
- Within the framework of the Organization as a Systems Model, compare each decision's change, impact, and fit, with organization's direction, mission, and strategies.
- Ask, "Where are we now?" (Keep the Rollercoaster of Change in mind)
- Use responsibility charting to clarify roles.
- Celebrate successes, even little ones as feedback and a guide to future success.
- Have each team member accept 100% responsibility for meeting~ success. Check for clarity on what this means.
- Use system thinking question #1: "What's the purpose of this meeting?"
- Ask, "What is the best use of our time right now?" when a meeting is off-track
- Clarify roles: leader, facilitator, gatekeeper, timekeeper, and action recorder; then give feedback on them.
- Use visual reinforcement and feedback: flip charts, overheads, etc.

- Increase meeting effectiveness with meeting management surveys.

Questions to Ponder...

- What three - five renewal mechanisms do you prefer? Why?
- Are "SKEPTICS - your best friends"? Why? Why not?
- Do you believe "knowledge is only an input? How do you view skills and attitudes vs. knowledge regarding keys to professional success?

Annual Strategic Reviews

Another area that is a veritable feedback bonanza for organizations is that of the Annual Strategic Review (Step #10 in our Reinventing Strategic Management model). In our imperfect world, organizational performance and system information will never be fully free of politics or fully available from all levels of the organization. For that reason, strategic planning, implementation, TQM, re-engineering, and desired outcomes, visions, and all other changes should be subject to an independent yearly audit—similar to the familiar, ongoing financial audits by CPA's.

The goals behind the Annual Strategic Review concept we have researched, copyrighted, and used with all our clients are two-fold:

> *Goal #1) Management attention to the Strategic Management Process itself*
> *Goal #2) Management attention to the strategic plan achievements*

This type of feedback ensures the continual updating of the organization's strategic plan in a changing environment. Strategic plans should be living, breathing documents (most are too rigid). It also clarifies the annual planning and budgeting priorities for the following year, and problem-solves issues *before* they arise.

Included in the annual strategic review is a Strategic IQ Audit that has the following purposes. It includes a focus on both:

- Your Strategic Direction, Customer Focus, Operational Excellence, and Financial results versus Best Practices to Achieve Business Excellence and Superior Results
- Your yearly Strategic Management System and Cycle that is Customer-Focused and generates these results, year after year (an integrated approach)

The question is whether you have a yearly financial audit and certification of your organization.

- Financial Audits look at the past – The Financials and Operations
- Strategic IQ™ Audits look at Strategy, Positioning, and a Future-Oriented Customer-Focus

Only the Haines Centre has researched proven best practices in Strategic Management building on the Baldrige Quality Award for Performance

Excellence. We created a Strategic IQ™ Audit and Certification that begins where the Baldrige leaves off. A *free* article about it is available at www. HainesCentre.com.

The Strategic IQ™ Audit is a comprehensive Enterprise-Wide Audit that includes an integrated suite of assessments, including:

1. Strategic Management results, direction, and marketplace positioning audit.
2. Yearly Strategic Management System, process, and capabilities audit.
3. Customer-orientation and customer-focus audit.
4. Economic analysis and financial results audit.
5. Operational Excellence: plans, accountability and culture (values) audit
6. Strategic business design, productivity, and efficiencies audit
7. Organizational Capacity for Change—five components audited.
8. (Optional) Enterprise-Wide Assessment vs. the Baldrige Quality Criteria for Performance Excellence (either a face-face or on-line assessment available).

All of this is based on the Proven Best Practices, Research of Organizations, using the Best 21st Century Integrated Organizing Framework and Language there currently is, The Systems Thinking Approach®.

Environmental Scanning Systems

To ensure your learning outcomes are the desired ones, being open to the environment and its constant changes is crucial. Probably the best way to start establishing ongoing environmental scanning is with the SKEPTIC framework, shown below:

> **S**ocio-demographics,
> **K** (c)ompetition,
> **E**conomics/Ecological,
> **P**olitical,
> **T**echnology,
> **I**ndustry/Substitutes, and
> **C**ustomer.

The beauty of SKEPTIC is that it takes all aspects of the environment into consideration. This, along with the identification of key stakeholders (see below), is key to an organization's environmental scanning process.

Stakeholder Analysis—the world as a complex system

Figure 10.1: Stakeholder Analysis

This chart is an excellent example of stakeholder analysis, as it shows the 360° perspective from which organizations should view their stakeholders. Many organizations don't comprehend the broad, literal definition of just what a stakeholder *is*—*any* group or individual who can affect or is affected by the achievement of the organization's objectives—and they lose sight of the fact that their success is often affected by less-than-obvious stakeholders.

Organizations must follow six key steps in establishing a Strategic Environmental Scanning System (SESS):

1. Identify the organization's environmental scanning needs, especially for the next round of strategic planning and/or annual strategic reviews.

2. Generate a list of information sources that provide core inputs (i.e., trade shows, publications, technical meetings, and customers).

3. Identify those who will participate in the environmental scanning process.

4. Collect data on a regular basis.

5. Disseminate the information in a large group meeting—both on a yearly basis and quarterly at the Strategic Change Leadership Steering Committee meeting.

6. Create an action plan based on this—revise your strategic plan.

Key Success Measures

Another great feedback mechanism are Key Success Measures (KSM). A Key Success Measure is a way in which to measure your organization's outcome measures of success in achieving its vision, mission, and values.

Measuring is the first step that leads to control and eventually to improvement

If you can't measure something, you can't understand it

If you can't understand it, you can't control it

If you can't control it, you can't improve it

KSMs are outcomes measures of success and are marvelous vehicles that, properly developed, can give your organization a tangible way in which to measure its progress and continuous improvement year after year. It's also crucial, when developing your organization's KSMs, to concentrate on developing ways to measure what's important, not just what's easy (input or process feedback, usually).

It's important to focus on a small number of overall KSMs—in such categories as customer, employee, owner satisfaction, etc.—so keep your organization's KSMs to roughly ten or less. More than this can take your eye off the ball and confuse people as to what is important.

As with all other renewal and feedback mechanisms we have looked at, establishing an organization's reinforcement mindset means creating a formal, ongoing reinforcement *system*. Examples of what could be included in such a system are:

- Once a month, teams will hold team meetings to re-examine their "living agreements", (i.e., continue, more of, less of)
- Each quarter, hold organization-wide meetings to problem-solve key issues and to review the organization's direction and values.
- Conduct a "52-week" training reinforcement program of the initial training (i.e., thirty minutes per week)
- Create visual posters for the top 5-10 training models/concepts, with applicable quotes posted throughout the organization.
- Use a visual control board to track the status of results.
- Encourage the buddy system, lunches, etc.
- Have small groups and teams teach and review each section for what is working and what's not.
- Build free-floating agendas in meetings.

What? So what? Now what?

Finally, optimize each of the feedback mechanisms you have in place—as well as the ongoing meetings to focus on reinforcing the learning from feedback—by always posing these three adult learning theory questions:

1. What happened? *(What did we see and feel...what trends are we observing?)*

2. So what did we learn, generalize, or figure out?

3. Now what are we going to do or apply as a result of this?

Note: In adult learning theory, these three "what", "so what", "now what" questions are the key focal point of learning. So are the next three questions:

The three questions—"continue", "more of", "less of".

It is in continually asking these key questions, and mapping out a plan of action based on the three questions, that true learning organizations can successfully create ongoing renewal and growth through the use of feedback. Use these anywhere, any time, and any place to generate spontaneous, "real time" feedback in 2-3 minutes (be sure to use them in this order, though).

A final word on feedback....rewards and recognition

Though we've previously discussed rewards and recognition it deserves mention here because of what it, in fact, is—the ultimate external form of feedback. Up until recently, rewards systems have pretty much become fixed in the standard, work-for-pay tradition. While there's nothing particularly wrong with this, the truth is that rewards programs as feedback would be infinitely more valuable if they were tied to the *consequences* of what we do.

To truly experience growth through change, it is crucial that we accept the consequences that result from our actions—both positive and negative. As long as conventional work-for-pay rewards programs provide our only feedback, however, there is no real incentive to act in new and different ways or to change the consequences of what we do.

To be truly effective, rewards and recognition systems need to devise ways in which people are positively rewarded when they support needed change, and negatively impacted when they don't. Research has shown that people primarily want three things:

1. Recognition for a job well done

2. Opportunities for freedom of action

3. Opportunities for learning and growth

When researching the top job needs of employees, Dr. H. Migliore, former Dean of Oral Roberts University's Business School, found that these were consistently the three priorities cited by employees nationwide. It's interesting to note that, out of the many desires employees stated, higher salary and/or more benefits only rated about mid-way through the list.

Research tells us that people are motivated by far more than mere external incentives, such as financial gain. What it also tells us is that rewards and recognition programs can be based on both external *and* internal motivators—thus proving the point that we respond to feedback that is linked to the consequence of our actions.

A well-thought out rewards, recognition, and consequences system can go a long way toward cementing motivation and ongoing commitment to change. In the end, to successfully create a true learning organization, rewards—both financial and non-financial—for individuals and teams that are timely, meaningful, and personally significant will be key.

Summary

What feedback boils down to, finally, is the question: “Do we want to follow disciplined Systems Thinking...or is it all just empty rhetoric?” To survive and thrive in the 21st century’s System Age, we must not only make feedback “the breakfast of champions”, but our best friend and tool for success.

Even San Diego’s pro-football team, the Chargers, are big believers in the need for feedback, as witnessed in their newsletter, *Chargers Powerline:*

“Training camp and preseason has been described by some as the world’s longest job interview. It’s a time of intense preparation forr both coaches and players. Players study and perform to the best of their abilities in hopes of being chosen to the final roster. And coaches spend hours and hours teaching the playbook and evaluating the players.”

There are many, many examples, in almost any organization you can think of, of the value of feedback. Unfortunately, this doesn’t often hold true for families or social groups.

In renewal—which, we saw, was about systems design and redesign—it’s clear that as soon as a design is implemented, its consequences indicate a need for redesign...and what is redesign about, if not feedback? T o make feedback a part of our ongoing conscious actions, our system redesigns must always include both a learning system and an adaptation process. This is a reality we must learn to accept in order to grow forward and succeed.

And, in all things, always remember that healthy growth and learning are the real goals...*not* perfection.

The best we can hope for, then, is an inexact, adaptive-learning, ideal-seeking system, based on real time feedback.

Chapter 10
Feedback...Breakfast of Champions

Summary of Key Concepts

1. Feedback...The Breakfast of Champions"...is the key to improvement everywhere—at all Levels of Living Systems. Entropy and degradation take over otherwise as a standard and natural system dynamic.

2. Giving and receiving feedback—"Seek first to understand then be understood". To influence, we must be willing to be influenced.

3. Feedback is a gift...allow others to give it to you. Leave your shield at the door. *Skeptics are my best friends.*

4. Keep in mind how we really communicate—words—7%, tone—38%, and body language—55%.

5. Good communications and retention = repetition, repetition, repetition (four times minimum). Use stump speeches over and over again.

6. Planned organization renewal is hard but has tremendous benefits—use the many mechanisms listed in this chapter.

7. The Annual Strategic Review and its Strategic IQ Audit are key to organizational renewal. There are many other organizational level ideas as well—environmental scanning, annual meetings, Key Success Measures, etc.

8. Effective management (and all) development requires a feedback/ reinforcement system—to challenge you, recognize and support you, and to help with repetition/practice.

9. Adults learn best by doing—the three key learning questions in order are "what—so what—now what."

10. The three key questions at the end of all meetings are: what do we want to continue—do more of—do less of?

11. Finally—rewards and recognition with feedback for positive performance are crucial to individual, team, and organizational success.

CHAPTER 11

Epilogue...last thoughts

> Our Level of Thinking
> To raise new questions, new possibilities, to regard old problems from a new angle, requires
> creative imagination and marks real advance in science.
> —*Albert Einstein*

Life on a living system—planet Earth

Despite the enormous change and positive direction that technology is bringing to our work and lives in the new millennium, America is continuing to decline in my view.

It is this random possibility of injury and death that is more frightening to Americans these days than just crime statistics. Government yearly deficits and the overall deficit are still with us and we find ourselves in political messed with neither party having good answers. We also see nuclear weapons being held by more and more nations—an immense global concern. There seem to be no fundamental ways to deal with any of society's issues in a positive manner.

Organizations are not immune to this either as our employees come from this society. The research on successful organizational change of all types is pretty dismal.

We need, however, some fundamental changes and new approaches in society and organizations if we are to resolve these issues. Like all things, it starts with each of us. I believe that the purpose of all of our institutions should include helping each of us be clear on our purpose in life. This purpose needs to include: (1) service to others and (2) to leave the world a better place than when we found it.

Such a purpose today, though, is an unpopular contrast to what often goes on in organizations and society where hedonism or self aggrandizement win the day. We need to see ourselves as helping to build civilized organizations and society with the kinds of strong values that one finds in all religious walks of life and Not-for-Profits, too. In fact, we might consider adopting the Cousteau society's purpose as our own:

> The Cousteau Society
> *"To protect and improve the qualify of life
> for present and future generations."*

*How we think...is how we plan...is how we act
...is how we are.*

Pursuing our individual life purpose as articulated above starts with being a leader in Systems Thinking. There is "no one best way" and the old "either/or polarization" is often obsolete. However, if we can change the way we think and look at life and its issues with a systems perspective, then the "butterfly effect" has a chance to work. This effect is about how small changes "up front" in how we think can make massive changes later on in implementation. Throughout this book we have tried to use Systems Thinking in a pragmatic yet simplistic way to help the reader understand how it and the systems age is coming quicker than we know. In fact, almost all scientific disciplines are converging on Systems Thinking, its time is really coming.

This convergence on Systems Thinking includes the disciplines of: 1) Cybernetics, 2). Chaos Theory, 3) Gestalt Therapy, 4) General Systems Theory, 5) Complexity Theory, 6) SocioTechnical Systems Theory, 7) Project Managers, 8) Information Systems, 9) TQM, 10) Operations Research, 11) Geodesic Domes, 12) Tao of Physics, 13) Mind and Nature 14) Systems Thinking versus Analytic Thinking, 15) The Structure of Scientific Revolution, 16) Organization Development, 17) Human Resource Management, 18) Biology, 19) Physics, 20) Mathematicians, 21) Astronomers, 22) Neuroscientists, 23) Philosophers, 24) Economists, 25) Futurists, 26) Educators, 27) Modern Artists, 28) Architects, 29) Mythology, 30) Leadership, 31) Business/Management, 32) Atmospheric and Oceanographic Sciences, 33) Strategic Planning, 34) Government, 35) Psychology, 36) Community Development, 37) Spiritual, 38) and many others. (For further details on these other disciplines, see the Bibliography).

We have tried to summarize Systems Thinking in a clear way throughout this book. In following Systems Thinking and its "Rule of Three", we can summarize Systems Thinking in three main concepts:

1. The Seven Levels of Living Systems—especially the levels of the individual, team or family, organization, and communities

2. The Systems Model, using A-B-C Phases (input, throughput, output and feedback in the environment)

3. The predictable systems dynamics that flow from the 12 basic General Systems Theory characteristics

These three basic Systems Thinking concepts are in turn complemented by a fourth concept:

4. The natural cycles of change —such as the ebb and flow of day and

night, of the tides, and of the seasons—we call it the 'Rollercoaster of Change™".

This crucial Rollercoaster of Change™ is how systems go through the implementation of new ideas and of changes in every walk of life. Overall, these four concepts summarize the key aspects and concepts presented in this book. It is the framework upon which to change how we think, how we act, and how we are—leading us toward obtaining the results we want to achieve in dealing with both our organizational issues and those of society.

Two last thoughts...

#1 "Think globally—we are all inter-connected

It is never more true than today that the seventh Level of Living Systems— the earth—must become the universal framework for how we think. Ever since the astronauts took pictures of earth from hundreds of miles in space, "thinking globally" has been our true reality. The earth—as our Seventh Level of Living Systems—is *a living organism with natural laws that we already have to follow; knowingly or not, reluctantly or not.*

We need to learn and recognize the earth's self-organizing principles, as translated by General Systems Theory and its 12 characteristics and standard dynamics. They can be applied to deal with many of today's organizational problems if we begin to understand that the chaos of today's world is a natural part of the movement from the past to the future. In looking at the globe, it should be clear to us all that "everything everywhere effects everything else" in today's world. Our air, our land, and our water all function in interrelated global patterns that affect every aspect of our lives.

The air from the nuclear explosion in Chernobyl circled the earth, in measurable ways, a total of six times. We find water from the South Pacific and its El Niños affecting the weather patterns of the entire world. The gulf stream from the Gulf of Mexico influences weather patterns as far away as Norway, and the Japanese current affects weather patterns all the way down to San Diego and South America. In fact, the central core of the earth spins at a slightly slower rate than the surface; creating the gravity and magnetism much as if the earth was one big electric, motor. The earth's tectonic plates move across the earth's surface, resulting partly from the molten lava that bubbles up from the sea floor. The lava and its hot molten core also has an effect on the El Niños and the earth's water temperature as it forces the plates to continue to move, leading to earthquakes and the Pacific's "ring of fire".

We are one earth and one living system. We need to fully understand this and its enormous implications for our lives. As Margaret Mead said on March 21, 1977,

Pledge of Allegiance

"The Earth Flag is my symbol of the task before us all....we are the custodians of the future of the Earth. Unless we check the rapacious explorations of our Earth and protect it, we have endangered the future of our children and our children's children. It reminds us how helpless this planet is...something that we must hold in our arms and care for."

We are also recognizing, on a scientific basis, that natural and regional 'geographic systems' exist. As a matter of survival, we need to focus upon these ecosystems. For instance, according to the Sierra Club, there are twenty-one ecosystems existing across North America, each requiring regional governance beyond communities, provinces, and states. In addition, regional alliances that deal with economic cooperation and development are flourishing—i.e., from NAFTA (in the U.S., Mexico, and Canada), MERCOSUR (in South America), to ASEAN (in Asia), and the European Union. Alliances across the continents with China and India are now becoming a new way of life.

Further, we now have satellites that deal with world-wide global positioning, and global information systems, as well. The Internet covers the world. We have personal communications and telephone systems that follow us everywhere across the globe.

English is becoming more and more the world's language. World-wide English—which began out of necessity in World Wars I and II, and led to post-war air traffic controller/ship's Captains and Harbor Pilots having to speak English worldwide—is now enhanced by both the computer and by the Internet. English is the world language.

Biotechnology is in its infancy. For the first time in human history, we are actually seeing the mapping and splicing of the human genes, as well as the mapping of the human gnome. We're also seeing natures' own computer development in the simplicity of DNA and nanotechnology, which could potentially exceed anything we could do with artificial intelligence. The human body and the human being is, in fact, a computer system—we just have to figure out how to utilize it as such. Gene therapies will continue to develop. Biotechnology should outstrip even computers and telecommunications as leading the next wave of massive change...another part of recognizing and applying our thinking to "humans-as-systems".

We are even now searching beyond the earth for the 8th Level of Living Systems somewhere in space. We continue to look for life on other planets and in other civilizations. However,...

#2 *"Act locally"—Let's improve our lives*
Team by Team, Organization by Organization...naturally

While we need to *think* globally, we must truly learn to *act* locally. We must use all the forces at our command and influence to build leadership and alliances in order to improve each and every organization, as well as each person and team within them. We need to better understand how our teams and organizations change, with integrative leaders voluntarily and willingly serving the individuals and teams they contain. *Systems Thinking is the only methodology that deals with these interdependencies and the need for integration in a natural and realistic way.*

The organization is the 21st Century's entity of change—not big government, and not just individuals and teams. We need true, committed involvement—at the level of each organization and each team—to achieve our desired future visions. We need to focus individuals, teams, and organizations of all types on integrated change—and it will start with each of us as leaders. We must be leaders who understand integration, interdependence, and the involvement of others if we are ever going to have organizations leading their own systemic changes. We need leadership teams that tie all parts of the organization together, all its individuals and all its teams. It's at the local level that most of us can "make a difference".

Summary

The earth is a natural system and the General Systems theorists have identified the key dynamics and characteristics of the earth's Living Systems that we all can apply examples. I believe strongly that it is only when we learn to apply these Systems Thinking concepts that we will find better solutions to today's complex organizational and societal problems.

As we've said repeatedly, moving beyond our fragmented, analytic thinking to Systems Thinking is about thinking in new ways. It's not about knowledge for the sake of knowledge—there are an abundance of 'knowledgeable idiots' in this world already—we certainly don't need more. Rather, it is about adopting the Systems Thinking Approach™, a more natural way of thinking about change and rededicating our revolutionary new leadership toward restoring vibrant and healthy organizations.

As revolutionaries throughout history have done in revolution after revolution, our organizations similarly need their own revolutions. They need to grab hold of the same three fundamental change levers that revolutionaries do. We have described practical Systems Thinking applications for these levers throughout this book:

Change Leverage #1: The police/controls...*in order to help with controlling the rewards, reinforcements, and accountability through individuals, teams, and organizations.*

Change Leverage #2: The media/communications...*to ensure the strategic communications and visibility we need to achieve such change are present and reinforcing the desired changes*

Change Leverage #3: Education/learning and leadership development... *at all levels and ages, to ensure the necessary education and life-long learning that will make a real, tangible difference, year after year*

These three leverage points are crucial in developing change, individual by individual, team by team, and organization by organization. Systems Thinking recognizes that for all Levels of Living Systems it is a more natural way to think, act, and change. It really does "take a village to raise a child"—and it takes the "cultural attunement of peoples hearts and minds to change organizations and their economic alignment". It takes ongoing commitment from leaders at all levels to *rededicate ourselves to their future.*

The major forces of the universe are invisible
and
you can use them for free:

Systems Thinking is one!

Thoughts rule the world.

—*Ralph Waldo Emerson*

"Preparation, discipline, and talent—
working within a system—
is the **winning playoff formula**."

— *Michael P. Mitchell, St Louis*
Sporting News, May 1994

Bibliography
Strategic and Systems Thinking Resources

Ackoff, R. (1974). *Redesigning the Future: A Systems Approach to Societal Problems.* NY: John Wiley & Sons, Inc.

Ackoff, R. (1999). *Ackoff's Best: His Classical Writings on Management.* Chichester, England: John Wiley & Sons, Inc.

Alban, B. & Bunker, B. (1997). *Large Group Interventions: Engaging the Whole System for Rapid Change.* San Francisco, CA: Jossey-Bass.

Baldwin, J. (1996). *Bucky Works: Buckminster Fuller's Ideas for Today.* NY: John Wiley & Sons.

Banathy, B. A. (1991). *Systems Design of Education: A Journey to Create the Future.* Englewood Cliffs, NJ: Educational Technology Publications, Inc.

Bateson, G. (2002). *Mind and Nature: A Necessary Unity (Advances in Systems Theory, Complexity, and the Human Sciences).* Cresskill, NJ: Hampton Press.

Bateson, P. (2001). *Design for a Life: How Biology and Psychology Shape Human Behavior.* NY: Touchstone

Beatty, J. (1998). *The World According to Peter Drucker.* NY: The Free Press.

Boardman, J. T. & Sauser, B. J. (2008). *Systems Thinking: Coping with 21st Century Problems.* Boca Raton, FL: CRC Press.

Boulding, K. E. (1964). *The Meaning of the 20th Century.* NY: Prentice-Hall.

Brinkerhoff, R. O. & Gill, S. J. (1994). *The Learning Alliance: Systems Thinking in Human Resource Development.* San Francisco, CA: Jossey-Bass Publishers.

Brown, L. R. (2001). *Eco-Economy: Building an Economy for the Earth.* NY: W. W. Norton & Company, Inc.

Capra, F. (2002). *The Hidden Connections: A Science for Sustainable Living.* NY: Anchor Books.

Checkland, P. (1999). *Systems Thinking, Systems Practice: A 30-Year Retrospective.* NY: John Wiley and Sons

Churchman, C. W. (1979). *The Systems Approach and Its Enemies.* NY: Basic Books.

Covey, S. (1989). *The Seven Habits of Highly Effective People.* NY: Simon & Schuster.

Covington, W. G., Jr. (1998). *Creativity and General Systems Theory.* Parkland, FL: Universal Publishers.

Cummings, T. G. (1980). *Systems Theory for Organization Development.* NY: John Wiley & Sons.

Daellenbach, H. & McNickle, D. (2004). *Management Science: Decision-Making Through Systems Thinking.* NY: Palgrave MacMillan.

Dannemiller, K. and Associates. (2000). *Whole-Scale Change.* San Francisco: Berrett-Koehler Publishers, Inc.

Davidson, M. (1983). *Uncommon Sense, the Life and Times of Ludwig Von Bertalanffy.* Los Angeles, CA: J. P. Tarcher, Inc.

deBono, E. (1999). *Simplicity.* London, England: Penguin Books

DeGeus, A. (1997). *The Living Company.* Cambridge, MA: Harvard Business School Press.

Dettmer, H. W. (2003). *Strategic Navigation: A Systems Approach to Business Strategy.* Milwaukee, WI: ASQC Quality Press.

Diamond, J. M. (1999). *Guns, Germs, and Steel: The Fates of Human Societies.* NY: W. W. Norton & Company, Inc.

Drucker, P. (1995). *Managing in a Time of Great Change.* NY: Dutton.

Dryden, G. & Vos, J. (1999). *The Learning Revolution: To Change the Way the World Learns.* Torrance, CA: The Learning Web.

Emery, F. E. [Ed.]. (1969). *Systems Thinking: Selected Readings, Vols. 1 and 2.* NY: Penguin Books.

Feldman, D. A. (2002). *Critical Thinking.* Boston, MA: Course Technology

Flood, R. L. & Romm, N. R. A. (1996). *Critical Systems Thinking: Current Research and Practice.* NY: Plenum Publishing Corp.

Forrester, J. W. (1971). *Principles of Systems.* Norwalk, CT: Productivity Press.

Frankel, V. (1959). *Man's Search for Meaning.* Boston, MA: Beacon Press.

Galbraith, J. R. (1993). *Organizing for the Future: The New Logic for Managing Complex Organizations.* San Francisco, CA: Jossey-Bass Publishers.

Gell-Mann, M. (1995). *The Quark and the Jaguar.* NY: W. H. Freeman.

George, C. (1968). *The History of Management Thought.* Englewood Cliffs, NJ: Prentice Hall.

Georgiou, I. (2007). *Thinking Through Systems Thinking.* London, England: Taylor and Francis.

Gharajedaghi, J. (2005). *Systems Thinking, Second Edition: Managing Chaos and Complexity: A Platform for Designing Business Architecture.* Burlington, MA: Butterworth – Heinemann, an imprint of Elsevier.

Haines, S. G. (2007). *Reinventing Strategic Planning.* San Diego, CA: Systems Thinking Press.

Haines, S. G. (2005). *Strategic Planning Simplified.* San Diego, CA: Systems Thinking Press.

Haines, S. G. (2005). *The ABCs of Strategic Life Planning.* San Diego, CA: Systems Thinking Press.

Haines, S. G. (2007). *Strategic Thinking Handbook #2: The Simplicity of Systems Thinking.* San Diego, CA: Systems Thinking Press.

Haines, S. G. (1998). *The Managers Pocket Guide to Systems Thinking and Learning.* Amherst, MA: HRD Press

Haines, S. G. (2000). *The Complete Guide to Systems Thinking and Learning.* Amherst, MA: HRD Press.

Haines, S. G. (2006). *Strategic Thinking Handbook #1: The Top 10 Everyday Tools for Daily Problem-Solving.* San Diego, CA: Systems Thinking Press.

Haines, S. G., Aller-Stead, G, & McKinlay, J. (2005). *Enterprise-wide Chang: Superior Results through Systems Thinking.* San Francisco, CA: Jossey-Bass Publishers.

Hamel, G. (2000). Leading the Revolution: How to Thrive in Turbulent Times by Making Innovation a Way of Life. Boston, MA: Harvard Business School Press.

Hammond, D. (2003). *The Science of Synthesis: Exploring the Social Implications of General Systems Theory.* Boulder, CO: University Press of Colorado.

Handy, C. (1994). *The Age of Paradox.* Cambridge, MA: Harvard Business School Press.

Handy, C. (1998). *The Hungry Spirit: Beyond Capitalism: A Quest for Purpose in the Modern World.* NY: Broadway Books.

Hanna, D. P. (2001). *Leadership for the Ages: Delivering Today's Results, Building Tomorrow's Legacy.* Provo, UT: Executive Excellence Publishing.

Hanson, B. G. (1995). *General Systems Theory Beginning with Wholes: An Introduction to General Systems Theory.* Washington, DC: Taylor and Francis.

Hock, D. (1999). *Birth of the Chaordic Age.* San Francisco, CA: Berrett-Koehler Publishers, Inc.

iThink. (2001). *An Introduction to Systems Thinking.* Lebanon, NH: High Performance Systems, Inc.

Jackson, M. C. (2003). *Systems Thinking: Creative Holism for Managers.* Hoboken, NJ: Wiley.

Jantsch, E. (1980). *The Self-Organizing Universe.* Oxford: Pergamon Press.

Jaques, E. (1989). *Requisite Organization: The CEO's Guide to Creative Structure and Leadership.* Alexandria, VA: Cason Hall & Co. Publishers.

Jensen, W. D. (2000). *Simplicity: The New Competitive Advantage in a World of More, Better, Faster.* NY: Perseus.

Johnson, R. A., Kast, F. E., & Rosenzweig, J. E. (1963). *The Theory and Management of Systems.* NY: McGraw-Hill.

Jordan, Bishop E. B. (2007). *The Laws of Thinking: 20 Secrets to Using the Divine Power of Your Mind to Manifest Prosperity.* Carlsbad, CA: Hay House.

Kauffman, S. (1995). *At Home in the Universe*. NY: Oxford University Press.

Klir, G. (1969). *An Approach to General Systems Theory*. NY: Van Nostrand.

Klir, G. [Ed.]. (1972). *Trends in General Systems Theory*. NY: Wiley-Interscience.

Kuhn, T. (1970). *The Structure of Scientific Revolutions (2nd ed.)*. Chicago, IL: University of Chicago Press.

Laszlo, E. (1972). *Introduction to Systems Philosophy*. NY: Gordon & Breach.

Laszlo, E. (1972). *The Advance of General Systems Theory*. NY: George Braziller, Inc.

Laszlo, E. (1996). *The Systems View of the World*. Cresskill, NJ: Hampton Press, Inc.

Levinson, H. (1976). *Psychological Man*. Cambridge, MA: The Levinson Institute

Meadows, D. & Booth Sweeney, L. (2001). *The Systems Thinking Playbook*. Durham, NH: the Institute for Policy and Social Science (University of New Hampshire).

Mesarovic, M. [Ed.] (1967). *Views on General Systems Theory*. NY: John Wiley & Sons, Inc.

Midgley, G. & Ochoa-Arias, A. (2004). *Community Operational Research: OR and Systems Thinking for Community Development*. NY: Kluwer Academic/Plenum Publishing.

Miller, E. J. & Rice, A. K. (1967). *Systems of Organization*. London: Tavistock Publications.

Miller, J. G., (1995). *Living Systems*. CO: University Press of Colorado

Mingers, J. (2006). *Realising Systems Thinking: Knowledge and Action in Management Science*. NY: Springer Science and Business Media, Inc.

Norbert, W. (1998). *The Human Use of Humans: Cybernetics and Society*. NY: Da Capo Press.

O'Connor, J, & McDermott I. (1997). *The Art of Systems Thinking: Essential Skills for Creativity and Problem Solving*. Hammersmith, London: Thorsons.

Olson, E. E. & Eoyang, G. H. (2001). *Facilitating Organization Change: Lessons from Complexity Science*. San Francisco, CA: Jossey-Bass Publishers.

Oshry, B. (1999). *Leading Systems: Lessons from the Power Lab*. San Francisco, CA: Berrett-Koehler Publishers.

Prigogine, I. & Stengers, I. (1984). *Order Out of Chaos*. NY: Bantam Books.

Sanders, T. I. (1998). *Strategic Thinking and the New Science: Planning in the Midst of Chaos, Complexity, and Change*. NY: The Free Press.

Seddon, J. (2003). *Freedom from Command & Control: A better way to make the work work.* Buckingham, UK: Vanguard Education.

Senge, P. M. (1990). *The Fifth Discipline: The Art and Practice of the Learning Organization.* NY: Doubleday/Currency.

Senge, P. M., Cambron-McCabe, N., Lucas, T., Smith, B., Dutton, J., Kleiner, A. (2000). *A Fifth Discipline Resource: Schools that Learn.* NY: Doubleday/Currency.

Sherwood, D. (2002). *See the Forest for the Trees: A Manager's Guide to Applying Systems Thinking.* Yarmouth, ME: Nicholas Brealey Publishing.

Shrode, W. A. & Voich, D., Jr. (1974). *Organization and Management: Basic Systems Concepts.* Homewood, IL: Irwin, Inc.

Snyder, R. (1980). *Buckminster Fuller: An Autobiographical Monologue/Scenario.* NY: St. Martin's Press.

Stacey, R., Griffin, D., & Shaw, P. (2000). *Complexity and Management: Fad or Radical Challenge to Systems Thinking.* London, UK: Routledge.

Sterman, J. D. (2000). *Business Dynamics: Systems Thinking and Modeling for a Complex World.* NY: McGraw-Hill Higher Education.

Trist, E. & Emery, F. (1973). *Toward a Social Ecology.* London and NY: Plenum.

Vickers, G. [Ed.]. (1972). *"A Classification of Systems".* Washington, DC: Yearbook of the Society for General Systems Research/Academy of Management Research.

von Bertalanffy, L. (1967). *Robots. Men and Minds: Psychology in the Modem World.* NY: George Braziller, Inc.

von Bertalanffy, L. (1998). [Revised Edition]. *General Systems Theory: Foundations, Development, Applications.* NY: George Braziller, Inc.

Waldrop, M. M. (1992). *Complexity: The Emerging Science at the Edge of Order and Chaos.* NY: Touchstone.

Weinberg, G. (2001). *An Introduction to General Systems Thinking (Silver Anniversary Edition).* NY: Dorset House Publishing, Company, Inc.

Wheatley, M. J. & Kellner-Rogers, M. (1996). *A Simpler Way.* San Francisco, CA: Berrett-Koehler Publishers, Inc.

Wilson, E. O. (2002). *The Future of Life.* NY: Alfred A. Knopf.

Note: For a complete Bibliography, go to www.HaineCentre.com and click on the words Systems Thinking.

INTEGRATED ORGANIZING FRAMEWORKS ARE KEY:

They give people the conceptual tools, frameworks, models, and language to organize their evidence, their experience, their learning, and their issues.

Otherwise, adults do **NOT** learn best by doing things.

The **best** conceptual, **integrated organizing framework** that exists
is
The ABCs Systems Thinking Approach®
because
it is the natural way the world works.

The world is composed of living, human systems